Endorsements

As a growing consensus emerges that the church today needs a "Second Reformation," one that reshapes the church and not just doctrine, we need to take a closer look at the Believers Church tradition. That is exactly what this new book by Dr. Barry Callen does, and in a very helpful way. Never was [this study] more relevant than now, as Christendom ends and a new millennium begins.—*Howard A. Snyder, Professor of the History and Theology of Mission, Asbury Theological Seminary, Wilmore, Kentucky (Wesleyan tradition)*

As William Faulkner said: "The past is not dead—it is not even past." There is great value in the way Barry Callen lifts up for us in a clear and informed way the thrilling history of the Believers Church tradition. It can only have the effect of inspiring us all to treasure the gifts we have been given and to be faithful.—*Clark H. Pinnock, Professor of Theology, McMaster Divinity College, Hamilton, Ontario, Canada (Baptist tradition)*

Here is a splendid introduction to the identity, history, theology, and mission of the Believers Churches. While commending the vision of these "radical" Christians to the conscience of mainstream Christianity, the author also challenges those within the heritage to confront the erosion of their commitment to the Christ who ministered on the margins of society. The book probes as well as informs.—*Luke Keefer, Professor of Church History, Ashland Theological Seminary, Ashland, Ohio (Brethren in Christ tradition)*

Barry Callen's most welcome synthesis of Believers Church history and thought marks the emergence of a new stage in Believers Church understanding. Many have assumed that central Christian doctrines, such as Christology and atonement, are developed and appropriated in the same way by all Christian traditions. By contrast, Callen demonstrates that the Believers Church tradition is more than an ecclesiological concept; it has the potential to become a distinctive theological lens for interpreting all of Christian thought and history.—*J. Denny Weaver, Professor of Religion, Chair, Department of Religion and History, Bluffton College, Bluffton, Ohio (Mennonite tradition)*

How is the church to respond to the call to radical commitment to Christ that has come to it from its biblical foundations? Dr. Callen provides a wealth of historical background and theological perspective on how the Believers Church tradition responds to this central question. This book is a must for those seeking to understand the many-faceted tradition and mission of the Believers Church as Christianity enters the twenty-first century.—*Kenneth F. Hall, Retired Chair, Department of Religious Studies, Anderson University, Anderson, Indiana (Society of Friends and Church of God, Anderson, traditions)*

RADICAL

Christianity

The Believers Church Tradition in Christianity's History and Future

Other books by Barry L. Callen and
published by Evangel Publishing House

GOD AS LOVING GRACE:
The Biblically Revealed Nature and Work of God

FAITHFUL IN THE MEANTIME:
A Biblical View of Final Things
and Present Responsibilities

SEEKING THE LIGHT:
America's Modern Quest for
Peace, Justice, Prosperity, and Faith

RADICAL
Christianity

The Believers Church Tradition in Christianity's History and Future

Barry L. Callen

Evangel Publishing House
Nappanee, Indiana 46550

Publisher's Cataloging-in-Pubication
(Provided by Quality Books, Inc.)

Callen, Barry L.
    Radical Christianity : the Believers Church tradition in
Christianity's history and future / Barry L. Callen — 1st ed.
    p. cm.
    Includes bibliographical references and index.
    LCCN: 99-63734
    ISBN: 0-916035-63-8

    1. Free churches. 2. Dissenters, Religious. 3. Protestantism.
4. Church—History of doctrines. I. Title

BX4817.C35 1999   280'.4
                          QBI99-803

Printed in the United States of America

9 0 1 2 3 EP 5 4 3 2 1

Dedications

To Todd, my son, and to Beth, my daughter-in-law, young Christians reared in and now voluntarily participants in the Believers Church tradition. For them, the Christian heritage is a rich resource, not a restrictive prison of ideas, structures, and practices. Christian faith invites the believer to get at the root of things, to be "radical" for the sake of present meaning and integrity. May their personal quests for spiritual wholeness and relevance flower into all that they desire and all that they are meant to be. So may the quest of today's church which needs her apostolic roots, Spirit-life, and ability to be herself, free of domination from anything beyond the distinctiveness of her own divine nature and mission.

To six precious Christian brothers and sisters who have been pioneers in the work of living out the Believers Church vision and linking it constructively to the larger Christian community. These prophetic voices are: Edward L. Foggs; Harold L. Phillips; James Earl Massey; John W. V. Smith; Susie Cunningham Stanley; and Gilbert W. Stafford. They represent well the commonality, the diversity, and the divinely-inspired courage necessary to bring to greater reality the intent of Jesus Christ for today's church and world. May what they represent so well flourish in the earth!

Table of Contents

Introduction

This book is historical in nature, at least in part. Information about the past often is lacking in the craze for newness that characterizes our times. Why is the past not summarily discarded here? Because yesterday and tomorrow probably should be linked in significant ways. G. K. Chesterton once said that remembering one's tradition is the way we invite our forefathers and foremothers to cast a vote about the kind of people we believe God now is calling us to be. Among other things, then, one will find in these pages the careful and respectful remembering of key Christian people and events of other centuries. They are recalled and recorded to help enable the process of their casting a vote about our tomorrows. The two appendices, for instance, capture some of their pivotal events and observations that no longer are easily available to most readers. There is no apology made for some looking back. Wisdom from select yesterdays may be one significant access to the door of God's intended tomorrow.

The important thing, of course, is not excessive preoccupation with the past, but contemporary relevance. So we ask this question. What is needed by today's church? If the past is to be considered in the process of answering this question, for what do we look so that the present will be served effectively? We choose here to look especially at the Believers Church tradition on the assumption that this relatively small but vigorous current in the river of Christian church history offers much that will serve today's church very well—but only if the church at large is willing to pay the high price required. "Mainstream" Christianity is faced with more than merely adding on to its evolved nature a helpful insight or two that happens to come from this more "radical" church tradition. Indeed, it may have to reconsider its very nature. Also, contemporary church bodies that are rooted directly in the Believers Church tradition have some of their own soul-searching to do. To what degree have they now blended into the general "Protestant" landscape and subtly abandoned their own distinctive heritage?

This book, then, is not intended merely as an academic exercise. It is a challenge to fresh Christian authenticity, a plea on behalf of Christian faithfulness whatever the cost.

To be found in what follows are: a brief history of the Believers Church tradition; discussion of the core theological and discipleship dimensions of this tradition; and exploration of the tradition's current relevance. The key emphases of the Believers Church focus on experienced spiritual reality, committed lives of genuine obedience to Christ, and the fostering of communities of faith that function visibly, voluntarily, and in Christlike ways, thus witnessing to the living Word of God by being present expressions of God's coming reign. Featured are the priority of an authentic visible manifestation of the believing community, the mounting of a significant critique of the institutional church, the high valuing of the daily life and practice of believers, and a vibrant community of faith in which obedience, discipline, and mutual support and service are constant concerns. The apostrophe (Believers') often used in the literature of this tradition has been removed here to avoid the subtle suggestion that the church is somehow the possession of its members.[1] This tradition would vigorously argue otherwise. The church is God's unique creation and possession, the realm of the divine rule, the body of obedient disciples who are yielded to Christ and not to themselves or the political structures of established church or unbelieving world.[2]

This emphasis on the priority of God's rule can be found clearly in numerous Anabaptist works dating from the sixteenth century, as well as in the work of John Wesley in the eighteenth century and in contemporaries like Clark Pinnock and M. Robert Mulholland, Jr. Pinnock is a Canadian Baptist theologian whose provocative voice in the last third of the twentieth century has sounded much like the

---

[1]Presumably the apostrophe has been used in the past as a way of emphasizing the community ideal of this tradition. Christians are believers together in a disciplined fellowship of the faithful. While this certainly is an appropriate emphasis, the device of the apostrophe can easily be misleading and has been eliminated here.

[2]Note, e.g., that the title of the biography of the primary pioneer of the Church of God (Anderson) movement, Daniel S. Warner, is *It's God's Church!* (Barry Callen, Warner Press, 1995).

prophetic positions of "radical" Christians across the centuries. Pinnock has come to value function as much or even more than form in the areas of biblical authority and interpretation, looking with disfavor at any excessive intellectualism and abstraction that detracts from concrete Christian discipleship and mission. The important question for him is how Scripture can be an authoritative guide for practical Christian living and witnessing. The Christian agenda, in his view, should be less a preoccupation with theological theories or denominational structures and much more with a healthy concern for a spiritual power enabled by the Spirit of God who both speaks through ancient Scripture and illumines the contemporary reader for real life and mission.[3] Such views reflect much in the Baptist and related Believers Church traditions.

Mulholland resonates with such a Christian agenda. Himself in the Wesleyan tradition, he has authored the classic book *Shaped by the Word: The Power of Scripture in Spiritual Formation*.[4] There he identifies as central for Christians the call to be spiritually formed toward the image of Christ by encounters with the Word of God. This involves a joining of knowledge and vital piety that leads to a wisdom that has its roots in the experience of the indwelling presence of God through the Holy Spirit. Of central concern is a special mode of being in the world. This spiritual shaping, the resulting special community of Christ, the focus on openness, obedience, and living the very life of God—visibly, voluntarily, together, and now—are all emphases of the historic Believers Church tradition. They all are needed very much by the church of today and tomorrow.

If indeed the Christian community is trying to find its way in the strange newness of a "post-modern" time,[5] some longstanding

---

[3]See, e.g., Clark Pinnock, *Flame of Love: A Theology of the Holy Spirit* (Downers Grove, Ill.: InterVarsity Press, 1996).

[4]M. Robert Mulholland, Jr., *Shaped by the Word: The Power of Scripture in Spiritual Formation* (Nashville: The Upper Room, 1985).

[5]See, e.g., Millard Erickson, *Postmodernizing the Faith: Evangelical Responses to the Challenge of Postmodernism* (Grand Rapids: Baker Books, 1998) and Stanley Hauerwas, *After Christendom?: How the Church is to Behave if Freedom, Justice, and a Christian Nation are Bad Ideas* (Nashville: Abingdon Press, 1991).

emphases of the Believers Church tradition can function as important guideposts across the unknown horizon now being faced. At the beginning of the twenty-first century, when the worldwide church is concerned about its scandalous divisions and needed renewal, this tradition holds important potential. The choice is between a church that accommodates itself to the world at the peril of its own identity and mission, and a church that derives a distinctive life from God's Christ and thus can stand as a distinctive and credible witness to the world.[6] Therefore, if the "mainstream" traditions of today's Christian community choose to listen and learn from the Believers Church witness, they will have to do more than merely add this "radical" witness to their more establishment patterns of faith and practice. They will have to seriously rethink their very natures in relation to the Spirit's will and the world's ways. The sixteenth-century Anabaptists, for instance, recognized themselves as neither Roman Catholics nor Evangelicals (later called "Protestants"), but rather as "brethren" boldly seeking Christ's way for themselves and God's mission in the world. They were committed to citizenship in the realm where God rules, whatever that would cost or come to mean. So must it be for contemporary Christians who intend to make a difference in the world in the wonderful wake of the difference Christ has made in them.

I express my profound appreciation for having been enriched personally by the particular Christian tradition emphasized here. I have grown up and ministered in the fellowship of the Church of God (Anderson). Both my wife's family and my family have deep roots in the Free Methodist Church, where the word "free" has several significant meanings. It was my privilege to gain my formal education in various settings that were alive to this tradition, including Anderson University School of Theology, Earlham School of Religion, Asbury Theological Seminary, and Chicago Theological Seminary. It also has been my privilege to participate in a decade-long dialogue with the

---

6See, e.g., John Howard Yoder, "A People in the World," in Michael Cartwright, ed., *The Royal Priesthood: Essays Ecclesiological and Ecumenical* (Grand Rapids: Eerdmans, 1994), 65-101. For Yoder, the medium (church) cannot be separated from the message (the good news in Jesus Christ).

Christian Churches/Churches of Christ[7] and now in a publishing partnership with Evangel Press, representing the Brethren in Christ denomination. The Believers Church tradition is varied in its expressions and rich in its resources.

What I have written in these pages has benefited greatly from all of this heritage, and from the wisdom of several wise and generous individuals who represent different streams within the Believers Church tradition. Each took time to review and critique the first draft of this book. My sincere appreciation is extended to: Dr. Jeff Bach (Church of the Brethren) of Bethany Theological Seminary, Kentucky; Dr. Luke Keefer (Brethren in Christ) of Ashland Theological Seminary, Ohio; Dr. Kenneth Hall (Society of Friends and Church of God, Anderson) of Anderson University, Indiana; Dr. Clark H. Pinnock (Baptist) of McMaster Divinity College, Ontario; Dr. Howard A. Snyder (United Methodist) of Asbury Theological Seminary; and Dr. J. Denny Weaver (Mennonite) of Bluffton College, Ohio. As the Believers Church tradition would have it, these committed believers and competent scholars have joined me voluntarily, for the sake of Christ, in seeking to be obedient disciples in what we choose to remember, believe, and do with our lives in every present moment.

As the Believers Church tradition also would have it, what follows is done cooperatively, under Christ, for the sake of the church's mission, and is not thought of as the last word on the subject. Believers are to continue their journey together under the guidance of the Holy Spirit, seeking ever fuller realization of their intended maturity in Jesus Christ. May what follows contribute something toward that end.

---

[7]See the published results of this dialogue between the Christian Churches/Churches of Christ and the Church of God (Anderson) in Barry Callen and James North, *Coming Together In Christ* (Joplin, MO: College Press, 1997).

1

On the Margin
with the Master

And whatever their individual origin, in the Messiah Jesus they
sensed that they together had inherited a momentous calling.
They were to be nothing less than God's "holy nation" (1 Peter
2:9). In them God was keeping a promise which he had made
many centuries earlier through Isaiah; he was forming a new,
transnational nation that would be "a light for the nations"
(Isa. 49:6; Acts 13:47; 26:23).[1]

One of the overlooked themes of Acts is how God repeatedly
decenters the world of the Christian community, calling its
members into relationship with God at the margins of their
"safe" structures of life.[2]

The idea was hardly typical, but it turned out to be especially productive. C. Leonard Allen chose to take a fresh look at the history of
his own church tradition (Churches of Christ) by doing other than the
usual. The usual is to review the mainstream voices, the standard
historians, the more influential theologians, staying carefully within

---

[1]Alan Kreider, *Journey Towards Holiness: A Way of Living for God's Nation* (Scottdale,
Pa.: Herald Press, 1987), 178.
[2]M. Robert Mulholland, Jr., "Life at the Center—Life at the Edge," *Weavings: A
Journal of the Christian Spiritual Life* XIII:4 (July/August, 1998), 27.

1

the set boundaries of generally accepted interpretation about the past. But listening to the powerful, the history-shaping voices, may not always be the wisest way to go. Allen decided that "important insights may reside at the margins of a tradition as well as at its center, among the minority as well as the majority." He rightly judged that "it helps to hear some of the 'distant voices,' those...whose views have been remembered selectively, screened out, or simply forgotten."[3]

In a similar way, these pages are dedicated to providing fresh and serious attention to one "minority" stream within the history of the whole church over the centuries. The "radicals" of the Believers Church tradition too often are only "distant voices" rarely heard by the large majority of Christians. They are sources of Christian wisdom seldom taken seriously by the mainstream church establishments and histories. In what follows here, however, we are prepared to listen, really listen, and potentially learn lessons from a family of prophetic voices that often is screened out and even forgotten. By moving to this margin, wisdom may be found that will help shift the center in a good direction. It will also remind us that Jesus himself was on the margin most of the time. In part, being a faithful Christian is choosing to be on the margin with the Master.

God may again be choosing to "de-center" the settled life of the Christian community. When Christians become established, comfortable, welcomed by the host culture, they tend to drift into a status-quo mode that can quietly threaten the integrity of their faith. Moving to the center of things usually means adjusting to the prevailing values of the whole society and functioning in ways typical of that environment. In other words, when the church is deeply in the world, the world so easily gets deeply into the church. Such a congenial compromise happens so easily and so often. When it does, prophetic voices in the church begin calling for the faithful to start moving back toward the margin where Jesus was in his day and where the work of Jesus may be in this day. Otherwise, Christ might again come to his

---

[3]C. Leonard Allen, *Distant Voices: Discovering a Forgotten Past for a Changing Church* (Abilene, Tex.: Abilene Christian University Press, 1993), 5.

very own people and they would continue failing to recognize or receive him (John 1:11).

Primary Allegiance

Conflict and suffering are hardly very comfortable places to begin. Nonetheless, the fact is that Jesus offered a paradoxical promise to his first followers. He assured them of God's knowing love and enduring provision and protection. He also promised them conflict and suffering if they were to be faithful. His intent was to send his followers as "lambs in the midst of wolves" (Luke 10:3). They would be in the honorable tradition of the Jewish prophets who, committed to the word and way of Yahweh, collided with priests and kings alike. Joining this tumultuous tradition would not be optional, according to Jesus, but it would be a source of blessing and even rejoicing (Matt. 5:10-12). Disciples, commanded Jesus, should "deny themselves and take up their crosses and follow me" (Mark 8:34). As Alan Kreider puts it: "For them, God's provision and protection thus did not mean the assurance of a happy old age in a Hebron retirement home; it meant that God would supply everything necessary as they followed their Teacher into conflict."[4]

The fact is that Christians are first and foremost to be citizens of God's realm and rule (Philippians 3:20). To be faithful citizens of the heavenly realm will lead to conflict with ultimate demands that often are made by the "principalities and powers" of this world that tend to consider all who inhabit their realms as citizens who owe loyalty to themselves. Notice what Paul says in Colossians 1:13-18. God "has rescued us from the power of darkness and transferred us into the kingdom of his beloved Son, in whom we have redemption, the forgiveness of sins.... In him all things in heaven and on earth were created, things visible and invisible, whether thrones or dominions or rulers or powers—all things have been created through him and for him.... He is the head of the body, the church; he is the beginning, the firstborn from the dead, so that he might come to have first place in everything."

---

[4]Ibid., 169.

Consequently, the church which is faithful to her Lord is to know and be fully committed to her Lord and work with him for the redemption of the world. The principalities and powers often think and act like they are the final rulers in their own right, becoming a terrible beast as described in Revelation 13. When they do, the church knows herself to be a stranger and pilgrim on the earth.

To be God's "peculiar people" means to walk in faith, daring to be loyal to God's reign, always recalling what Jesus said when being questioned by Pilate: "You would have no power over me unless it had been given you from above" (John 19:11). To be a pilgrim people empowered "from above" is what Rodney Clapp had in mind when he pictured the church as itself a distinctive culture in today's "postmodern" society. He wants a theology "that will help me survive, and survive Christianly, the Powers That Be." Decrying "hypercommercialized" Christianity and a rationalism that sees Christianity primarily as a set of right ideas, Clapp announces that his primary allegiance is to "lived faith, or actual Christian community."[5] The Believers Church tradition is characterized well by pilgrim people, church as distinctive culture, surviving a wayward Christian establishment, avoiding rationalism in favor of lived faith, and real Christian community.

What is the intended role of the faithful church in relation to the visible kings, princes, presidents, giant corporations, highly organized church denominations, and other power structures that, in varying degrees, root in this world? Probably no clearer answer has been given than the one by the anonymous writer of the Epistle to Diognetus in the second century after Christ (an obvious commentary on the "our citizenship is in heaven" words of Philippians 3:20). In part this ancient writing reads:

> Christians cannot be distinguished from the rest of the human race by country or language or customs.... Yet, although they live

---

[5]Rodney Clapp, *A Peculiar People: The Church as Culture in a Post-Christian Society* (Downers Grove, Ill.: InterVarsity Press, 1996), 12-13.

in Greek and barbarian cities alike, as each man's lot has been cast, and follow the customs of the country in clothing and food and other matters of daily living, at the same time they give proof of the remarkable and admittedly extraordinary constitution of their own commonwealth. They live in their own countries, but only as aliens.... It is true that they are "in the flesh," but they do not live "according to the flesh." They busy themselves on earth, but their citizenship is in heaven. They obey the established laws, but in their own lives they go far beyond what the laws require.... They are reviled, and yet they bless; when they are affronted, they still pay due respect.... To put it simply: What the soul is in the body, that Christians are in the world.... The soul dwells in the body, but does not belong to the body, and Christians dwell in the world, but do not belong to the world.[6]

Christians certainly are to be on mission in the world, but without being merely more of the world. They are to be disciples of the Jesus who disrupted conventional Jewish wisdom of his time, ministered in the wilderness, sometimes had nowhere to lay his head, demonstrated how one can reign even from a cross, and made clear that his was a kingdom not *from* or *of* but *for* this world. The challenge of this call to primary allegiance still remains. Concludes Clapp:

There is a place for Christians in the postmodern world, not as typically decent human beings but as unapologetic followers of the Way. There is a place for the church in the postmodern world, not as a sponsorial prop for nation-states but as a community called by the God explicitly named Father, Son, and Holy Spirit.[7]

Accepting such a challenge is the "radical option," the Jesus way, the way of the cross. It is what it means to be truly Christian—so the Believers Church tradition has said for centuries.

---

[6] As quoted by C. Norman Kraus, "Toward a Theology for the Disciple Community," in J. R. Burkholder and Calvin Redekop, eds., *Kingdom, Cross and Community* (Scottdale, Pa.: Herald Press, 1976), 276.

[7] Clapp, op. cit., 32.

Destabilizing Movements

Only occasionally does a movement surface in Christian church history that is prepared to undergo the most severe of persecutions on behalf of what it judges to be authentic New Testament Christianity. When it does surface, it unfortunately has tended to be a marginalized phenomenon within the larger body of believers in Jesus Christ. Sometimes the restricting and even persecuting force is the prevailing social leaders who are staunchly committed to the status quo and relegate religion to an incidental role that is carefully controlled. Religion is to be no more than a conservative and stabilizing element of society, a comforting chaplain that puts the affirmation of a religious stamp on what is the official establishment view—official and often wrong. Sometimes, ironically, the limits are laid on the disciples of Jesus by other Christian believers who themselves are, or at least who are in league with, the prevailing political powers.

Within only sixty or seventy years after John's apocalyptic visions on the Isle of Patmos that became formalized as the last book of the New Testament, the first renewal movement began to stir among the early Christian communities. Later called "Montanism," it believed that God's Spirit was presently active in the church as at the beginning and that purity and discipline should thus be present as marks of the church's integrity. This destabilization was, in the words of Howard Snyder, "the first charismatic movement," "the first widespread outbreak of renewal currents and the first serious challenge to the institutionalizing tendencies in the church."[8] It is typical that the dynamic of God's Spirit, if welcomed and honored, will yield life and a lively and often awkward relationship between the community of divine life and the surrounding culture of unbelief.

God has been faithful throughout the centuries. Often the church has yielded to the temptations of the world and become only a shad-

---

[8]Howard A. Snyder, *Signs of the Spirit: How God Reshapes the Church* (Grand Rapids: Academie Books, Zondervan, 1989), 15, 18.

ow of her true self. In the midst of these accommodations with the world, God has continued to love and move and always has found those who would be faithful. There now has accumulated a long heritage of the appearances of renewal thrusts, destabilizing Christian movements that have proceeded under various names, usually designations assigned to them by their established and resisting opponents. There were, for instance, early monastic movements and the eventual evolution of various specialized church "orders" within the large orbit of the Roman Catholic Church. Sometimes the monastic motive was retreat in search of perfection. Typically the precipitating context was one of growing laxity within a church which was too much at peace with its setting, imperially patronized, culturally compromised, and increasingly dominated by a centralized hierarchy. It can be argued that over the centuries the existence of such movements and orders functioned as escape valves for church renewal needs and efforts, thus enabling the Roman Catholic Church to avoid an early and formal splintering into numerous separate entities. Viewed this way, the renewal movements "on the margin" actually served to protect the integrity and unity of the institutional church.[9]

Western proto-Protestantism has its roots at least from the Waldensians (Peter Waldo, twelfth century) who "became the first post- and anti-Constantinian[10] 'free church,' thereby beginning the line of resistance that later surfaced as what we here call 'Radical Protestantism' within the Reformations of the fifteenth and sixteenth centuries...."[11] Names like "Free Churches," "Nonconformists," "Dissenters," "Baptists," "Methodists," "Quakers," and "Disciples" have developed, each emphasizing that some believers, for whatever reasons, were believing and functioning in ways unacceptably disruptive to the reigning

---

[9]See Jane Elyse Russell's doctoral dissertation titled *Renewing the Gospel Community: Four Catholic Movements with an Anabaptist Parallel* (University of Notre Dame, 1979).

[10]This phrase relates to the Roman Emperor Constantine (c. 275-337). See chapter two for an explanation of his relationship to the "fall" of Christianity.

[11]John Howard Yoder, in Michael G. Cartwright, ed., *The Royal Priesthood* (Grand Rapids: Eerdmans, 1994), 246-247.

establishment. The phrase "Radical Reformation," for instance, was assigned to the sixteenth-century outbreak of this destabilizing type of movement by one analyzing scholar, the German sociologist of religion Max Weber (1864-1920). He sought to isolate and describe one stream of early Protestants who chose at great cost to distance themselves from state-sponsored church establishments in Europe. Soon also known as "Anabaptists,"[12] these sincere European Christians of a few centuries ago had a keen sense of separation from what they judged the "fallen" church, both in its Roman Catholic and even its newer Protestant forms (even the "protesters" were thought to have failed to protest enough). Indeed, some scholars argue that these disrupting visionaries represent a "third type" of Christianity, a type quite relevant to the "post-Christian" era into which the West appears to have entered in the last decade of the twentieth century. In 1962, for instance, George Williams of Harvard University presented what then was a new picture of sixteenth-century church history by speaking of the "Radical Reformation," rather than the "Left Wing of the Reformation" as Roland Bainton had been doing earlier.[13]

These "radicals" were diverse in several ways, to be sure, but at least those who have comprised this tradition have had something "free-church" in common. The liberating instinct has centered in a determination to maintain strong and biblically-based Christian beliefs and lifestyles that are lived apart from the suffocating control of humanly-dominated civil and church governments. The point has hardly been independence for its own sake; rather, it has been believed

---

[12]This derisive term means baptizing again or re-baptizing, an unacceptable and even seditious act as judged by both political and church establishments at the time. While such reform-minded Christians insisted that only the baptism of believers was valid (thus not recognizing as "baptism" an involuntary act done to an infant and thus not seeing themselves as rebaptizing anyone), the name was laid on them by opponents, both civil and church. Probably the term "Mennonite" (after Menno Simons) eventually replaced "Anabaptist" among some of the "radicals," at least in America, because in the larger society it lacked the negative theological and political connotations. See chapter three for discussion of the life and ministry of Menno Simons.

[13]George H. Williams, *The Radical Reformation* (Philadelphia: Westminster Press, 1962).

that there is a normative biblical model of how the church should be. It should be formed around the belief that Jesus Christ alone is Lord of the church.[14] Such "Anabaptists" or "radicals" of any time are attracted to biblical metaphors like "pilgrim," "sojourner," even "alien" to designate the earthly people of God.[15] Why? It is because they believe that true disciples of Jesus are, first and foremost, to be loyal to God's rule, not to the values, goods, and kingdoms of this world. The central calling of Christians is to live together as obvious first-fruits of the Spirit's regenerating ministry, the early inbreaking of the ultimate rule of God that one day will be all in all. When Jesus insisted on identifying himself with a kingdom that is not of this world (e.g., John 18:36), he was misunderstood, persecuted by many of the religious establishment, and finally murdered by the civil authority. Truly loyal disciples of Jesus risk the same in any age.[16]

In recent centuries, this risking and often persecuted tradition has been pioneered primarily by the Anabaptist-Mennonites in the sixteenth century, the Baptists and Quakers of England in the seventeenth century, and the Brethren of Germany in the eighteenth century.[17] Among today's denominational families recognizing themselves as largely within the general Free or Believers Church tradition are the various Baptist and Brethren bodies, the American Campbellite tradition of the Disciples, Christian Churches, and Churches of Christ, the Church of God (Anderson) and other Wesleyan/Holiness bodies, the Society of Friends, Mennonites, Pentecostals, and oth-

---

[14]See, e.g., Barry Callen, *It's God's Church! The Life and Legacy of Daniel Sidney Warner* (Anderson, Ind.: Warner Press, 1995).

[15]For a widely-circulated contemporary statement, compare Stanley Hauerwas and William Willimon, *Resident Aliens: Life in the Christian Colony* (Nashville: Abingdon Press, 1989).

[16]The God known in the Bible is a God prepared to take real risks in relation to a fragile and now fallen humanity because of the depths of divine love and faithfulness. See John Sanders, *The God Who Risks: A Theology of Providence* (Downers Grove, Ill.: InterVarsity Press, 1998).

[17]Earlier dissenting movements carrying in differing settings similarities to the general Believers Church tradition were the Montanists (second century), Waldensians (thirteenth century), and Lollards (fifteenth century).

ers.[18] Weber intended his term "radical" to refer to those Christians who sought "a community of personal believers of the reborn and only those."[19] A designation of this kind comprises all Christians committed to voluntary church membership,[20] choosing to belong to the community of Christ's disciples, the true church, by a conscious faith decision and life change. The primary question is: To what realm does one grant primary allegiance in all of life? This is a vital and enduring question, one that Christians of all times and cultures must face and somehow answer.

A New Beginning

Recent decades have witnessed a remarkable shift in church historiography. Previously the radical reformers of the sixteenth century were known primarily through the writings and interpretations of their persecutors—the way most history comes to be written and then believed (those in control interpret the circumstance from their privileged position and usually for their own purposes). Comments Michael Novak:

> Who were the Anabaptists? They were the "full-way" reformers, the radical reformers. Their characters, their intentions, and their doctrines have long been misunderstood. They aroused the fears, hatred, and wrath of [Martin] Luther and [John] Calvin. Catholic authorities joined the classical reformers in putting them to death: by the sword, by fire, by torture with heated tongs, and—in parody of their own belief in adult baptism—by

---

[18]While the Mennonites are direct heirs of sixteenth-century Anabaptism, for many others the connection to Anabaptism is less direct historically and more direct in terms of commonality of certain Christian perspectives and practices. For example, Baptists seem most closely related to seventeenth-century English Separatists in terms of direct historical continuity; but Baptists clearly are at least indirect heirs of the sixteenth-century "Radical Reformation."

[19]Max Weber, *The Protestant Ethic and the Spirit of Capitalism*, trans. T. Parsons (N. Y.: Charles Scribner's Sons, 1958, originally 1930), 122, 144.

[20]See William Brackney, ed., *The Believers Church: A Voluntary Church* (Kitchener, Ontario: Pandora Press, and Scottdale, Pa.: Herald Press, 1998).

drowning. Hunted and imprisoned in life, they were blackened also in death by historians among their enemies.[21]

Then came scholars like Harold Bender, Roland Bainton, Franklin Littell, and George Williams who went back to original sources and evolved a more diverse and appreciative view of the sixteenth-century radicals. The beginning of a new era in the study of Anabaptism may be dated to December 1943, when Harold Bender[22] presented the presidential address to the American Society of Church History. Titled "The Anabaptist Vision,"[23] the address vigorously countered the then standard view that such sixteenth-century reformers were violent radicals worthy of being generally discounted. Bender called for a redefinition that would understand them primarily as peaceful Protestants worthy of contemporary admiration because they took it upon themselves to complete the Reformation begun but left unfinished by Martin Luther in Germany and Ulrich Zwingli in Switzerland.

Maybe many of the old stereotypes and diatribes were not universally applicable after all. In fact, in addition to instances of excess that certainly did arise among some Anabaptists in the midst of their enthusiasm and under the pressure of their frequent persecution, there was among the radicals an admirable biblical vision of Christian faith and life that still is very worthy of careful inspection and possible imitation by any believer who cares about truly prophetic, biblical, missionary Christianity. We seek in these pages to recover, explore, and commend the contemporary implications of this vision. Such has become increasingly possible because of research and other developments since the middle of the twentieth century.

---

[21]Michael Novak, "The Conception of the Church in Anabaptism and in Roman Catholicism: Past and Present," *Journal of Ecumenical Studies* (Fall 1965), 428. Novak notes that "socialists and marxists claim it [Anabaptist vision] as an early version of their revolution" (429).

[22]Harold Bender (1897-1962) was a leading worldwide Mennonite spirit of his time. From 1924 to 1962 he was at Goshen College (Indiana) teaching church history, Bible, and sociology. He also was dean of Goshen College (1931-1944) and of Goshen College Biblical Seminary (1944-1962). In 1927 he founded the influential journal, the *Mennonite Quarterly Review*. See the substantial biography by Albert Keim, *Harold S. Bender 1897-1962* (Scottdale, Pa.: Herald Press, 1998).

[23]Later published in *Church History* 13 (March 1944), 3-24.

The 1950s in North America was a post-war decade of economic growth accompanied by significant church growth. The general religious atmosphere of the nation tended to be a mixture of blandness and uniformity. There were sometimes ominous political overtones to the standard but rather stale Christian establishment. The FBI director in the United States was J. Edgar Hoover, who once urged this: "Since Communists are anti-God, encourage your child to be active in the church." Sunday Schools were full, although men were less inclined to get involved. American GIs, now the heads of growing households, often equated religion with mere church-going and a "true believer" with fanaticism. Reinhold Niebuhr, preacher-professor at New York's Union Theological Seminary, lashed out at the "undue complacency and conformity" that he saw as a stance woefully inadequate to address the ills of modern society.[24] Will Herberg complained about the secularization and homogenization of religion in his book titled *Protestant-Catholic-Jew* (1955). These three major faith families, he argued, had for most practical purposes become functionally equivalent in social life. Americans appeared to be moving away from sharp religious distinctions to a common ground for national identity, one that, according to Herberg, encouraged a deeper commitment to an American way of life based more on materialism and consumerism than on a vital religious faith.

The National Council of Churches was formed in 1950. Its concern for Christian unity was judged by many as furthering the decline of denominational loyalties and thus further weakening religious commitments. Its intent, however, was to weaken the scandal of rampant division among Christians and strengthen a united Christian witness. Many Christians questioned this "ecumenical" impulse, fearing that it was really trying to build one "super church" that would force a uniformity on all believers, undermining the sovereign role of God in the

---

[24]One of Niebuhr's classic books is *Moral Man and Immoral Society* (N.Y.: Charles Scribner's Sons, 1932). He argues the thesis that a crucial distinction must be drawn between the moral and social behavior of individuals and of social groups—national, racial, and economic. This necessary distinction is said to justify and in fact necessitate political policies which a purely individualistic ethic must always find embarrassing.

face of all human structures, churchly or otherwise. The 1950s, then, was more a priestly than a prophetic time, with people having their felt needs met by the caretakers of a tradition (priests) more than their questionable values challenged by insightful and courageous voices (prophets).[25] At the end of the decade the movie *Elmer Gantry* played to packed theaters, dramatizing a hypocritical, silver-tongued, skirt-chasing, boozing evangelist who, unfortunately, became almost as well known to the public as the real and highly respected evangelist Billy Graham. The society at large was oriented to public order, family stability, conformity, institution building, and a belief in progress. Nonetheless, throughout this national "high," America "lacked any adult generation focused on inner spiritualism."[26] Such a time is both comfortable for a well-acculturated faith and dangerous for a marginalized minority of believers who are prepared to focus on the demands of citizenship under God's rule and abandon the routines of a compromised establishment faith.

Beginning in 1955, there emerged a new term to help focus the heart of the church's radical nature and role in such a time. The focus was the same one found at other times in church history, especially in times of general apostasy when prophetic voices and actions arose from a quickly marginalized minority of protesting believers. How should committed Christians respond in a time of tolerance and "ease in Zion," a time of religious accommodation with the establishment—whether of state or church? A new phrase, the "Believers Church," was coined to refer to the ongoing tradition of those who resist the broad and bland way of being Christian in this world. Since 1955 this phrase has become widely used as a more precise designation than "Free Church" for at least two reasons. In the United States and some other modern nations, all religious bodies technically are "free churches" in the sense that church and state are separated legal-

---

[25]For a more extensive treatment of the 1950s in the United States, see Barry L. Callen, *Seeking the Light: America's Modern Quest for Peace, Justice, Prosperity, and Faith* (Nappanee, Ind.: Evangel Publishing House, 1998), chapter three.

[26]William Strauss and Neil Howe, *The Fourth Turning: An American Prophecy* (N.Y.: Broadway Books, 1997), 169.

ly in contrast to the state-church tradition in Europe. Additionally, some groups like the Unitarians tend to be pleased with a free-church designation for themselves since it can convey the idea to some people of considerable flexibility (freedom), allowing room for all manner of heterodox theology that is quite out of touch with biblical teaching.

After World War II, the tradition now increasingly being called the Believers Church saw some of its scholars enter the academic fields of Bible, theology, and church history as full-fledged participants in schools of the dominant ("mainstream") church culture. Discovering there that the tradition they represented faced heavy bias, even hints of heresy charges, they sought to re-read church history from the perspective of their own tradition and to develop an apologetic that would more fairly represent the origins and essence of their tradition. A prominent example within Mennonite historiography was Harold S. Bender's classic work, *The Anabaptist Vision*.[27] Part of this effort at a more favorable and fair historical recovery was focused in a new series of Believers Church conferences that still continue. An early example came in the 1950s.

A well-organized study conference on the Believers Church tradition was convened at the Mennonite Biblical Seminary in Chicago in August, 1955. Its intent was to contribute to the well-being of the General Conference Mennonite Church. This body was seeking crucial clarity on many practical issues of contemporary church life, but only within "the larger discussion of basic beliefs concerning the church." Recognized as basic was the contrast between the Believers Church and the "church type" of territorial ecclesiastical institutions "whose membership is more clearly co-extensive with society covering either a given geographic area...or a given cultural group." Central on the conference agenda was the enhancement of contemporary Christian discipleship, including "the radical commitment to a life

---

[27]Harold Bender, *The Anabaptist Vision* (Scottdale, Pa.: Herald Press, 1944). Later studies would argue that Anabaptist origins were somewhat more complex than Bender first suggested.

of love and nonresistance." There arose for this conference one persistent question: "What kind of a church must we have to produce this type of Christian?"[28] This question soon was being asked by more Christians than those associated with this one Mennonite body. Its broadened addressing is to be seen in part by a series of multi-denominational gatherings in subsequent years that would explore various dimensions of the Believers Church tradition, especially as it offers important insights for living as authentic Christians in today's kind of world. See Appendix A for a historical listing of these conferences.[29]

The series of recent Believers Church conferences began modestly with two discussions. The first was initiated by Johannes A. Oosterbaan, a Dutch professor of theology at the Amsterdam Mennonite Theological Seminary. He had become active in the ecumenical work of the World Council of Churches, attending the 1961 Third Assembly in New Delhi, India. Increasingly he was convinced that the several contemporary inheritors of the "Radical Reformation" had an important contribution to make to world Christianity in the late twentieth century, but first they needed a fresh awareness of and appreciation for their common heritage. They also needed some way of uniting their concerns and entering into the ecumenical dialogue with strength, as the churches descended from the magisterial Reformation (classical Protestantism) already were doing. Following his attendance at the 1963 meeting of the Faith and Order Commission of the WCC in Montreal, Oosterbaan held conversations with various colleagues in Canada and the United States and gathered support for his concern and vision. It was a modest but real beginning.

The second scene of early conversations occurred at a peace-testimony session hosted in 1964 by Wilmer A. Cooper at Earlham College, a Quaker institution in Richmond, Indiana. Two questions emerged there: "What about a pattern of conferences focused on the

---

[28]Elmer Ediger, "Statement of Our Task in This Study Conference," in *Study Conference on the Believers' Church* (Newton, Kan.: The Mennonite Press, 1955), 5-7.

[29]See John Howard Yoder, "The Believers' Church Conferences in Historical Perspective," *Mennonite Quarterly Review* (January 1991), 5-19.

Free Church?" and "Should they include only 'Peace Church' scholars?" After all, several bodies in the Believers Church tradition were historically pacifist in commitment and a few were not. The first question was answered with a "Yes" and the second with a "No." A key conversation partner from the beginning, for instance, was Franklin Littell, the prominent Methodist author of *The Anabaptist View of the Church* (1952, 1958, 1964) and *The Free Church* (1957).

It was time for more concrete action. It would come through the suggestion of John Howard Yoder, a young Mennonite theologian, that Professor Oosterbaan's concern and vision be picked up and initially carried forward by a prominent Baptist seminary in the United States. James Leo Garrett took the next initiative by calling the first formal Believers Church Conference, which convened at Southern Baptist Theological Seminary, Louisville, Kentucky, in 1967. Two planning sessions in 1966 developed a prospectus for the coming 1967 Conference, including this hypothesis to be tested by the participants:

> ...there exists in the heritage of those Christian groups which have insisted upon the baptism of believers, on confession of faith, into visible congregations, an apprehension of the nature of the gospel and of the church which is specific and coherent; which constitutes a theologically valid option and a needed contribution in ecumenical debate.

In other words, whatever the historical, cultural, and other differences, is there such a thing as a distinctive, coherent, and significant Believers Church tradition? And if there is, is this tradition still important?

The 1967 Conference at Southern Baptist Theological Seminary involved some 150 representatives from a range of Believers Church bodies, as well as observers from the National Council of Churches of Christ in the USA, the World Council of Churches, and the Roman Catholic Bishops' Commission for Ecumenical Affairs. This is the *Resolution of Consensus and Commitment* that emerged from this first major conference on the concept of the Believers Church.

> Being assembled in conference on the concept of the Believers'
> Church and understanding ourselves as heirs of various Free
> Church traditions, we profess to have discovered in history and
> in our present fellowship a common scripturally based heritage,
> which is relevant for contemporary life and which is developing
> in churches of other traditions.
>
> By study and comparison we have noted that this heritage
> includes the following acknowledgments: the Lordship of Christ,
> the authority of the Word, church membership regenerated by
> the Spirit, the covenant of believers, a need for a perpetual resti-
> tution of the church, the necessity for separation from the world
> and proclamation and service to the world, and a special con-
> ception of Christian unity.
>
> We, therefore, commit ourselves this day to study together our
> common heritage, to remember one another in prayer, to pro-
> mote a wider awareness of our common stance, and to seek to
> multiply contacts with one another in days to come.

This Believers Church tradition may have had a long, sturdy, and
sometimes dramatic history, much of it predating the twentieth century, but the 1950s and especially the 1967 conference was a new
beginning in many ways. The tradition's history was being widely
noticed and appreciated again and the obvious question was at least
beginning to be addressed: What from the honored past of this tradition should and can endure for a needed future? The momentum
started by the successful and well-publicized Louisville meeting in
1967, including the resulting book *The Concept of the Believers' Church*
edited by James Leo Garrett, Jr., was carried on by a Committee on
Continuing Conversations coordinated by Donald F. Durnbaugh and
John Howard Yoder. Now, more than three decades later, this study-
ing, remembering, promoting, and seeking still continues in Canada
and the United States. A series of major Believers Church study conferences have been sponsored, mainly by educational institutions
representing church bodies ranging from Southern and Canadian
Baptists to the Church of the Brethren, Mennonites, Churches of
Christ, Church of God (Anderson), and the United Church of

Christ.[30] A complete record of these conferences is found in Appendix A, including the location, date, theme, and subsequent publication emerging from each.

Center of a Living Heritage

What is at the center of the Believers Church heritage that has continuing relevance for contemporary Christian life? While the remainder of this volume seeks the best answer to this question, a beginning overview can be previewed here. According to the fresh retrieval of understanding in the 1950s and 1960s, whatever the center of this heritage is, it at least will focus on the lordship of Jesus Christ and be based on the authority of the Word of God. It will be a living faith in the Spirit of Christ who establishes membership in the Body of Christ through the regeneration of sinners. These new creations in Christ then become committed disciples who choose voluntary covenant with each other, thus forming communities of the Spirit.[31] Such communities will seek to stand apart from the world in order to nurture their distinctive Christ-identity, which in turn enables them to be sent savingly by the Spirit into the world. Whatever the diversity among these Spirit communities, they will foster a special conception of Christian unity—a unity realized by life in the Spirit rather than by any formal and forced uniformity of creed or structure.

In the setting of the sixteenth century in Europe, free-church leaders often were persecuted, sometimes because their view on believers'

---

[30]Mennonites have found the concept of the Believers Church tradition helpful in providing self-understanding. They have used it as an organizing principle for courses or whole curricula in schools like the Associated Mennonite Biblical Seminaries, Goshen College, Eastern Mennonite College, and Bluffton College. They have used it as the theological basis for Christian education materials ("Foundations Series" and "Jubilee: God's Good News") and for a series of Bible commentaries. This *Believers' Church Bible Commentary* is published by Herald Press in Scottdale, Pennsylvania, and says it represents a specific set of theological understandings "such as believers baptism, commitment to the Rule of Christ in Matthew 18:15-18 as part of the meaning of church membership, belief in the power of love in all relationships, and a willingness to follow the way of the cross of Christ."

[31]See C. Norman Kraus, *The Community of the Spirit: How the Church Is in the World* (Scottdale, Pa.: Herald Press, rev. ed., 1993).

baptism was considered seditious. Such a radical view implied voluntary church membership, religious freedom, and separation of church and state—an intolerable radicalism in the midst of strict church-state establishments. Franklin Littell once judged that the heritage's center is the vision of the true church as "a voluntary association of convinced believers."[32] Nadine Pence Frantz says this about the heart of the radical heritage: "Suspicious of creeds and doctrines which were used as tests of faith against them, the emphasis in the tradition has been on an active, living faith, one that is demonstrated by the lifestyle of the believers rather than by their doctrine."[33] According to C. Arnold Snyder:

> …the heart and soul of the Anabaptist movement is found in its *soteriology*; and central to that soteriology is the integral linking of the inner and outer lives of believers…. Human beings must yield to the inner working of the Spirit of God (*Gelassenheit*), they must assent to this grace (exercise human free will) and, thanks to the regeneration by the Holy Spirit, they will live lives of visible obedience and discipleship.[34]

At the opening of the twenty-first century, we dare to accept by faith Franklin Littell's judgment that "the flowering years of the Free Church tradition lie before us" and that, essential to such flowering, there is the clear need to "work out both the definition and the terms of our obedience."[35] This present volume hopes to be one modest tool

---

[32]Franklin Littell, *The Free Church* (Boston: Starr King Press, 1957), 2.

[33]Nadine Pence Frantz, "Theological Hermeneutics: Christian Feminist Biblical Interpretation and the Believers' Church Tradition" (doctoral dissertation, Divinity School, University of Chicago, 1992), 144.

[34]C. Arnold Snyder, *Anabaptist History and Theology* (Kitchener, Ont.: Pandora Press, 1995), 384. While affirming this emphasis of Snyder, J. Denny Weaver critiques Snyder's general approach of defining Anabaptism by what its early constituents presumably held in common in the sixteenth century. Since they did not agree on the relation of the sword to the faith, for instance, Snyder moves this topic to the periphery of Anabaptist theology—something that Weaver sees as a modern synthesis being read back historically in an inappropriate way that damages today's "peace" churches (Weaver, "Reading Sixteenth-Century Anabaptism Theologically," *The Conrad Grebel Review* 16:1, Winter 1998, 37-51).

[35]Franklin Littell, "The Historical Free Church Defined," *Brethren Life and Thought* IX (1964), 4:78.

that assists in the process of that working out. Chapters two through five explore the essential building blocks of "definition." Chapter six then focuses on the dialogue that now is seeking to establish "the terms of our obedience"—the attitudes and actions called for if the Believers Church tradition is to persist as a distinctive and significant witness within the larger Christian community and to the unbelieving world of the twenty-first century.

Now is an especially good time to recall this Free Church or Believers Church heritage and thereby nurture a fuller integrity of Christ's church in today's world. While secularism and religious pluralism are very real characteristics of modern society, and certainly can be dismaying, "the loss of Christendom gives us a joyous opportunity to reclaim the freedom to proclaim the gospel in a way in which we cannot when the main social task of the church is to serve as one among many helpful props for the state."[36] In other words, when Christianity no longer carries the role of the "official" faith of the culture, it is freed from the temptations that come with the power of controlling establishments, freed to be herself, Christ's prophetic body and witness in the world. Should Christians choose to accept this challenge and opportunity, then it appears that the timing is right for a serious reconsideration of the Believers Church tradition. The judgment of Donald Durnbaugh in 1968 is still and even increasingly true:

> In a time in which are heard calls for a theology of revolution, for a church stripped for action in the world, for a ministry *by* the laity, *for* the laity, and *of* the laity, the major concerns of the

[36]Stanley Hauerwas, William Willimon, *Resident Aliens: Life in the Christian Colony* (Nashville: Abingdon Press, 1989), 39. This loss of "Christendom" refers back to Emperor Constantine's Edict of Milan in 313 when the young Christian faith was itself "baptized" in the Roman Empire, became part of the political establishment, and in the eyes of many interpreters thus began to "fall" from its distinctive countercultural self. Modern secularization of what had been Western societies that previously had been dominated by the Christian faith tradition is seen as the end of the Christian establishment. Comment Hauerwas and Willimon: "The demise of the Constantinian world view, the gradual decline of the notion that the church needs some sort of surrounding 'Christian' culture to prop it up and mold its young, is not a death to lament. It is an opportunity to celebrate.... We American Christians are at last free to be faithful in a way that makes being a Christian today an exciting adventure" (18).

Free Church, first initiated by the Anabaptists of the sixteenth century and mediated through left-wing Puritanism, speak clearly to the needs of our day.[37]

Our "modern" world has not shed its inclination to totalitarianisms, both political and religious. Christians in many countries now face either active persecution, because of their lack of conformity to accepted public norms, or they face aggressive acculturation by a dominant secular culture that tends to apply successfully its pervasive principles of pluralism and tolerance to virtually any value or belief system (except one that persists in claiming exclusive truth in the face of all alternatives and dares to live out in a credible way the implications of such a claim). Remembering Menno Simons (1496-1561) is one good way to bring focus and courage back into the community of today's Christian faith. For two decades Menno moved secretly among the Dutch Anabaptist congregations of the sixteenth century. The Empire of that time had a heavy bounty on his head. Many of his humble ministerial colleagues died in baptisms of blood, the price then of practicing a life of faith characterized by volunteerism and liberty of conscience. His conviction put him at the margins of the reigning establishments, but at the center of the Master's will and way in the world. His faith insisted that his real citizenship ultimately lay in the realm of Jesus Christ and under the rule of Christ's Spirit. The need for such perspective and commitment persists to this hour.

Menno and numerous other Anabaptists were not social anarchists, only loyal citizens of God's realm—which in important ways was found to be in conflict with the prevailing political and church arrangements of the time and place. They were biblical radicals who, among other things, were even accused of dissolving the Christian ministry itself since they often condemned the attitudes and actions of those who held high office in Christendom as priests, theologians, and canon-lawyers ("Roman doctors"). The concern was that many

---

[37]Donald Durnbaugh, "Theories of Free Church Origins," *Mennonite Quarterly Review* (April, 1968), 95.

church leaders preached "for hire" and held more tightly to their commissions from town council or prince than they held to the call of God and the needs of common believers. They did as they were paid, not as they were compelled by the Spirit and love of God. But there were and always are believers who will listen to the voice of God's Spirit and risk whatever is necessary to obey what is heard.

In a more recent context, for example, one finds the same set of Believers Church concerns vigorously expressed. Daniel Warner (1842-1895) walked out of what he judged unacceptably closed denominational settings, leading to the Carson City (Michigan) Resolutions. One "Resolved" said in part that we "adhere to no body or organization but the church of God, bought by the blood of Christ, organized by the Holy Spirit, and governed by the Bible." Another "Resolved" insisted that "we ignore and abandon the practice of preacher's license as without precept or example in the Word of God, and that we wish to be 'known by our fruits' instead of by papers."[38] For such radical and risking Christians of any century, the fruit of Spirit-life necessarily involves a Spirit-community, which itself is to be a Spirit-witness to the world by virtue of its very existence and faithfulness. Writes John Howard Yoder:

> The political novelty that God brings into the world is a community of those who serve instead of ruling, who suffer instead of inflicting suffering, whose fellowship crosses social lines instead of reinforcing them. This new Christian community in which the walls are broken down not by human idealism or democratic legalism but by the work of Christ is not only a vehicle of the gospel or only a fruit of the gospel; it is the good news. It is not merely the agent of mission or the constituency of a mission agency. This is the mission.[39]

---

[38]This walkout and related events in October 1881 led to the formation of the Church of God (Anderson) movement. The Carson City Resolutions are found in Barry L. Callen, ed., *A Time To Remember: Teachings* (Anderson, Ind.: Warner Press, 1978). A description of the concerns and developments surrounding these Resolutions is found in Barry L. Callen, *It's God's Church!: The Life and Legacy of Daniel Sidney Warner* (Anderson, Ind.: Warner Press, 1995), chapter six.

[39]John Howard Yoder, "A People in the World," in Michael Cartwright, *The Royal Priesthood: Essays Ecclesiological and Ecumenical* (Grand Rapids: Eerdmans, 1994), 91.

In other words, true Christian community is faithful life together on the margin with the Master. Within the borders of such a Jesus community, the Spirit of God is free to renew, gift, break down destructive social barriers, transcend burdensome structures, and thus create a Spirit-community that is a credible witness by its very presence in the world, and especially by the lived reality of its distinctive Spirit life. The true origin of authentic church renewal is beginning again with life in the Spirit.

2

Starting with the Spirit

If any would come after me, let them deny themselves, take up their crosses, and follow me (Jesus, Luke 9:23). When the day of Pentecost had come, they were all together in one place. And suddenly from heaven.... (Acts 2:1).

The gospel proclaims a present reality. That is of the essence. The gospel announces something which both happened in the past and is happening in the present.... What happened at Pentecost provided the connecting link between past and present. The continuity between the historical presence of Jesus and our present salvation was disclosed in the living presence of the Spirit of Christ.[1]

At the beginning of the twenty-first century, we Christians have come full circle in some ways. It was in the sixteenth century that "radical" Christians protested against ecclesiastical deadness and a replacing of the life of the Spirit with the excessive and intolerable burden of human traditions and controls on civic and church life. With the opening of the twentieth century there came the beginnings of a "pentecostal" movement that now has placed a major mark on world

---

[1]C. Norman Kraus, *The Community of the Spirit* (Scottdale, Pa.: Herald Press, 2nd ed., 1993), 12-13.

Christianity. On January 23, 1959, Pope John XXIII, announcing plans for the Second Vatican Council of the Roman Catholic Church, prayed that the windows of that church be opened to God's breath in the hope that the Divine would sweep away deadness and unleash refreshing renewal in the Christian community. The common prayer seems to be: Welcome, Holy Spirit. Come anew and bring your own life that will set us free to be all that God intends.

Jesus made it very clear a long time ago. His disciples were to wait before they were to work for him in the world. The work to be done would put them on the world's margins; thus the only effective way to accomplish the task was to be instruments shaped and directed by the Spirit of the Christ. Jesus could live on the edge because he was firmly centered in the love and purpose of God for a lost and resistant creation. Paul came to know that, although faithful followers of Jesus risk being viewed as the rubbish of the world (1 Cor. 4:13), they nonetheless can do all things that God intends when they are divinely strengthened (Phil. 4:11-13). The required strengthening, inspiring, and gifting of willing disciples is the work of the Spirit, the work for which we are to wait.

One might say that the Believers Church tradition is a Spirit-centered and ongoing reformation stream in the life of the larger church. It seeks to reform (re-form) what has lost its proper shape. It insists on waiting for the Spirit and then serving through the insight and energy of the Spirit. Usually, then, the attempt at reformation begins with a fresh focus on the Spirit of God. Jesus' disciples, once aware of his resurrection, knew that it was really just the beginning of the work of God. However rich their Jewish heritage and however dramatic the saving events of God in the life, teachings, death, and resurrection of Jesus, God also was propelling believers into the future. They were learning that "to be a Christian was [is] to be a risk-taker. Every day they could expect that God's Spirit would do creative things in making Jesus' presence real."[2] To live in Christ is to live by God's loving grace, through the ever-present Spirit of God, as an extension

---

[2]Alan Kreider, *Journey Towards Holiness: A Way of Living for God's Nation* (Scottdale, Pa.: Herald Press, 1987), 204.

of the emerging post-resurrection life of Jesus. To do so together as the body of Christ is to be the church, the on-mission community of the Spirit of the Christ. To really begin on this divine journey is necessarily to begin with the Spirit.

A Springtime Tradition

The Anabaptists of the sixteenth century have been best known, at least to Roman Catholics in America, through the caricature provided by Ronald Knox in his book *Enthusiasm*.[3] The portrait found there is one of an eccentric people who immaturely allowed themselves to be swept up in a wild current of mere emotion—a waiting on the Spirit somehow gone wrong. At least prior to the Second Vatican Council in the 1960s, Catholics "were often inwardly constrained from learning from the Anabaptists...first by prejudice, next by ignorance, and third by condescension."[4] The time for such prejudice, ignorance, and condescension, however, is now long past; this is the time to re-examine "enthusiasm" for its many contributions to the church and not primarily for its occasional pitfalls. Without question the Anabaptists in general, following the basic Protestant critique of medieval Roman Catholicism, were agreed that neither priests nor the "sacraments" administered by them were capable of conveying God's grace or of initiating the Christian life. This was the work of the Spirit alone.

To be oriented to the presence and work of the Spirit is not necessarily to be mired in subjectivism or committed to anarchy in church life, although these are criticisms often heard. Spirit orientation is the conscious determination of Christian believers to be free of artificial and forced structures of belief and church life and, conversely, to be committed to the present spiritual reality, serious discipleship, and credible covenant community which God surely intends. The Colossian believers were instructed not to "let anyone condemn you in mat-

---

[3]Ronald Knox, *Enthusiasm* (Oxford University Press, 1950).
[4]Michael Novak, "The Conception of the Church in Anabaptism and in Roman Catholicism: Past and Present," *Journal of Ecumenical Studies* (Fall 1965), 427.

ters of food and drink or of observing festivals, new moons, or sabbaths. These are only a shadow of what is to come, but the substance belongs to Christ" (Col. 2:16-17). Particularly the Quaker element of the Believers Church tradition so focuses on the inner reality of Christ that, in the spirit of this Colossians passage, it relegates outward structural and liturgical forms, including baptism and the Lord's Supper, to a secondary status—or to no status at all. This opting for reality in place of signs and symbols is one instinct of the Believers Church tradition, although many in the tradition would not go as far as the Quakers by eliminating classic Christian worship practices.

It is understandable that Anabaptists or Spirit-oriented reformers in general are often critiqued as immature, emotional "enthusiasts,"[5] institutionally unrealistic, and even eccentric. Such a pattern of critique reflects a perception rooted in part in the late 1100s when a Roman abbot, Joachim of Fiore, had a vision that led him to a dramatic and influential conclusion. He concluded that human history was unfolding according to a trinitarian scheme of three successive ages, the ages of the Father, then the Son, and finally the Holy Spirit. In the final age God would remove all impediments to perceiving God's will and God would reveal himself directly. By the sixteenth century, the "Radical Reformation" tended to the view that believers were living in the endtime, the third age, and that the most important feature of their time was a renewed outpouring of the Holy Spirit.[6] This naturally encouraged vigorous objections to, and even disdain for, the large body of church tradition and its heavy network of controlling institutions and priestly agents.

The early Anabaptists believed themselves to be a movement

---

[5]The charge of being an "enthusiast" was leveled at John Wesley, for instance, despite his commitment in many respects to "high-church" Anglicanism.

[6]It should not be assumed that the Believers Church tradition is heavily dominated by speculative eschatology to the near exclusion of focus on the historic teachings of Jesus and the call to present discipleship. To the contrary, historic roots of the faith and present relevance of the reign of God's Spirit are prominent features of this tradition. See, e.g., Barry Callen, *Faithful in the Meantime* (Nappanee, Ind.: Evangel Publishing House, 1997) and Walter Klaassen, *Armageddon and the Peaceable Kingdom* (Scottdale, Pa.: Herald Press, 1999).

inspired freshly by the Spirit of God. In fact, it may not be too much to say that "pneumatology" was the *sine qua non* of the early Anabaptist movement. This emphasis on the active working of the Spirit meant that the movement's strong emphasis on the central authority of the Bible was mediated by the accompanying expectation that the Spirit would illuminate and provide the proper understanding. Thus, "although the Anabaptists accepted the 'scripture principle' as a point of departure, it would be more accurate to say that, in their view, divine authority needed to be based on '*Scripture and Spirit together,*' rather than the 'Scripture alone' of Luther."[7] The ever-present work of the Spirit was assumed to be basic for proper biblical interpretation and the conversion and rebirth that lead to baptism and the life of discipleship. This Spirit focus soon changed, however. Note the explanation of C. Arnold Snyder:

> But it is no mystery why the pneumatic/spiritualism side of Anabaptism fell out of favour within the movement: the spectacular failures of specific prophecies and apocalyptic projects certainly led to sober second thoughts; and, the more individualistic and spiritualistically oriented Anabaptists lost the battle to convince others to make their Anabaptism a predominantly interior one, and withdrew (or were expelled) from the movement. As the sixteenth century progressed, the general tendency in the surviving movement—the part of the movement that passed on the Believers' Church tradition—was thus to limit or even suppress pneumatic expression: letter took priority over spirit; conformity to outer ecclesial rules of behaviour took priority over experiences of inner regeneration; visible lines of demarcation separating church from world were defined with increasing precision.[8]

---

[7]C. Arnold Snyder, *Anabaptist History and Theology: An Introduction* (Kitchener, Ontario: Pandora Press, 1995), 88.

[8]Ibid., 379-380. After the sixteenth century, various streams of the Believers Church tradition sought to reintroduce the Spirit focus by conscious involvement in another reforming movement that has come to be called Pietism. This was true of the Brethren in Christ, for instance (see Luke Keefer in the *Wesleyan Theological Journal*, Fall 1998), and the Church of the Brethren (see Dale W. Brown, *Understanding Pietism*, rev. ed. 1996, Evangel Publishing House).

Central to the Believers Church tradition, which includes and extends well beyond the Anabaptists, is the issue of proper allegiance. There is to be no question that a committed Christian is, above all else, one yielded to the reign of God. Christian life is life in a community that is in covenant with Christ and fellow believers. This citizenship in the divine realm, with its corporate church focus, derives from a voluntary act of the individual who freely chooses to receive the grace of Christ and thus the life of a disciplined discipleship in the community of believers. The beginning point of Christian life is the Spirit of God coming, convicting, redeeming, commissioning, gifting, and comforting. The Spirit always remains, working through the community on behalf of the community and its mission in the world. Summarizes Clark Pinnock: "Being a Christian is knowing Father and Son and walking along the pathway of cross and resurrection through the power of the Spirit." And further, the church is best seen from the standpoint of the Spirit, meaning that it is "a continuation of the Spirit-anointed event that was Jesus Christ."[9] All things from creation to redemption to consummation start with the Spirit of God.

The very concept of the Believers Church is based on yieldedness to God's Spirit by the knowing decision of the uncoerced person. One reason that the practice of infant baptism was discarded by most of the sixteenth-century Anabaptists was that it was seen as a coercion of conscience and an instrument of the civil authorities intruding inappropriately into church life (divine grace and political citizenship supposedly being conveyed simultaneously and apart from the child's informed participation). Both the Christian Churches/Churches of Christ and the Church of God (Anderson), for example, are committed to the concept of a Believers Church. For them, this means in part that infants and very young children are not considered fit subjects for baptism. Why? Because such very young persons have not yet been able to confront their own need and make a personal faith com-

---

[9]Clark Pinnock, *Flame of Love: A Theology of the Holy Spirit* (Downers Grove, Ill.: InterVarsity Press, 1996), 47, 113.

mitment.[10] God wants no compulsory service, no supposed admissions to the church by virtue of national citizenship or the faith and actions of others. The joyous task of being one of Christ's faithful children and loyal followers is to be a task freely chosen and seriously pursued within a committed community ruled by God's Spirit.[11] Very young children cannot confess their faith or participate in the discipleship of the community of faith.

There is a mission for the people of God, a divine task to which they are called. This task is nothing less than being a "light to the nations," an embodiment in this world of a life derived from and reflective of another. What other? The realm of God, the life of the Spirit. Those who truly believe in the Christ of God are called to be loyal and productive citizens of the realm where God reigns. There is to be no higher loyalty than obedience to God, no citizenship that supersedes the ultimate demands of the divine rule. Such citizenship requires sturdy commitment and extensive preparation. In the midst of it all, God's Spirit leads, enables, rules, sends.

The heritage of the Believers Church, therefore, is a springtime tradition in the history of Christians. The season of spring usually is identified as the annual time of renewal, cleansing, and preparation. In nature, there is rebirth, fresh flowers, a greening of the dormant

---

[10]See, e.g., Barry Callen and James North, *Coming Together In Christ* (Joplin, Mo.: College Press, 1997), 91ff.

[11]In early Anabaptism the central role granted to the calling of the Holy Spirit was assumed to function equally for men and women. There was assumed to be no gender discrimination on God's part. However, it also became typical to assume that the Spirit restricts to men the divine calling to "official" leadership positions in the church's life. Societal norms of the time surely were significant here as, in paternalistic settings, Anabaptist leaders moved away from the flexibility of the early pneumatic beginnings to increasing reliance on a literal interpretation of the Bible to provide the "rule of life" for the church (including statements of Paul about the proper role of women in the congregation). While the result was hardly a "golden age" for gender equality in the church, in many ways "Anabaptist women were empowered to choose for themselves, contravening common societal restrictions on their gender" (C. Arnold Snyder, op. cit., 269). The Spirit's crossing of human barriers was to be seen more dramatically in the nineteenth-century Holiness Movement, especially in the Church of God (Anderson) movement (see James Earl Massey, "Race Relations in the American Holiness Movement," *Wesleyan Theological Journal* 31:1 [Spring 1996], 40-50).

ground. In homes, there is spring cleaning. The garage is cleared of accumulated debris and the windows cleansed of winter's assorted grime. In baseball, there is spring training. Fat is run off, skills are sharpened, and team identity and spirit are built before the long and demanding summer ahead. The issues are new life, identity formation, fresh dedication, and careful preparation. The springtime changes can be dramatic. Frozen ground gives way to soft and fertile earth and impressive new displays of delicate beauty. What seemed the stillness of death yields to the vibrancy of life.

One might say that Christianity is a springtime faith. Death gives way to life. Fallenness yields to risenness. The death and then new-life resurrection of Jesus suddenly became the foundation, the hope, the model of faith fulfilled and a future promised. The core reality, then, centers in Pentecost.[12] The key theological problem addressed by the Book of Acts involves what form of life Israel should assume in the post-Jesus era. After the ascension of the resurrected Jesus came the Spirit, the principal agent of God's current work of salvation and revelation within the faith community (cf. John 14:16-17, 25-26). It would be by the Spirit that the apostles and other ministers would be empowered to witness to the risen Jesus (Acts 4:28-31) and by whom the word of God "increases" to the end of the earth (6:7). It is to be by the Spirit that the faith community of Jesus would emerge as a distinctive, vigorous, witnessing, and sometimes suffering people who would be faithful to God in an anti-God world (Acts 2:46-47; 5:40-42; 7:51-59; etc.).[13] A resurrection from the dead signaled springtime for a chilled and otherwise hopeless world; the dramatic arrival of Christ's

---

[12]In the context of a Trinitarian understanding of God, aspects of God's work on behalf of human salvation can be attributed properly to God the Father, Son, and/or Holy Spirit. All is of God. Nonetheless, while the work of God the Spirit is emphasized here, some bodies such as the Church of the Brethren are inclined to be more Christocentric in focus. Jesus is the incarnation of God, even though admittedly it is the Spirit of Christ who interprets, equips, and applies all that Jesus was and did. We see no conflict here, only choice of focus.

[13]For a more extensive discussion, see Barry Callen, *God As Loving Grace* (Nappanee, Ind.: Evangel Publishing House, 1996), chapters 6 and 7.

Spirit then brought the divine sunshine and rain necessary to enable the growth and power essential for the church's mission ahead.

Barton Stone (1772-1844) and Alexander Campbell (1788-1866) were key pioneers of the Restoration Movement in the United States. Stone was convinced that Christian unity will never come to reality by all believers finally confessing a common set of doctrines. The only real hope is a "Fire Union," the fire of the Spirit by which hard and unloving hearts are softened and filled with a supernatural love. Unity emerges as God's presence transforms people into new creations and then those people together form new communities of faith, love, and witness.[14] Campbell, however, was more rationally oriented and merged the restoration philosophy which he had inherited from the Reformed and Puritan traditions with the Enlightenment approach inherited from the Age of Reason. He thus surrounded Stone's Spirit orientation with "a rational perspective according to which the Bible itself became a sort of scientific manual, a constitution, or a technical blueprint."[15] So Robert Richardson (1806-1876) soon became a prophetic voice to this same reforming tradition when, despite its vision, it was generating its own rationalism and fragmentation. During the 1840s and 1850s he feared that a superficial and heartless formalism was overtaking the movement, causing a denial of any significant present-day role for the Holy Spirit. Emotional excess in religion, he readily admitted, clearly is a negative; but he went on to

---

[14]See C. Leonard Allen, *Distant Voices: Discovering a Forgotten Past for a Changing Church* (Abilene, Tex.: Abilene Christian University Press, 1993), 19. Stone believed that heresy involves less the believing of wrong doctrines and more the lack of love and a rending of the body of Christ. In choosing "Fire Union" as the most appropriate basis for authentic Christian unity, he was rejecting what he called "Book Union," "Head Union," and "Water Union" (unity founded on the doctrine of immersion of believers in water). The Church of God (Anderson) tradition resonates with the heart of Stone's analysis and prescription for bringing about true Christian unity. One beloved song from this tradition is "The Bond of Perfectness." The repeating chorus affirms: "Beloved, how this perfect love, Unites us all in Jesus! One heart, and soul, and mind: we prove the union heaven gave us" (as in *Worship the Lord: Hymnal of the Church of God*, Anderson, Ind.: Warner Press, 1989, 330).

[15]C. Leonard Allen and Richard T. Hughes, *Discovering Our Roots: The Ancestry of Churches of Christ* (Abilene, Tex.: Abilene Christian University Press, 1988), 82.

insist that a Spiritless faith is an even greater evil.[16] Christ arose and the Spirit came. These twin facts are both the historic foundation and the present dynamic of the church.

The uniquely Christian identity and power resident in this resurrection-pentecost reality is essentially what comprises the seeds of the springtime Believers Church tradition. At the tradition's most formative roots lie the wonder of new life, a power beyond human origin or manipulation, and a willingness to yield in humble obedience. There also is willingness to be nurtured in the faith, to be voluntarily part of a communal reality in Christ, and to retain intolerance for that which obstructs and detracts from the life of Christ now available through the gracious ministry of God's Spirit. Accordingly, this focus on formative roots, this biblical and "radical" inclination led John Howard Yoder to argue that the Believers Church concept "is not a mere midpoint on a scale between establishment and chaos, not a *via media* between too much tradition and too little."[17] The issue is more fundamental. It involves full allegiance to the Spirit within a Spirit-formed community that is to function as a foretaste in this world of the coming reign of God. In fact, "a fault-line of geological proportions runs throughout Protestantism since the 16th century. The free churches are not simply marginal or corrective to mainline Protestantism,… [they] represent a fundamentally different view of church history, theology, ethics and Christian living."[18]

This crucial claim sets an important and demanding agenda. Definitions are needed. What "fault-line"? What is a "free church"? What "fundamentally different view" do we mean? In this chapter and the next there are attempts at offering answers to such questions. After the basics are clarified, chapters four and five then explore how such a free-church vision affects an understanding of the substance of Chris-

---

[16]See, e.g., Pat Brooks, "Robert Richardson: Nineteenth Century Advocate of Spirituality," *Restoration Quarterly* 21 (1978), 135-149.

[17]John Howard Yoder, "The Believers' Church Conferences in Historical Perspective," *Mennonite Quarterly Review* (January 1991), 12.

[18]Franklin Littell, "The Contribution of the Free Churches," The Chicago Theological Seminary *Register* (September 1970), 49.

tian faith and the tasks of Christian discipleship. The final chapter looks to the present time and asks how the springtime of God's grace and serious dedication to God's reign in this present world can allow the church to be her true self as the vehicle of the good news of Jesus Christ to the lost world. Might lessons from the tradition of the Believers Church be helpful guides as the whole church seeks its identity and mission for the opening years of the twenty-first century? We think they can.

Such preparing for the church's future is aided by a careful look at the church's past. For instance, God's providence was seen at work two centuries ago in England. John Wesley observed the widespread undermining of life-transforming Christianity and judged that this religious deterioration could (should) be seen as a way in which nominal Christians could be prepared to tolerate and even finally receive *real Christianity*. He saw eighteenth-century English society "causing a total disregard for all religion" and in the process opening the way "for the revival of the only religion which was worthy of God!"[19] More recently, Wesleyan interpreter Howard Snyder has seen a similar divine providence at work in the secularizing process of contemporary Western societies. He also longs for the emergence from the ashes of discredited religion of a fresh Christian faith and renewed church truly worthy of bearing God's name. It is his hope that "the collapse of the present order will lead to a new outbreak of revolutionary Christianity."[20] "Revolutionary" Christianity points toward what has been envisioned as central for centuries. The revolution in view is one of divine grace, new creation, and faithfulness to the reign of God, not the taking or forcing of anything inside or outside the Christian community. The way is one of peace; those involved are all and always volunteers.

This impassioned and perennial hope that collapse of the compromised can launch a new beginning assumes the potential existence of a "radical" form of Christian faith, the only form that can bring the

---

[19]John Wesley, in his sermon titled "Of Former Times."
[20]Howard Snyder, *The Radical Wesley* (Downers Grove, Ill.: InterVarsity Press, 1980), preface.

human and social transformation God intends and is willing to enable. In each generation some spiritual seekers are prepared to ask the pivotal questions once posed by Wesley, and addressed in a Believers Church tradition that, by Wesley's time, already had a long history. These questions include: What does it mean to live according to the full expectation of the gospel of Christ? What about resurrection power and the Spirit's current ministry? How is the church to live out its life in the face of a fallen world that does not understand, care, or sometimes even tolerate those who take seriously the implications of a divine Christ and his servant way of life? What about the fallenness of the church itself? How can God live in and work through church structures that, often in spite of their own best intentions, allow low human motives and very human means to dominate their lives? What is the price of daring to be prophetic—and who is prepared to pay?

The quest is to find and live out a strong doctrine of both God's Spirit and God's church. Authentic Christian life requires a vital and growing relationship between the believer and God; it also requires a responsible relationship between the believer and other believers. The historians of two of the Believers Church traditions have each captured this essential duality in the very titles of their denominational histories. Carlton O. Wittlinger of the Brethren in Christ uses the title *Quest for Piety and Obedience*, while John W. V. Smith of the Church of God (Anderson) employs *Quest for Holiness and Unity*. By "piety" Wittlinger means "a personal, heartfelt relationship with God through Jesus Christ" and by "obedience" he refers to "the definition of Christianity as the outward expression through faithful discipleship of the inner experience of regeneration."[21] Smith sees the personal relationship with God (holiness) as basic, and its faithful and loving expression in the fellowship of believers (unity) as the divinely intended outcome. These, Smith says, were judged by the pioneers of this movement as the two vital characteristics of the church which should be "related each to the other as being inextricably bound together in

---

[21]Carlton O. Wittlinger, *Quest for Piety and Obedience: The Story of the Brethren in Christ* (Nappanee, Ind.: Evangel Press, 1978), ix.

producing the kind of church Christ intended."[22] To be newly alive in the Spirit is surely springtime in the church. To be responsibly accountable to other believers in the unity of the faith is to translate new birth into effective mission in the world.

Rebirth and Radical Discipleship

The Christian faith is not simply about *knowing* the truth in Christ; it also is about being *transformed* by that truth. Such is the case both for the awareness and transformation of individual believers and the community of believers, the church. According to Norman Kraus:

> Promise has become reality. That is the essential message of the New Testament.... It is not that the *correct philosophical formula* has been found to demonstrate that "God is there" after all. Neither is it that a new *ethical principle of agape love* has been given to free men and women from the tyranny of legalism. The gospel is this: the promised "power of God for salvation" (Rom. 1:16) has become reality for all who have eyes to see and ears to hear![23]

If, beginning in the fourth century, Constantianism perverted the church with a crippling inclusiveness, the Enlightenment beginning in the eighteenth century added to the burden with a deadening rationalism. Since the 1980s there has been a growing reaction to the negative aspects of the Enlightenment ethos,[24] a reaction that newly opens the way for serious consideration of the ancient insights of the Believers Church tradition.

A radical discipleship is at the core.[25] If Lutheranism is a tradition focused primarily on the search for a merciful God despite the ugly

---

[22]John W. V. Smith, *The Quest for Holiness and Unity: A Centennial History of the Church of God* (Anderson, Ind.: Warner Press, 1980), xiv.

[23]C. Norman Kraus, *The Community of the Spirit* (Scottdale, Pa.: Herald Press, 2nd ed., 1993), 12.

[24]See, e.g., Millard J. Erickson, *Postmodernizing the Faith: Evangelical Responses to the Challenge of Postmodernism* (Grand Rapids: Baker Books, 1998).

[25]See Harold Bender, "The Anabaptist Vision," *Mennonite Quarterly Review*, 18 (1944), 67-88.

face of human sin (how can we humans be saved?), Anabaptism "developed around the central idea of a righteous walk with the Lord after the experience of repentance and rebirth"[26] (how should we humans then live?). Menno Simons stubbornly insisted that the new birth in Christ is more than a private experience of sins being forgiven. There is a necessary link between the *new birth* and the *life of a newborn Christian*. If Christian faith is to be considered authentic, discipleship must give tangible evidence of the gift of saving grace. Menno challenges the temptation to preach any gospel of grace which fails to declare the community dimension and serving responsibility of that grace.[27] Put another way, any true reformation of the church must include the quest for, and fruit of, holiness.

True Christian faith is not merely what church members believe, although that is very important (see chapter four). It also and significantly is *who believers are* and *how they live*, especially as a committed faith community in contrast to "the world." Howard Snyder paraphrases the thought of John Wesley as he insisted on the following in relation to his own eighteenth-century renewal movement in England and then in America: "Men and women do not truly *believe* the gospel without a moral change which enables them to live the gospel. Faith not only believes; it *works*—in both senses."[28] The fundamental work of God's Spirit at Pentecost was the formation of a new community of the Spirit. This community, the church, when faithful would act like the Spirit and thus itself become part of the "incarnation drama."[29]

This necessary visibility of effectual grace has been affirmed consistently by the Believers Church tradition in relation both to individual disciples and to the integrity of the life of the church itself. For example, in 1939 church historian Charles Brown wrote *The Church*

---

[26]John Oyer, *Lutheran Reformers Against the Anabaptists* (The Hague: Martinus Nijhoff, 1964), 212.

[27]Note Randy Maddox, *Responsible Grace: John Wesley's Practical Theology* (Nashville: Kingswood Books, Abingdon Press, 1994) which views the whole of the theological burden of John Wesley within this emphasis of Menno.

[28]Howard Snyder, op. cit., 147.

[29]C. Norman Kraus, op. cit., 11.

Beyond Division, as exposition of the biblical picture of Christ's people united and visible in the world as intended in the Spirit. This book puts into prose the vision of the church that Charles Naylor and Andrew Byers earlier had shared poetically and musically in one of the loved heritage hymns of the Church of God (Anderson):

> The church of God one body is,
> One Spirit dwells within;
> And all her members are redeemed,
> And triumph over sin.
>
> O church of God! I love Thy courts,
> Thou mother of the free;
> Thou blessed home of all the saved,
> I dwell content in Thee.[30]

Believers need the inspiration of such a vision that "sees the church" in a way that fits the grace-filled idealism of the New Testament and leads to a visible expression that encourages the world to believe. All members of the church, by definition, "are redeemed" and "dwell content" in divine courts that function as the "mother of the free." The "triumph over sin" is a commitment to holiness, being like God as God's people through the Spirit in the church and in the world.

According to Menno Simons: "The true evangelical faith sees and considers only the doctrine, ceremonies, commands, prohibitions, and the perfect example of Christ, and strives to conform thereto with all its power."[31] The Believers Church tradition, accordingly, differs sharply from what is at least the common Protestant perspective on Roman Catholicism—that it is institutional at heart—and from all Protestant scholasticisms that are propositional at heart. Idealized in the Believers Church tradition are the transformed lives of individual Christians and the distinctive life of the whole church together, a life

---

[30]Hymn "O Church of God" in *Worship The Lord: Hymnal of the Church of God* (Anderson, Ind.: Warner Press, 1989), 289.

[31]Menno Simons, *The True Christian Faith* (c.1541), as in *The Complete Writings of Menno Simons* (Scottdale, Pa.: Herald Press, 1956), 343.

focused on Christ that exceeds structural considerations, transcends rational and creedal barriers, and is in contrast with and thus potentially a witness to the world. Clark Pinnock puts well the central truth:

> ...the effectiveness of the church is due not to human competency or programming but to the power of God at work. The church rides the wind of God's Spirit like a hawk endlessly and effortlessly circling and gliding in the summer sky. It ever pauses to wait for impulses of power to carry it forward to the nations.... The main rationale of the church is to actualize all the implications of baptism in the Spirit.[32]

Cleansing the Sanctuary

One of the core elements of the Believers Church tradition, according to that first Believers Church Conference in 1967, is recognition of the "need for a perpetual restitution of the church." If the church on earth is viewed as God's sanctuary, that sanctuary needs occasional cleansing (as Jesus himself found out in Jerusalem). It has been typical of this tradition to recognize this need and be willing to engage in the necessary reform, costly to itself as that activity may be.

New birth in Christ followed by a radical discipleship is viewed in the Believers Church tradition as central both to the Christian life and a proper understanding of the nature and mission of the church. Believers are to be holy, as are the congregations comprised of such believers. In the face of all church compromises with surrounding establishments, whether of a church or secular nature, this tradition represents a distinct and daring view of Christianity. In the sixteenth-century European setting:

> Other reformers, such as Luther and Calvin...understood the visible church as coextensive with the local community wherein people must live and worship in harmony. The Anabaptists, however, focused not on the whole community, but on local

---

[32]Clark Pinnock, *Flame of Love: A Theology of the Holy Spirit* (Downers Grove, Ill.: InterVarsity Press, 1996), 113-114.

congregations of voluntary members who regarded themselves as altogether set apart from the state. For them, the one true church consisted only of true believers, whose status could be ascertained by tests of conduct and belief. Those not meeting their standards for church membership were expelled and banned.[33]

Typically, congregations intentionally composed only of committed believers (Believers Churches) have viewed the institutionalized establishment churches as seriously compromised with the world, being bound more to their own traditions and power arrangements than to the living Christ. This negative judgment often has led to an isolationist and restorationist mentality in the process of reformers insisting that any adequate church renewal must make God's sanctuary a holy place again. Biblically speaking, a sanctuary is a holy place, one set apart for the divine. God's original plan was to have a pure and holy people (Eph. 1:4), a people serving as a sanctuary, a light to the world. So, after humankind's fall into sin, God chose Israel, intending that it be a distinctive people separated to and for God's purposes.[34]

Given its failures of faith and practice, however, there finally came into being a new covenant sanctuary. God's church now is (or should be) the appointed sanctuary. This church was prefigured by the tabernacle and temple of the Jews, early shadows of the truths about the person, salvation, and church of Jesus Christ. God now desires to indwell this new spiritual house (church as sanctuary), organizing and tempering the body together, preserving it in peace and unity, and gifting it to operate effectively in its saving mission in the world. But even the church often has failed in its faith and practice, thus also requiring a restoration to its "primitive glory" by a cleansing "from all sin and unrighteousness, and from all rubbish of creeds, traditions, and

---

[33]Howard Clark Kee, et. al., *Christianity: A Social and Cultural History,* second edition (Upper Saddle River, N.J.: Prentice Hall, 1998), 278.

[34]See Alan Kreider, *Journey Towards Holiness: A Way of Living for God's Nation* (Scottdale, Pa.: Herald Press, 1987). Rather than focusing primarily on a personal spiritual experience, Kreider views "holiness" as an intended central characteristic of the people of God who are to be a holy nation for God in the world.

inventions of sectism which the dark ages of the past have heaped upon her, and which the people have been blindly educated to identify with her."[35]

The "dark ages" resulting from the "fall" of the church, as commonly conceived in the Believers Church tradition, is symbolized well by the Roman emperor Constantine and centers in a subtle co-opting of the church by a nation-state. One of the more negative aspects of the downward shift was that the church chose to stop confronting the social order of the Roman Empire and came increasingly to accommodate it, even focus on working through it and organizing itself in reflection of it. The notion of the church as a voluntarily gathered and visible community of committed believers gave way to the publicly endorsed church-is-everybody view. Believers came to be understood as all of the baptized, with baptism and political citizenship blending in meaning. Persecution of the church subsided; but the major fact is that there was an unnatural fusion of what are two different realities, the church and the non-church. The world was "baptized" as the church was tamed. The church over the following centuries came to see itself largely as the official clergy more than the people. The church's liturgy, controlled by the clergy, subtly shifted to the service of the values and even policies of the state.[36]

In the sixteenth century it finally was the Anabaptists who dared to again conceive of the church as a voluntary community of believers disciplined according to New Testament standards, functioning freely apart from surrounding secular and even church traditions and powers. They sought to restore the true church as it was before the "fall,"

---

[35]Daniel Warner and Herbert Riggle, *The Cleansing of the Sanctuary* (Moundsville, W.V.: Gospel Trumpet Publishing Co., 1903), 229-230.

[36]This "fall" is described well by John Howard Yoder in "The Otherness of the Church," *Mennonite Quarterly Review* 35 (October 1961), and in "The Constantinian Sources of Western Social Ethics," in *The Priestly Kingdom* (Notre Dame, Ind.: University of Notre Dame Press, 1984), 136ff. See also Rodney Clapp, *A Peculiar People: The Church As Culture in a Post-Christian Society* (Downers Grove, Ill.: InterVarsity Press, 1996), 23-27.

before "the pride of the hierarchs, the arrogance of the professional theologians, and the ambitions of temporal rulers had enhanced its outward show of prestige and weakened its true inward strength."[37] Restorationism was a common goal among early Anabaptists and also among various other Believers Church traditions since. Steven Land, for instance, explains Pentecostal spirituality as an "apocalyptic vision" that includes a recovery in the last days of the faith and power of the apostolic church.[38]

This radically "charismatic" and restorationist view of the church might be thought a noble and sometimes needful exercise in ecclesiastical idealism. But, admittedly, those who engage in such idealism too often are, as Howard Snyder puts it, "naive concerning institutional and sociological realities and blind to the institutional dimensions of their own movement. In their concern with present experience they may fall prey to bizarre apocalyptic, dispensational, or millennial views which are unbiblical and unrealistic and may lead to extreme hopes, claims or behavior."[39] Snyder suggests that John Wesley offers a helpful synthesis of the institutional and charismatic in that he came to regard Methodism as a movement of authentic Christianity within the larger church (the Church of England and beyond), an "evangelical order" with its own institutional identity, but nonetheless intentionally functioning within and on behalf of the universal church.[40] For Believers Church adherents, such a synthesis can be viewed either as a practical maturing of the ideal or a subtle deviation,

---

[37]Franklin Littell, *A Tribute To Menno Simons* (Scottdale, Pa.: Herald Press, 1961), 24.

[38]Steven Land, *Pentecostal Spirituality: A Passion for the Kingdom* (Sheffield, England: Sheffield Academic Press, 1993), chapter 2. See also D. William Faupel, *The Everlasting Gospel: The Significance of Eschatology in the Development of Pentecostal Thought* (Sheffield, England: Sheffield Academic Press, 1996).

[39]See chapter three for a brief recounting of the Münster debacle (1534-35), one of several sad examples of this very real danger.

[40]Howard A. Snyder, *The Radical Wesley and Patterns for Church Renewal* (Downers Grove, Ill.: InterVarsity Press, 1980), 128-129, 133. Snyder even observes: "If Methodism had been born two centuries earlier within Reformation Protestantism, it would likely have been forced to become a separate believers' church" (151). Those that were so forced in the sixteenth century should somehow not think of themselves or function as bodies totally separated from the life of the whole church.

the first step back to fundamental compromise. At a minimum, it is crucial at least to start with the central significance of the Spirit's presence and transforming work and be aware that ideal visions are vulnerable to their own perversions.

In the United States, the Stone-Campbell movement of the nineteenth century arose out of a profound disenchantment about the church's compromised past. Since that past was viewed largely as the sordid scene of confusion, compromise, sectarian strife, and deadening traditionalism, the renewing goal became a determination to sweep this past away, abandon it, and resort to a renewed linking with the pure stream of the original church of the New Testament. Pursuit of this goal seeks a partaking of the presumed perfections of the early church in a relatively tradition-freed atmosphere. The hope is to participate in a fresh and unfettered move of God. However, according to C. Leonard Allen representing one wing of today's Stone-Campbell (Disciples) movement, emerging in the restoring process usually are "exhilarating and damaging illusions." He says that the reformer's "sense of historylessness works in powerful and subtle ways," including making "our leaders larger-than-life figures, religious geniuses, people who never mixed eternal truth with temporal clay. And so we often constructed romantic chronicles, pitting unmixed Truth against the hosts of ignorance and Untruth. It was an exciting story, almost the stuff of epics and legends."[41]

There has been, however, more than a no-history sense in the larger Believers Church tradition. This tradition stresses the priority of an authentic and very visible expression of the believing community of Christ, accompanied by a particular view of history. Typically the tradition has mounted a radical critique of the institutional church and argued vigorously for the integrity of the daily life and practice of believers in terms of community, obedience, discipline, mutual support, and service in the ministry of Christ. It begins with the assumed presence and current work of the Spirit of God, and is impatient

---

[41]C. Leonard Allen, *The Cruciform Church* (Abilene, Tex.: Abilene Christian University Press, 2nd ed., 1990), 4-7.

with any demeaning of this work by accommodations with the surrounding church or non-church cultures. It presents a renewal movement model that features a distinctive biblical-theological-historical
approach. This approach is

> ...biblical in that it sees the New Testament teachings and
> believing community as providing the normative model of what
> the church is always to be; theological and historical in that it
> interprets church history in the light of this model, usually view-
> ing Constantinianism as the fall of the church and calling for its
> restitution to the New Testament pattern.[42]

Righteous renewal crusades are understood by their leaders to be
instruments for cleansing God's sanctuary in the face of a deeply
troubled past of the church. The irony to be faced is that the refor-
mationist or restorationist mindset tends to develop its own powerful traditions (relatively uninstitutionalized, at least at first) in the
midst of its rhetoric against tradition and the unwitting illusion that
it now exists without its own rapidly evolving tradition. For agents of
renewal to serve well their own calling, they always must maintain an
appropriate humility about their own roles and long-term accom-
plishments.[43] Even so, the radical call remains.

Serious response is required if a believer's commitment is really to
the full reign of God in one's life and in the church. Salvation is
thought to be interpreted best in relational terms rather than sacramental forms. The emphasis is on a faith identification with the risen
Christ, that is, walking in the resurrection.[44] The call is from the Spirit of the Christ who wants preeminence in the church over kings, leg-
islatures, denominational structures, official liturgies, and human

---

[42]Howard A. Snyder, *Signs of the Spirit: How God Reshapes the Church* (Grand Rapids: Academie Books, Zondervan, 1989), 40.

[43]For an excellent treatment of the typical lack of the appropriate humility of perspective, see Richard Hughes and C. Leonard Allen, *Illusions of Innocence: Protestant Primitivism in America*, 1630-1875 (Chicago: University of Chicago Press, 1988).

[44]See Myron Augsburger, "Concern for Holiness in the Mennonite Tradition," *The
Asbury Seminarian* (October 1981), 28-44.

"lords" of any kind. The Christian church is to be a distinctive culture, a way of life, the community of Christ through the presence and power of Christ's Spirit.[45] There is to be no "political" vision other than that of the reign of God. The issue of the citizenship of the believer is to be clear to the believer and the world. Jesus Christ and he alone is Lord.

Reflecting the Fullness

Jesus asks all who would be his followers to live lives guided by the priorities of the now come—and yet coming—reign of God. We are to pray continually for God's kingdom to come, meaning that God's will is being done on earth as it is in heaven (Matt. 6:10). We are to pray for the kingdom's arrival and prepare for that arrival by actually living the life of the coming of the kingdom through the power of the already present Spirit of Jesus Christ. Sensitivity to the priority of God's reign requires that we who would be Christ's children and agents in this world will be experiencing *now* the first fruits of the kingdom through the Spirit. Participating by grace in "the powers of the coming age" (Heb. 6:5) will enable life in a responsible faith community that is tasting and reflecting in the present the reality of the divine rule that is not yet in its fullness.

In the meantime, lives are to be changed, sanctuaries cleansed, risks gladly taken. Believers should dare to be separate from the compromised positions of establishment churches which are defined as much by their accommodations to the values and structures of this world as they are by their relatedness to the ongoing incarnation drama begun in Jesus and now to be carried on by God's Spirit through the faithful church. Whether separating from compromised circumstances often found in the established church should include a denial of the necessity and legitimacy of the institutional church

---

[45]Rodney Clapp argues that the United States has so thoroughly been Constantinian "that it does have a true 'old-time' and civil religion, but this religion is not Christianity. It is instead that eminently interiorized and individualized faith called gnosticism" (*A Peculiar People*, 1996, 34).

itself is a central and continuing question.[46] What is not in question for the Believers Church, however, is the primary fact that the church which God intends is nothing other than the church generated by the Spirit of God, the one founded, filled, gifted, and sent by the Spirit. If one does not start and stay here, one is in the wrong regardless of what else may be right.

The vitality of the received tradition of the Believers Church rests on a continuing encounter with the living Christ. It is the grafting of lifeless twigs onto the living Vine that first brought into being a "church of believers." However, Believers Churches are now more like venerable old plants, with deep roots and sometimes rather wilted leaves. The challenge for today in this tradition is to have the wisdom and resolve to prune with care and patience whatever hinders lives and congregations from being lived in and by the Spirit of God. It is important to begin with the Spirit, the source of divine life. It then is important to recall the vision that originally gave existence and rationale to the Believers Church tradition. Chapter three seeks to recover and explore this vision.

---

[46]Contemporary Roman Catholic theologian Rosemary Ruether speaks favorably of the constructive reforming role of the "free churches," but sees them as properly interrelated to the institutional church. On the one hand, she sees the institutional church as secondary to the immediacy of the Spirit's life and work; nonetheless, the established church is viewed as essential for perpetuating the church's tradition from generation to generation. Thus, ideally in Ruether's view, "the two are interdependent polarities within the total dialectic of the church's existence" ("The Free Church Movement in Contemporary Catholicism," in Marty and Peerman, eds., *New Theology No. 6*, Macmillan, 1969), 286-287.

3

Seeing the Vision

So in John's Gospel we have a new language of friendship, a language of participation instead of management. Cruciform and subversive friendship, as opposed to managerial friendship, is attentive rather than manipulative, organic rather than technical, relational rather than rational, open-ended rather than calculating.... In this light, the church's immediate and extended task on behalf of friendship is the freeing task of proclaiming and embodying the gospel and, in so doing, teaching and cultivating an alternative language, a contrast culture, for friendship....[1]

While accepting the "Sola Scripture" of the Reformers, it may be said that their emphasis was Sola Christus, for Jesus as the Christ is the center of faith. For the Anabaptists the Christian life meant discipleship in the freedom of Christ, an identification of the total life with Jesus Christ, and a commitment to walk in the Spirit.... And so, for them, holiness of life meant discipleship, an obedience to Christ, a separation of the life of the believer from the world in an active pursuit of the priorities of the Kingdom of Christ.[2]

It has been said wisely that an especially dangerous time in the life of any reforming movement is when the vision inspiring that move-

---

[1]Rodney Clapp, *A Peculiar People: The Church as Culture in a Post-Christian Society* (Downers Grove, Ill.: InterVarsity Press, 1996), 209-210.

[2]Myron A. Augsburger, "Concern for Holiness in the Mennonite Tradition," *The Asbury Seminarian* (October 1981), 28.

ment is being carried out by leaders who have never seen it. Without question the earlier generations of the Believers Church tradition did see something significant; it may be well worth all of us seeing it again. Roland Bainton once made the significant observation that the worth of the Anabaptists "is not to be judged in the light of their contribution to history. They took their stand in light of eternity regardless of what might or might not happen in history."[3] What was the stand that was worth risking whatever might happen? The task of this chapter is to identify the vision that captured and motivated these "radical" reformers and provided for them a special way that they would follow regardless of the cost.

A particular context surrounds our search for this vision at the opening of the twenty-first century. The above quote of Rodney Clapp on friendship in John's Gospel presumes that it now must be implemented in a "post-Christian society." There is, then, a pervasive problem and a fragile possibility. The problem is that the contemporary North American church is inordinately shaped by the society's rampant materialism and consumerism. As Walter Brueggemann once put it, Christian consciousness "has been claimed by false fields of perception and idolatrous systems of language and rhetoric." The possibility, according to Brueggemann, involves a "prophetic imagination" and ministry based on the Christian prophet being, not a child of the culture, but a child of the faith's tradition who is shaped by its memory, language, and perceptions, and dares to highlight the incongruity between the faith and its current cultural captivity. The central task of prophetic ministry is "to nurture, nourish, and evoke a consciousness and perception alternative to the consciousness and perception of the dominant culture around us."[4]

---

[3]Roland Bainton, *Studies on the Reformation* (Boston: Beacon Press, 1963), 206.

[4]Walter Brueggemann, *The Prophetic Imagination* (Minneapolis: Augsburg Press, 1978), 13. In this and other books, Brueggemann uses the Israelite exodus from Egyptian slavery as the primary paradigm of a people who, with the help of Moses, gained a prophetic imagination other than the dominant one of the controlling culture (symbolized by the presumably all-powerful Pharaoh), and thus found liberty through the action of a responding God who heard their cries.

Running through the whole of Christian church history has been a prophetic stream that has been a compelling alternative to a passing parade of dominant other-faith cultures. Central to this stream's defining countercultural dynamic has been a daring vision of the nature and implications of the Christian faith. This vision, confident of its distinctiveness and significance, fires a resolve in sincere believers to live out faith in Jesus Christ to the fullest extent in the midst of the world. Whatever this view is, surely it is not a mere extension of the world.

The problem for Christians arose early and dramatically. Jesus had been crucified as a possible threat to the stability of sole Roman authority in one of its eastern provinces. The first generations of his disciples were then viewed as a small minority of rather strange people functioning on the margins of mainstream society. But in the fourth century after Christ, the Roman Emperor Constantine helped to join the cause of the Empire and Christianity, an unnatural synthesis making Christians key threads in the very fabric of mainstream Roman society. Christianity now was becoming the established religion. Church and state were blending, with the church inevitably compromising something of its independent and distinctive nature.

The Believers Church tradition has arisen as a prophetic voice, and even a defiant faith community, in response to such loss of church distinctiveness. It seeks to recapture the vision of what it believes to be the New Testament way of being the church, the church that God intends in contrast to being the compromised religious community that this world is pleased to tolerate and even support. As God's church, and not merely an extension of the world's acceptable altruism, the Believers Church tradition has sought to be countercultural by its very nature. The church of Jesus is seen as a new beginning, a divinely-constituted society of its own within the human social structures that always surround and seek to control it. What has been envisioned is not merely some new wrinkle on things, but a whole new society, with its members committed to being fully obedient to God's rule.

Locating evidence of this Believers Church vision anywhere in church history can be done by finding the Christian believers who answer the following question in favor of the church: Does God choose to work in this world primarily through the world's established social and political authorities or through the divine creation of a new society, the church? This question focuses on the significant difference between the faithful community of Christ being understood as (1) a renewing force functioning primarily within and through the structures of human societies and (2) a new society in itself, a radical alternative to human societies, a source of renewal to this world made possible primarily by the church of God's Spirit being its distinctive self in the midst of the world. Thus:

> It is the difference between Christianity as a renewal movement from within a society which gradually transforms it into the kingdom of God and the idea that the church constitutes an alternative to the existing society, an outpost of the kingdom of God calling individuals to leave the existing society, at least symbolically, in order to join God's society.[5]

The Believers Church, then, is a tradition based on a conscious and committed decision. Christians associated with this "radical" way necessarily choose to join and belong to the church, the new-creation body of Christ in the world. To so choose requires that the chooser be of a responsible choosing age (thus no infant baptism) and a new creation in Christ by faith in the transforming presence of the Spirit of Christ (thus only those who have truly repented). This way of envisioning the faith and church is radical, in part because it denies the corrosive "Christendom" claim that the church is a religious estab-

---

[5]J. Denny Weaver, *Becoming Anabaptist* (Scottdale, Pa.: Herald Press, 1987), 21-22. For Weaver's more recent and complete discussion of the relation of church and society, see his chapter "The Socially Active Community: An Alternative Ecclesiology," in *The Limits of Perfection: Conversations with J. Lawrence Burkholder*, 2nd ed., Rodney Sawatsky and Scott Holland, eds. (Waterloo and Kitchener, Ont.: Institute of Anabaptist-Mennonite Studies, Conrad Grebel College, and Pandora Press, 1993), 71-94. The answer to the question posed above likely is not a strict either/or; even so, the Believers Church focuses significantly on the faithful church as the divinely chosen locus of God's work in the world.

lishment composed of all people living in a given nation or region that is officially designated "Christian." To the contrary, it is assumed that to be Christian is to choose God's gracious offer of new birth in Christ and then submit voluntarily to the privilege of membership in Christ's new community of faith. Being a Christian is not to belong by default to the faith tradition because of place of birth or prior political arrangements. Rather, a believer is such by divine grace and by personal choice. Being a citizen of God's realm is to accept citizenship status by faith, quite apart from the political and official church structures prevailing in any given time or place. The church, composed of such reborn and voluntary members, is free—free in Christ to be Christlike in the world.

Luther's "Impractical" Model

Such a model of freedom in and for Jesus Christ was pioneered by numerous communities of Christians in several countries at about the same time in sixteenth-century Europe. That, of course, was the very time of the famous Protestant reformers Martin Luther and John Calvin. Theirs was a new beginning, but much less "radical" in some ways than the freedom communities that came to be called "Anabaptists." A nineteenth-century example helps clarify the sixteenth-century status of Martin Luther in relation to the less celebrated and even more dramatic reforms of the Anabaptists.

Daniel Warner was a prophetic voice that emerged from within the American Holiness Movement in the late 1870s. He cried out against rampant division in God's church and insisted both that the division was hurtful to the church's mission and that a holiness experience for believers was the cure for the sinning and divisive spirit among Christians. This experience was to transform individual believers into genuine Christlikeness (holiness) and also impact the church by blending hearts together, enabling a unity of love, and thus enhancing the church's witness potential in the world. To employ the distinction made by one sociologist, Warner was the *prophet*, not the *reformer*. A reformer "would have cut the problem up into smaller pieces and tackled them one at a time. But the prophet sees only the vision of the

complete ideal which he seeks and he will accept no half-way mea-
sures."[6] Warner represented the birth stage of the reform he had in
view. He was in the pioneer position that soon would yield to the *constructive* stage in which the rhetoric of criticizing what is wrong gives
way to the rigor of implementing what is envisioned as much better.[7]
His was a "radical" voice in the Believers Church tradition.

Warner and many others of his time were standing on the reforming shoulders of the classic reformers of the sixteenth century. Martin Luther clearly had also been a prophet, a troubled and searching
Roman Catholic priest, a sixteenth-century German protester with
vision and passion. Following his open opposition to such things as
the abuse of indulgences, he finally had to oppose pope and emper-
or more broadly. His concerns were dramatized initially by the posting of his 95 theses at the church in Wittenberg, Germany, in October
1517. By 1520 he was defiantly calling the pope anti-Christ. Luther
and his key followers were now faced with the constructive task of
somehow organizing a new evangelical church. Luther went beyond
Warner in personally entering actively into some early aspects of the
constructive stage of the reforming process.[8] In 1526, for instance, he
published his own vernacular mass, incorporating the new teachings
into the traditional form. But, as Donald Durnbaugh has noted, what
Luther judged really needful was a "truly evangelical order" featuring

---

[6]Valorous Clear, *Where the Saints Have Trod* (Chesterfield, Ind.: Midwest Publica-
tions, 1977, a revision of his earlier University of Chicago doctoral dissertation), 41.

[7]For an extensive exploration of the teaching tradition of the Church of God (Ander-
son) movement that in part emerged from Daniel Warner's pioneering work, see Barry
L. Callen, *Contours of a Cause: The Theological Vision of the Church of God Movement*
(Anderson University School of Theology, 1995). For direct focus on Warner's vision, see
Callen, "Daniel Warner: Joining Holiness and All Truth," *Wesleyan Theological Journal*
30:1 (Spring 1995), 92-110.

[8]Luther's intent had not been to break with the Roman Catholic Church and found
his own "sect." He sought needed church reform, seeing himself as a faithful and obedient
servant of the church. As early as 1522, for instance, when he learned that Protestants in
England, France, and Germany were calling themselves "Lutherans," he issued a sharp
disclaimer. Luther preferred to see himself as a simple German monk being faithful to the
Word of God, not as an ecclesiastical revolutionary (although the Word of God itself
indeed was bringing major change to the church).

private gatherings for those people "who want to be Christians in earnest and who profess the gospel with hand and mouth."⁹

Luther, however, never managed to establish such an order of earnest Christians. He saw this goal, what would be at the heart of the more radical Believers Church vision, but did not get very far down the path toward it. The truly evangelical order became for him an impossible dream, both because of the lack of personnel for the implementation task and because of his conflicting desire to secure his reformation in a way that resulted in a church inclusive of those actively confessing faith *and* all those residing in a given geographic area (a "confessing" and a "territorial" church simultaneously). For this, Luther would turn to political authorities for the necessary tools of effective implementation. Thus, his reformation became "magisterial," that is, related to and even dependent on the political establishment (magistrates). This resulting state-church outcome was at odds with the core dynamic of the "truly evangelical order" that he had once envisioned. It would be the Anabaptists who shared this more radical vision and would go on with the daring task of seeking its actual implementation.

Durnbaugh judges that Luther's "impractical" model of a new and truly evangelical order is an excellent sketch of the central character and concerns of the Believers Church tradition. Luther's aborted vision of how such a group should be formed was explained this way by him. Those believers "who want to be Christians in earnest and who profess the gospel with hand and mouth" should

> ...sign their names and meet alone in a house somewhere to pray, to read, to baptize, to receive the sacrament, and do other Christian works. According to this order, those who do not lead Christian lives could be known, reproved, corrected, cast out, or excommunicated, according to the rule of Christ, Matthew 18 [15-17]. Here one could also solicit benevolent gifts to be willingly given and distributed to the poor, according

---

⁹Donald Durnbaugh, *The Believers' Church: The History and Character of Radical Protestantism* (Scottdale, Pa.: Herald Press, 1985 ed., originally 1968), 3.

to St. Paul's example, II Corinthians 9. Here would be no need of much and elaborate singing. Here one could set out a brief and neat order for baptism and the sacrament and center everything on the Word, prayer, and love.[10]

This and similar passages from Luther's writings were known to the first "Free Church" advocates of the sixteenth century. Having explored such writings, George Williams considers that

> ...despite his final acquiescence in the political oversight of a territorial ecclesiastical establishment, Luther nevertheless more than once and empathetically gave theoretical expression to his ideal preference for a gathered church based upon elective affinity.[11]

Unfortunately, when groups of earnest Christians did arise much as Luther had envisioned, he called them *Schwärmer*, people swarming like an uncontrollable buzzing of dangerous bees around a hive. Many reformers were more impatient and less tolerant of the political-religious establishment than Luther, who chose to settle for key elements of the status quo. The non-accommodationist "radicals" came to think of Luther, Zwingli, and Calvin as "half-way men," regretting that Luther and the others lacked either the fullness of their own vision or the necessary courage to step out and actualize the ideal.[12] Even so, during the 450th anniversary of Luther's posting of the famous 95 theses, George Williams recalled with appreciation:

---

[10]Ulrich Leupold, ed., *Liturgy and Hymns*, vol. 53 of *Luther's Works*, ed., Helmut Lehman (Philadelphia: Fortress Press, 1965), 53ff. Luther's *Deutsche Messe* was published in 1526.

[11]George Williams, "'Congregationalist' Luther and the Free Churches," *Lutheran Quarterly*, XIX (August 1967), 285. Williams notes further: "The wonderful thing about Luther's third form for the church was that it was never thought of by him as anything like a come-outers' church. So many a believers' church has, alas, been also a leavers' church."

[12]For a similar and more contemporary judgment, see William Mueller, *Church and State in Luther and Calvin* (Nashville: Broadman Press, 1954), 24-25. Adds Franklin Littell: The "principle of discontinuity, of separation, was the real offense which the political and religious leaders of Christendom could not bear" (*A Tribute to Menno Simons*, 30).

> But the wonderful thing about Luther was that he would image within a few short paragraphs an international Latin liturgy and church, a vernacular church of the masses, and a highly disciplined conventicle that might in other circumstances have met all the specifications of the Anabaptists he so haughtily opposed.... [Thus we should] honor Luther...for also having foreseen the place in the larger whole of the disciplined community of the devout, the Believers' Church.[13]

Soon, despite Martin Luther's broad vision, Lutheranism itself began moving toward a new establishment that feared being bothered and embarrassed by those it quickly stereotyped as non-conforming fanatics, enthusiasts, and rebels. One recent scholar referred to the "radical" reformation less judgmentally as a "reformation of the Reformation," a "correction of the correction of Catholicism."[14] It was the attempt to fulfill the vision of Luther himself, making practical at almost any price what he had backed away from as presumably impractical or at least an untimely dream. "In many ways," concludes church historian James Murch, "the Anabaptist movement was the culmination of the principles Luther espoused. He would have been the last to admit this, for he zealously opposed and even persecuted all Anabaptists until his dying day."[15] Even so, alongside the magisterial reformation of establishment Protestantism, there emerged and survived a more radical reformation.

Radical Reformation (Anabaptists)

The most prominent manifestation of the Believers Church tradition in recent centuries was the sixteenth-century European movement often called the "Anabaptist" movement. Under this broad designation were sometimes diverse groupings of "radical" Christians in

---

[13]George Williams, "A People in Community: Historical Background," in James Leo Garrett, Jr., *The Concept of the Believers' Church* (Scottdale, Pa.: Herald Press, 1969), 102.

[14]J. A. Oosterbaan, "The Reformation of the Reformation: Fundamentals of Anabaptist Theology," *Mennonite Quarterly Review* (July 1977), 171-195.

[15]James DeForest Murch, *Christians Only: A History of the Restoration Movement* (Cincinnati: Standard Publishing, 1962).

various parts of Europe, having in common at least a rejection of the concept of the church being legally tied to and dependent on civil authorities and an accompanying refusal to acknowledge as necessary or tolerable the Lutheran abandonment of his vision of a truly evangelical order. The pejorative name "Anabaptist" (rebaptizer) was given to them by critics on the basis of their most famous churchly practice, baptizing only confessing and committed believers. Such baptisms were done in spite of the fact that often the candidates already had been "baptized" as infants in conjunction with civil control of the church and concurrent recognition of the child's status as a citizen of the political entity in question. Those who re-baptized adult believers opened themselves to severe persecution from both the political and church authorities (in its Catholic and then new Protestant forms).

Anabaptists naturally rejected this designation of who they were since they did not consider their practice re-baptism (the infant occurrence being judged invalid, so the adult baptism was actually the first). They preferred a name like *Brüder* (Brethren) in the German-speaking areas or *Doopsgezinde* (baptism-minded) in the Low Countries. The first of the many rebaptisms probably happened in Zürich, Switzerland, in January 1525, when Luther's reformation was already in full motion.

Anabaptists and later also Pietists[16] featured a desire to carry the Protestant Reformation of the sixteenth century to what seemed to them its logical conclusion. That conclusion was a particular way of believers being together as the church. As J. Denny Weaver summarizes:

> The church was characterized as a voluntary brotherhood or community, which gave it a position as an alternative society both to the dominant society with its government which usurped authority in religious affairs, and to the established church which depended on the government and pretended to encompass all of that society.[17]

---

[16]Dale Brown, *Understanding Pietism* (Nappanee, Ind.: Evangel Publishing House, rev. ed., 1996), 17.

[17]Weaver, *Becoming Anabaptist*, op. cit., 117-118.

Such voluntary communities or "evangelical orders" believed that what makes the church "radical" is that it knows Jesus, and the world does not; and it intends that Jesus will really be Lord of the church and all of life, while much of "Christendom" intends this lordship only with certain significant reservations.[18] Beyond this commonality, however, there was much diversity among early Anabaptists. Such dissenters were no longer Roman Catholics and did not fit well into the diverse Protestant movement. They were a movement of spiritual and ecclesial renewal which stood on the margins of the major "territorial" churches, Catholic and Protestant alike. These daring reformers had no one theological leader unifying them and they had their differences on key issues, including even rebaptism in some cases. Regardless, the term "Anabaptist" has endured as a widely accepted designation. So has the essential integrity of the reforming tradition they fostered, the Believers Church.

The early sixteenth century was a tense and volatile time in Christian Europe. Martin Luther (1483-1546) and Ulrich Zwingli (1484-1531) led in breaking the religious-political dominance of Roman Catholic control of church belief and life, resulting in a diversity of vigorous religious opinion and political anxiety. In the words of Donald Durnbaugh:

> Stirred up by the preaching of evangelical freedom, excited by apocalyptic currents, frightened by the threat of Turkish invasion, caught between an ambitious, rising middle class and an increasingly desperate peasantry, Europeans found themselves in a veritable caldron.[19]

The Anabaptist beginnings, while complex, not clearly document-

---

[18]Being formally allied to political structures was, of course, one such reservation. See Stanley Hauerwas and William Willimon, *Resident Aliens: Life in the Christian Colony* (Nashville: Abingdon Press, 1989). These authors argue that in the contemporary setting "the political task of Christians is to be the church rather than to transform the world" (38). Such a task is undermined when the church is tied to and dependent on the non-church political arena.

[19]Donald Durnbaugh, *The Believers' Church: The History and Character of Radical Protestantism*, 64-65.

ed, and occurring in several European locations at nearly the same time, likely made their earliest appearance with a small band of Swiss "Brethren." They rejected Ulrich Zwingli's tendency to delay or impede what they considered needed church reforms in or near Zürich, Switzerland. In the city, Zwingli was willing to place in the hands of the city's council the task of implementing the reforms "appropriately and without disturbance." He thus tacitly reaffirmed the right of civil authorities to regulate the "outward" life of the church, although affirming Scripture as the sole authority for setting the goals of the church's reformation he was helping to initiate. In 1525, following a public disputation at which was debated the issue of whether the Roman mass was really a sacrifice, the less compromising of the reformers defied the authorities by doing their own baptizing. Conrad Grebel (1495-1526), one of their leaders who had been mentored by Zwingli, helped mark the beginning of the modern "Free Church" movement.[20] Once he and others with him saw that Zwingli was prepared to place the unity of Zürich above the immediate faithfulness of the church to its growing understanding of biblical truth,[21] a radical form of Anabaptism had become for them a necessity in principle, even though infant baptism was not yet an issue.

For some very dedicated Christians, then, biblical teaching, when bound to the restrictions of secular control, was an unworkable and unacceptable Christian compromise.[22] Summarizes Franklin Littell:

---

[20]Today, in his honor, one of the key Canadian centers of the Believers Church tradition is Conrad Grebel College in Waterloo, Ontario.

[21]A slightly alternate reading is that Grebel and his friends were not exactly the uncompromising radicals whose focus was impatience with Zwingli's not carrying out needed church reform in the city. Instead, Grebel and others wanted to institute their more radical view of needed reform in rural parishes around Zürich—in the process freeing those parishes from Zürich's control. Zwingli and the city's council would have nothing of it, inciting Grebel's initial irritation with Zwingli's more cautious approach to church reform (move only as fast as the system can bear). For discussion of recent revised versions of Grebel's role in the early Anabaptist movement, see *The Mennonite Encyclopedia*, vol. V, A-Z (Scottdale, Pa.: Herald Press, 1990), 354-356.

[22]See John Howard Yoder, "The Turning Point in the Zwinglian Reformation," *Mennonite Quarterly Review* (April 1958), 128-140.

For the Anabaptists the authority of the magistrate stopped at the door of the church: matters of faith were reserved for the governance of God the Holy Spirit in the congregation. For the state-church Reformers, religion was one dimension of a continuum still called "Christendom," and subjects were expected to obey with docility and silence in confessional matters as well as political.[23]

The Anabaptists were prepared to pay whatever price necessary to evolve independent and voluntary Christian groups dedicated exclusively to faith and life under biblical authority.[24]

Such groups had their considerable diversities, lacking a clear and common confessional norm aside from the brief Schleitheim Confession of 1527—perhaps the movement's most representative early statement of concerns and principles. Their variations may be seen in the following.

Swiss Brethren forsook control of Christianity by the civil government and convened churches not authorized by the Zürich city council, voluntarily becoming missionaries to their district and world.

Following Jacob Hutter (d. 1536), the Hutterites turned away from the capitalism and militarism overtaking Europe and experimented with collective ownership unprotected by any sword.

At Schleitheim, a village on the German-Swiss border, radical believers in 1527 abandoned independent efforts and voluntarily formed a "Brotherly Union" sealed in the atoning blood of Christ, pledging a distinct way of living. This is known as the Schleitheim Confession which consolidated the young Swiss and southern German Anabaptist movements.

---

[23]Franklin Littell, *A Tribute to Menno Simons* (Scottdale, Pa.: Herald Press, 1961), 40.

[24]Note the video dramatization of the early Anabaptists titled *The Radicals* (1989, distributed by Gateway Films, Worcester, Pa.). Featured is the moving story of Michael Sattler who had been Prior of a Benedictine monastery, became an Anabaptist, carried primary responsibility for drafting the Schleitheim Confession, and then was martyred on May 20, 1527 (burned at the stake, with his wife being executed by drowning two days later).

Waldshut, a town in South Germany, led by its parish priest Balthasar Hubmaier, abandoned corrupt clerical religion and volunteered to participate in a new pattern of life and thought summarized in Hubmaier's "Eighteen Theses."[25]

North German and Dutch baptists, motivated by the terrible experience of government by militant saints (the tragedy of Münster in 1535, see below), renounced the use of force. They followed an elder named Menno Simons by voluntarily forming communities of peaceable stability (Mennonites).

Radical Christians in England and then in its new American colonies shared similar renunciations and volunteered similar experimental communities of faith and life, giving rise to people called Puritans and Baptists.

Something of the commonalities among the early Anabaptists may be seen in these strong convictions that are part of the famous Schleitheim Confession originating from the village of Schleitheim, Canton Schaffhausen, Switzerland, February 1527.

Baptism shall be given to all those who have learned repentance and amendment of life, and who believe truly that their sins are taken away by Christ, and to all those who walk in the resurrection of Jesus Christ, and wish to be buried with Him in death, so that they may be resurrected with Him, and to all those who with this significance request it [baptism] of us and demand it for themselves. This excludes all infant baptism, the highest and chief abomination of the Pope....

---

[25]Balthasar Hubmaier was burned at the stake in 1528 and often is thought to have been the most eloquent spokesperson and profound theologian of sixteenth-century Anabaptism. One entire Believers Church Conference (1989) was dedicated to a study of his thought and influence (see Appendix A and the *Mennonite Quarterly Review,* January 1991, 5-53). While his writings on religious freedom, freedom of the will, and baptism became foundational, he was controversial. Not a strict pacifist, for instance, he is said to have envisioned a territorial Anabaptist church supported by the prince's coercive power. Put more charitably, he was open to the idea of a Christian magistrate, thinking such a person better than a non-believer in the implementation of secular power.

SEEING THE VISION   63

All those who wish to break one bread in remembrance of the broken body of Christ, and all who wish to drink of one drink as a remembrance of the shed blood of Christ, shall be united beforehand by baptism in one body of Christ which is the church of God and whose Head in Christ....

A separation shall be made from the evil and from the wickedness which the devil planted in the world.... He [the Lord] further admonishes us to withdraw from Babylon and earthly Egypt that we may not be partakers of the pain and suffering which the Lord will bring upon them. From this we should learn that everything which is not united with our God and Christ cannot be other than an abomination which we should shun and flee from. By this is meant all Catholic and Protestant works and church services, meetings and church attendance, drinking houses, civic affairs, the oaths sworn in unbelief and other things of that kind, which are highly regarded by the world and yet are carried on in flat contradiction to the command of God, in accordance with all the unrighteousness which is in the world.

A Third Way

With the above history, diversity, and commonality in mind, there emerges the general shape of a distinctive church tradition, a third way. It was a way between Catholicism and Protestantism—church alliance with the political world—and a violent, revolutionary Anabaptism—like at Münster. It is not possible to draw on any one person as an official representative of this third way. Even so, Menno Simons serves as a helpful source and model. He at least is a widely recognized spokesperson for one large and enduring branch of Anabaptism.

"Mennonites" are the most numerous twentieth-century representatives of sixteenth-century Anabaptism. Eventually the name of Menno Simons (1496-1561) would be used—especially in America—to designate large numbers of Anabaptists of Dutch, Swiss, and South German origin. Menno began as a loyal Roman Catholic. Born four years after Christopher Columbus had "discovered" America, son of a dairy farmer in the Dutch village of Witmarsum just a few miles from the North Sea, he was ordained a priest in 1524 and served faithfully, although not altogether selflessly. Soon he read some of the provocative work of reformers like Martin Luther and came to question privately the biblical appropriateness of the Roman teachings on infant baptism and transubstantiation (bread and wine of the Eucharist actually becoming the body and blood of Christ).[26] Now troubled in conscience, he nonetheless enjoyed the privileges of priesthood, even accepting a promotion to his home parish in 1531, led there he later admitted by the desire to obtain a great name for himself. The time soon came, however, when Menno would realize that such hypocrisy had to end.

His renouncing of the Roman Catholic Church was precipitated less by his doctrinal doubts and more by dramatic events in Leeuwarden (1531) and Münster (1534-35). Both incidents ended in bloody tragedy. The 1531 martyrdom of Sicke Freeriks Snijder, "a godfearing, pious hero," prompted Menno to read his Bible more carefully. Why would a good man believe so strongly in rebaptism that he would risk and then suffer beheading by civil authorities? The Münster fiasco played out much like the 1993 story of the Branch Davidians in Waco, Texas. Hundreds of Dutch-speaking Anabaptists converged on this city, driven by the conviction that Münster was about to become the New Jerusalem, the site for reestablishing God's reign on earth.[27] Although at first they were elected as a majority of the city council, the

---

[26]As Menno began to entertain doubts about Roman Catholic doctrine in 1525, that very year Conrad Grebel was organizing the first Anabaptist congregations in Switzerland. The Anabaptist movement may be said to have begun in Zürich when Grebel baptized Georg Blaurock and then Blaurock baptized others present, constituting a gathered church and bringing down the wrath of the city council. Grebel's life ended the next year, probably of plague after being weakened by imprisonment.

[27]Behind such expectation were the extravagant visions and prophecies of Melchior Hoffman (c.1495-1543), most significant early propagator of Anabaptism in northern Germany who had called for true believers to accept baptism into the pure church of Christ in preparation for Christ's return and the world's expected end in 1533. He declared Strasbourg as the locus of the final events. Magistrates of that city imprisoned Hoffman until his death, but his teaching fired the expectations of some others who shifted the locus of expectation to Münster.

circumstance degenerated into a morass of religious fanaticism, including Jan van Leyden naming himself king, taking twelve wives, eliminating private property, forcing the city's non-Anabaptist citizens to be baptized, and arming for the final battle in which the elect were to vanquish the godless. But that summer the army of a Catholic bishop stormed the city, bringing to a violent conclusion the whole sordid affair. The poor reputation of Anabaptists in the region now had become much worse, and for reasons they especially deplored.

Menno, then teaching Roman doctrines he considered false, was impressed by these Christians who, although clearly wrong on some beliefs and actions, gave their estates and lives for what they believed. Now he implored God for forgiveness of his own hypocritical life and got more daring by himself preaching the Reformation doctrine of repentance, using the Bible to oppose all sin, idolatry, and false worship. His earliest surviving tract is a 1535 polemic against Jan van Leyden in which he denounced private visions and the resorting to violence in the name of God. In 1536 Menno finally abandoned his priesthood to become an itinerant evangelist. He was baptized and newly ordained in 1537 by a leader of the beleagured pacifist remnant of Dutch Anabaptism. For the rest of his life he would exist mostly as a hunted heretic working to rally and mold into a unity the scattered Anabaptists of Holland and northern Germany. Apparently there was no way for a true Christian to avoid an almost daily cross in the circumstances of Menno's time.[28]

Following the Münster tragedy of 1535 and the discrediting of militant millenarianism, there were no further forceful Anabaptist attempts to restore the world to primitive Christianity. Now the focus was on strategic withdrawal from the corrupted worlds of both church and state. Under the leadership of Menno Simons, whose own brother was killed either in the Münster debacle or in another armed occu-

---

[28]Although limited by the state-church compromise of the mainline Lutheran reformation, the theology of Martin Luther himself focused strongly on the cross, both of Jesus and as a way of being a Christian in the world. See Alister McGrath, *Spirituality in an Age of Change* (Grand Rapids: Zondervan, 1994), chap. 5, "The Dark Night of Faith: Luther's Theology of the Cross."

pation in Friesland, the Anabaptist remnants in Holland and northern Germany were gathered into voluntary communities that sought to function in relative separation from the established and powerful civil and religious orders. In 1540 Menno published his most influential writing, *The Foundation of Christian Doctrine*. He made it clear that he spoke for non-resistant, pacifistic Anabaptists, explicitly condemning the characteristics of the Münsterites: "the sword, polygamy, an external kingdom and king, and other like errors on account of which the innocent have to suffer much."[29] His work was a rationale for those Anabaptists whose choice was the cross and not the sword. Menno, however, acknowledged the legitimacy of civil authorities and pledged obedience to them in all areas which did not violate the requirements of biblical faith.

How then should voluntary "evangelical orders" of "radical" Christians relate to the world? If one way was political alliance with the world, the old Constantinian synthesis being perpetuated newly by the magisterial Protestant reformers like Luther, and a second way was the Münster-like revolutionaries, Menno's was clearly a third way. Christians should concentrate on being Christians, servants of God's rule, first, fully, and peacefully; they then and only then should be obedient and supportive of the secular government to the fullest degree compatible with their faith. At his death in 1561, Menno left behind a biblically-rooted moderation that impacted the broader Anabaptist tradition among and beyond his own "Mennonite" followers.

The first decade of the "radical" reformation had been chaotic, diverse, and experimental; but by the time of Menno's death, and in significant part because of his ministry, the Anabaptist view of the true church and the pattern of free-church life had reached a certain historical, theological, and sociological maturity. Franklin Littell observes:

> The basic problem of the radicals, we may safely conclude, was to gather and discipline a movement, to effect a reasonable balance between the strong individualism of a fresh spiritual

    [29]John C. Wenger, ed., trans. Leonard Verduin, *The Complete Writings of Menno Simons* (Scottdale, Pa.: Herald Press, 1956), 107.

experience and the hard necessities of a community living in the world and in history.[30]

Menno's vision of the faith was a third option in at least one other way. The Radical Reformation in general was characterized by a decided emphasis on the interiorized process of salvation. An experience of new birth was understood to be a prerequisite for water baptism. But it also was taught clearly that inward and individual spiritual experience must not be restricted to private visions or a "spiritual" realm. Faith and its intended fruit are to be inseparable in all aspects of life. Menno, and with his help Anabaptists generally, did not accept Luther's forensic doctrine of justification by faith alone because the abstraction of such doctrine was seen as an obstacle to a "lively" faith which leads necessarily to holy living. Menno was disturbed by what he saw as latent tendencies to antinomianism in Luther's doctrine of justification, at least as that doctrine had been lived out by the Lutherans that he had observed. Menno once reported quite critically about Lutherans:

> They strike up a psalm…while beer and wine verily run from their drunken mouths and noses. Anyone who can but recite this on his thumb, no matter how carnally he lives, is a good evangelical man and a precious brother.[31]

Timothy George observes that "the Anabaptist's concept of discipleship as a deliberate repudiation of the old life and a radical commitment to Jesus as Lord could not tolerate such a lackadaisical abuse of the grace of God."[32] Robert Friedmann summarizes well. The sixteenth-century Anabaptists

> …ventured the hard and narrow way of non-conformity to the "world" that is a consistent life of earnest discipleship of Christ.

---

[30]Franklin Littell, *The Anabaptist View of the Church*, 2nd ed. (Boston: Starr King Press, Beacon Hill, 1958), 43.

[31]Wenger, op. cit., 333-334.

[32]Timothy George, *Theology of the Reformers* (Nashville: Broadman Press, 1988), 270.

It became in fact a "Christian revolution."...their primary concern was the keeping of the commandments of Christ, or to say it in one word, obedience.... The brethren, as they called themselves, tried to follow two great principles, well known to every Christian, but rarely actualized in history: Love and the Cross.... Love leads to brotherhood, to a close and permanent fellowship which is unknown in the world at large, while the Cross is the unavoidable consequence of such contradiction to the world as it was taught by Christ.[33]

Menno, to avoid a possible pitfall developing from such an emphasis on obedience, rejected rigid predestinarianism, trying rather to strike a balance between "works righteousness" and the theological determinism typical of the mainline Protestants of his day.[34] He was an advocate of toleration, insisting that the saving grace of God is for everyone, but should not be forced on anyone. The bottom line was a vision shorn of the temptations to make extreme apocalyptic pronouncements, a vision based instead on two fundamental biblical ideals. These had to do with a (1) practical holiness that is (2) practiced within the church, the company of the committed and the community of the Spirit.[35] Associated elements of this vision were the complete separation of the church and secular politics, toleration and freedom of conscience, high moral and social ideals, the preaching and practice of peace—all of these presuming the supreme sov-

---

[33]Robert Friedmann, "The Anabaptist Genius and Its Influence on Mennonites Today," in *Proceedings of the First Conference on Mennonite Cultural Problems* (Bethel College, Bluffton College, Eastern Mennonite School, Freeman College, Goshen College, Hesston College, Messiah Bible School, and Tabor College, 1942), 21.

[34]Intrinsic to Believers Church theology, ecclesiology, and ethics is a free-will assumption about humans, in contrast to Calvinistic predestination teaching that rests on a "bondage of the will" assumption. This whole tradition is premised on the belief that somewhere in the development of personhood one gains a knowledge of good and evil and the capacity and responsibility to respond to God's offered grace. This is the "prevenient grace" that God provides to enable human choice (taught so clearly in the later work of John Wesley).

[35]See Elton Trueblood, *The Company of the Committed* (N. Y.: Harper & Row, 1961), and C. Norman Kraus, *The Community of the Spirit* (Scottdale, Pa.: Herald Press, rev. ed., 1993).

ereignty of Christ over his children in this world.[36] Not an abandonment of this world, the Menno model was a call to really be the church in the world for the sake of both believers and the world. In neither the sixteenth nor twentieth centuries did Menno speak for all Christians of the Believers Church tradition on all subjects— nor did anyone else. He did, however, speak influentially, centrally, and well. Two contemporary interpreters of this tradition put one of his core concerns this way: the church "doesn't have a social strategy, the church is a social strategy."[37] To really be what she is called to be in the present, the church first must know what she was originally and should be ideally. Typically, for the Believers Church tradition, this quest for church self-awareness has resulted in an appreciative focus on the church's apostolic beginnings.

An Apostolic Idealism

More basic to the sixteenth-century Anabaptist movement than the occasional apocalyptic extremism was a biblical commitment that nurtured an apostolic idealism. The "radical" nature of the resulting Believers Church stream of tradition emerging from this sixteenth-century reformation had a meaning other than merely going to the limit in its "protesting" against the excesses of the Roman Catholic Church, the limitations of the work of the magisterial Protestant reformers, and certainly the occasional violence like happened in Münster. With the reactive was the proactive, driven by a particular vision of what ought to be. Once establishing an organizational break with the dominant church structures and having been instructed by the non-violent moderation of leaders like Menno Simons, the radicals set a course toward being "earnest Christians" together in a "truly evangelical order" (to borrow Luther's phrases). Moving beyond *reforming* the established church of the time, the intent became one of *restoring* in actual practice enduring elements of the earliest church of the New Testament.

---

[36]See the Schleitheim Confession of 1527 and Appendix B, the Report of the Findings Committee, Conference on the Believers Church tradition, 1967.

[37]Hauerwas and Willimon, *Resident Aliens*, 43.

Zwingli's biblical views moved him beyond Luther to a focus on Christian "primitivism." While Luther continued to be rooted deeply in the traditions of the established Roman church with their presumed authority alongside the Bible, Anabaptism shifted the accepted locus of authority more singularly toward the "biblical pattern." James Murch, a church historian of the Disciples of Christ, reports that "the Free Church has had an unbroken existence in Christendom from the first Christian Church in Jerusalem, A. D. 30, to the present day." He traces the path of this existence through the Waldensians, then the Anabaptists, to the left-wing Puritans, and eventually to the revival in Scotland led by the Haldane brothers, culminating in the Restoration sparked by Thomas and Alexander Campbell in the United States.[38] This American-born Restoration Movement began about the year 1800 to attempt a restoration of the church to the ideals that were understood to be pictured in the New Testament. What are these ideals? According to James North, they are "the concern for the unity of all Christians in the one body of Christ and the concern for the Bible as the only authority for the faith and practice of Christians."[39] Whatever the particular elements of restoration highlighted by different groups, the Believers Church stream generally has been intent on gathering and disciplining a "true church" based on the apostolic precedent, dynamic, and/or pattern, however this is understood.[40] Church historian Philip Schaff puts it this way: "The reform-

---

[38]James DeForest Murch, *The Free Church* (Restoration Press, 1966), 36-48. This, of course, is not to say that the Anabaptists were influenced directly by the Waldensians or that the Anabaptists necessarily understood themselves to be furthering the reforming stream of the Waldensians or others.

[39]James B. North, *Union In Truth: An Interpretive History of the Restoration Movement* (Cincinnati: Standard Publishing, 1994), 6. The 1975 Believers Church Conference was convened on the California campus of Pepperdine University that is associated with the Churches of Christ. It explored the theme of the restoration of apostolic Christianity. See the published report of this conference in the *Journal of the American Academy of Religion* 44:1 (March 1976), 3-113.

[40]The English Puritans, e.g., attempted to restore "true Christianity," were frustrated in England, but in America aspired to enable the new world to become the primordial kingdom of God. This and other restorationist streams, visions, and experiments were the focus of the 1975 Believers Church Conference at Pepperdine University. See Appendix A.

ers aimed to reform the old Church by the Bible; the radicals attempted to build a new church from the Bible."[41] The latter gathered and disciplined a "true church" on what was understood to be the apostolic ideal.

The restoration[42] envisioned by the Believers Church tradition has had at least three essential components. (1) The renewed church will be an alternative both to the currently established churches and to the dominant secular culture. (2) The norm of the renewed church will be biblical teaching, especially Jesus who is accepted as the norm of truth itself. (3) The form of the renewed belief and life of the church will be more than a mechanical imitation of any past. In fact, the Believers Church idea "works against the idea of straightforward recovery. As a set of regulative principles, an outlook, or an approach to the Christian life, the Believers Church idea is not an objective entity for imitation."[43] Restoration is a continuing process of renewal. To freeze creedal formulations or church structures and practices from any time period, including the early church, is to establish a post-biblical canon of authority. Even so, there has been a pervasive search for the restoration of something judged to be basic and original. This was and is the apostolic idealism of the Believers Church tradition.

A proper "apostolicity," according to most sixteenth-century Anabaptists, surely does not mean an unbroken line of ministerial ordinations from Peter to today. What it does mean is that the New Testament era is normative, that believers always should be true to the inspired biblical teachings of the original apostles of the Christ, and that some restoration clearly is required in order to return the church

---

[41]Cited by R. J. Smithson, *The Anabaptists* (London: James Clarke & Co., 1935), 14-15.

[42]For some the word "reformation" is preferred over "restoration" since the latter implies that the early church offers an ideal pattern that only needs to be duplicated in every later time. This pattern idea is thought to be too mechanical and too historically and culturally naive.

[43]Weaver, *Becoming Anabaptist*, 122. Franklin Littell affirms nonetheless that "the Anabaptists maintained that the New Testament was clear both as to the content of the Christian faith and the organizational procedures in the true Christian community" (*The Anabaptist View of the Church*, 46).

to the firmer footing it knew before its "fall." That is, believers need to recover what was basic before "the pride of the hierarchs, the arrogance of the professional theologians, and the ambitions of temporal rulers had enhanced its outward show of prestige and weakened its true inward strength."[44]

The biblical story of God in Israel and in Christ is foundational for Christian faith. But more than foundation is needed. According to the Believers Church tradition, an *orthodox* base is to be accompanied by *radical* relevance. The past is prologue. It is pivotal, but nonetheless preliminary. Believers are to be touched and transformed by a particular past so that they can be positioned to touch the present and future. The task is to gain true Christian identity, formed by the biblical revelation as understood in the earliest Christian community, for the sake of Christian life and mission today. Here is the key question: What is it that comes to us from ancient biblical times which can be considered the enduring essence of the Christian faith?

Millard Erickson lists five possible answers, each common in church history. The permanent essence may be: (1) institutional; (2) a sequence of the historical acts of God, especially the exodus in the Old Testament and the "Christ-Event" in the New; (3) abiding spiritual experiences, such as the universal hope of immortality; (4) a particular way of life; or (5) a set of enduring doctrines, biblically rooted theological propositions that are unchanging and authoritative.[45] The Believers Church tradition has actively sought the right choice among these alternatives and usually has been especially reluctant about the first and last in the list. Why? Because established church institutions and restrictive creedal statements tend to rely heavily on the abstract, rational, traditional, and structural—all easily honoring human establishments over the present dynamic of the

---

[44]Franklin Littell, *A Tribute to Menno Simons*, 24. Littell warns that in view here is no "sterile restorationism which later characterized one wing of the Campbellite [Christian Churches] movement" (28).

[45]Millard Erickson, *Christian Theology*, vol. 1 (Grand Rapids: Baker Book House, 1983), 108-112.

Spirit of God and all easily distracting the disciple of Jesus from primary commitment to the actual living of the faith.

Being "apostolic" is crucial. On the other hand, how can contemporary Christians be faithful to historic foundations without blindly romanticizing the past? How can church leaders be alert to the best of modern or ancient wisdom without idolizing either? The biblical revelation of God with us in particular past times, especially in Jesus Christ, is the believer's special revelation and guide. The past, at least as represented by the biblical narrative about the Christ, clearly should be definitive. Even so, Donald Bloesch warns that we must avoid one of the "pathways to evangelical oblivion," that of becoming "fixated on the past rather than [being] alive to the myriad possibilities that God brings to the church in the here and now."[46] It is no easy task to be both truly apostolic and currently relevant. Does a restorationist mind-set not lead to a rather mechanical, slavish, and unrealistic imitation of the past, one being remembered only in part and not wholly adequate for guiding what is yet an uncharted future?

Lillie McCutcheon of the Church of God (Anderson) once cautioned wisely: "The difficulty with pioneers is that all too soon they become settlers.... Even if it were possible to reproduce the church of the first century, it would obviously be immature and inadequate to serve today's world.... God is searching for a body of people who will be fashioned by the Holy Spirit to reveal His design for the church in this age."[47] The Findings Committee of the 1967 Believers Church Conference (see Appendix B, section 3B) agreed: "We are left with the temptation to exaggerate the possibility or desirability of imitating in particular details the cultural forms of New Testament church life."

If not by some mechanical duplication of words, forms, doctrines, or practices, just how is the apostolic church to function as the Christian standard for today? Church historian Charles Brown responds by

---

[46]Donald Bloesch, *The Future of Evangelical Christianity* (Doubleday, 1983), 86.

[47]As in Barry L. Callen, *The First Century*, vol. 2 (Anderson, Ind: Warner Press, 1979), 778-779. This observation was made about the Church of God (Anderson) movement as it reflected on its heritage in preparation for its centennial celebration in 1980.

employing the analogy of a healthy baby compared to a fully grown adult who is crippled by a disabling disease. The adult hardly needs to recover the ignorance or immaturity of childhood, but rather that childhood's health and normality. Today's church likewise should not imitate the apostolic church in ways not reflective of the massive cultural changes in the intervening centuries. However, "we are under a most heavy responsibility, so far as possible, to reproduce the spiritual life, the truth, the doctrine, the holy equality of the universal priesthood of believers; the warm, rich, deep fellowship; and the burning message of redemption, as well as the overwhelming experiences of the Spirit's complete control of our lives, which were known so well in the apostolic church."[48]

"Primitive" Christianity enjoyed the keen awareness that believers were living in the presence of the absolute future which had already arrived in the person of Jesus Christ. Therefore, the Believers Church tradition has tended to be comfortable with the view of a contemporary Lutheran theologian that "continuity with the apostles does not mean constructing an irreducible minimum of apostolic doctrines, nor does it mean connecting up with an unbroken chain of apostolic offices of leadership." What then does it mean? It means "to lay hold of the *original eschatological drive of the early Christian apostolate* and to trace its trajectory through the discontinuities of time and history."[49] This early eschatological drive was rooted solidly in the person and work of Jesus Christ. True primitivism leads back to the Bible, the faithful witness to Jesus Christ. God has spoken in Jesus Christ who, for the Christian, is the truth, the way, the life and hope. The biblical narrative about Jesus, when enlivened by the Spirit, is the primary avenue to touching and being touched by "apostolic" truth in a way that can inspire current relevance.

For the church to be truly apostolic in any present time, the church must be about Christ's business of extending the reign of God in the

---

[48]Charles E. Brown, *The Apostolic Church* (Anderson, Ind: Warner Press, 1947), 31.
[49]Carl E. Braaten, *Principles of Lutheran Theology* (Philadelphia: Fortress Press, 1983), 51.

enabling wake of the truth and power of the arrival of that gracious reign in Christ's first coming. What, then, is the task of Christian theology? In the words of Jürgen Moltmann, another contemporary Lutheran, theology "must 'make present' the fundamental historical recollection of Christ, in order to interpret the present in the light of that and to open up the future which is being headed for in that historical past."[50] Reports the Quaker philosopher-theologian David Elton Trueblood: "One of the most encouraging ideas which has entered my mind is that we are *early Christians*, still alive while the faith is fluid and capable of assuming new forms."[51] The faith, ever enduring as the one and only faith once delivered to the saints, is also to be ever fresh, definite while yet dynamic, capable of and often needing to assume newly articulated and embodied forms. We contemporary believers indeed are "early Christians" now living in a secularizing and multi-cultural world.[52] To be early, apostolic, is at once to be close to the origins of the faith and to be facing ahead to a large, unknown, and demanding future of sharing and living out the faith in new circumstances and probably in some new ways.

Although the New Testament was inspired by the Holy Spirit and therefore is uniquely authoritative for apostolically-oriented Christians, the images which appear in the New Testament were most certainly used "because they were needed to elucidate the work of Christ in some particular place and in some special situation."[53] Thus, to be authentically apostolic includes being able to distinguish between what is enduring substance and what is dated expression and application. It is to be faithful by seeking to be vitally relevant in needed new expressions and applications. It is being *orthodox* without being

---

[50]Jürgen Moltmann, *Theology Today* (Philadelphia: Trinity Press International, 1988), viii.

[51]D. Elton Trueblood, *While It Is Day: An Autobiography* (Harper & Row, 1974), 123-124.

[52]In fact, Justo González sees the situation of today's church as similar to that of its earliest centuries. See his *Christian Thought Revisited* (Nashville: Abingdon Press, 1989), chapter nine.

[53]John Driver, *Understanding the Atonement for the Mission of the Church* (Scottdale, Pa: Herald Press, 1986), 31.

rigidly locked into all aspects of a dated past; it is being *radical* without being blindly overwhelmed by all aspects of the shifting present.

An important breakthrough occured at the 1963 conference on Faith and Order of the World Council of Churches convened in Montreal, Canada. A crucial distinction was made there between church "traditions" and the Christian "Tradition." The delegates came to speak of the goal of ecumenical theology as a recovery of the "Tradition of the Gospel, testified in Scripture, transmitted in and by the Church through the power of the Holy Spirit." The proper task of Christian theology, then, "is not to compare twigs and branches of the Christian tree, but to explore *together* the common trunk.... The goal must be to struggle together to confess the Tradition of the Gospel, not simply to preserve intact our confessional traditions."[54] This fresh focus is similar in many ways to the gospel orientation and apostolic instinct of the Believers Church tradition. Such is the case, however, only if the "Tradition" is not viewed as a subtle affirmation of "establishment" Christianity (state churches or mainstream denominations closely allied with host cultures). Any church tradition reflects authentic Christian faith only as it truly reflects the heart, life, and mission of Jesus Christ.

Ecumenically speaking, the vision of the Believers Church tradition tends to be appreciative of such breakthroughs. Its own unity vision is significantly congregational and "visible" in character. As the 1967 Findings Committee of the Believers Church Conference affirmed, the

---

[54]As quoted in Michael Kinnamon in *Baptism and Church*, Merle Strege, ed. (Grand Rapids: Sagamore Books, 1986), 149-150. Kinnamon notes in his *Truth and Community* (Eerdmans, 1988) that biblical scholars Ernst Kasemann and Raymond Brown presented pivotal papers at this 1963 Montreal conference. They stressed the internal variety in the Bible itself, arguing that the Bible "actually canonizes the diversity of Christianity." The Bible, concludes Kinnamon, "frees us from a sterile preoccupation with recovering the shape of the New Testament church and opens us to the possibility of a unity that (following Scripture) is richly diverse and oriented toward the future leading of the Spirit" (1988, 3). Restoration of the apostolic church in our time may vary widely from the specifics of what actually existed in the first and second centuries, all without breaking continuity with that ancient, diverse, and itself developing church.

unity goal "is not the spiritualized concept of a purely invisible unity." But neither is the visibility sought to take the non-congregational form of "one agency…seeking or claiming to gather, represent, or lead all Christians." Unity will be a lived reality among Christians. While admittedly facing the danger of "anarchy, competitiveness, and isolationism," true unity will include a "passionate commitment to a freer, more fluid, more missionary, and more costly manifestation of the unity of Christ's body" than do the "higher" and more structurally-, creedally-, and liturgically-based versions.[55]

Donald Bloesch speaks eloquently of the "confessional theology" he personally affirms. It is "catholic" and not "reactionary." It advocates "not a return to the past but a critical reappropriation of the wisdom of the past." It espouses "continuity with tradition but is willing to subject even church tradition to the judgment of the Word of God." It, therefore, champions the ancient good news together with the whole community of faith ("evangelical" and "catholic") without being narrowly sectarian or mechanically restorationist.[56] Such confessional theology gladly embraces the message of the biblical revelation, confessing it as the necessary base for an authentic faith today. To this, the Believers Church tradition would insist on adding the following just to be sure that no theology or anything else is permitted to enslave the church: The church as a pilgrim people in this world must, at any cost, avoid allowing itself to be chained and then changed by compromise with a government, a secular way of life, or some "spirit of the times." When it *does*, it *dies*. Believers are to be chained to the biblical revelation of Jesus Christ and changed by Christ's Spirit. Only then is it authentically apostolic.

---

[55]See Appendix B, section 2D. From the numerous unity writings of the Church of God (Anderson) tradition within the Believers Church stream, see James Earl Massey, *Concerning Christian Unity* (Anderson, Ind.: Warner Press, 1979), and Barry L. Callen and James B. North, *Coming Together in Christ: Pioneering a New Testament Way to Christian Unity* (Joplin, Mo.: College Press, 1997).

[56]Donald Bloesch, *A Theology of Word and Spirit* (Downers Grove, Ill.: InterVarsity Press), 268. Often the adjective "confessional" suggests a more fixed and doctrinaire stance than this witness of Bloesch implies.

Five Critical Marks

A former Moderator of the Church of the Brethren helpfully identifies five critical marks of what it means to be Brethren—and, more generally, what it means to be part of the Believers Church tradition.[57] They are:

> 1. We are a people who have confessed our sin, accepted Christ as Lord, and have proposed to live in keeping with the spirit and teaching of the New Testament, have proposed to be faithful members of the Body of Christ, and have sealed those commitments in Christian baptism.
>
> 2. We are a people who work for integrity between word and deed. When persons asked Alexander Mack how the Brethren were to be recognized, he said, "By the manner of their living." Not a word about what they believed; no mention of creed.... I grew up looking for integrity between worship and life....
>
> 3. We are a people of unfinished faith. Brethren have no creed other than the New Testament. For some, that is not enough; they want it more defined; more clear; less open-ended; more manageable....
>
> 4. We are a people committed to living in community. Because faith is unfinished, always in process, our life together can never be judgmentally divisive, ought never to create fences which delineate who is in and who is out. We need each other in our quest to be faithful while remaining open to new leadings of the Spirit. That is, integrity in relationship with one another is as important as integrity between word and deed.
>
> 5. We are a people committed to service. "Inasmuch as you have done it to one of the least of these" are words to mature and grow by; words to test our own kingdom work; and not words to test the validity of another's faith conviction.

In light of such defining marks, truly Christian communities, churches, or denominations are those whose identities are forged less

---

[57]Earle W. Fike, Jr., in Emmert Bittinger, ed., *Brethren In Transition: 20th Century Directions and Dilemmas* (Camden, Maine: Penobscot Press, 1992), 20-21.

by creeds, confessions, traditions, and structural arrangements and more by the shared experience of faith in Jesus Christ and commitment to all that this faith implies for life as individuals and as the corporate body of believers. Recalling the quotation from Rodney Clapp that heads this chapter, the church, to be at her best, needs a language of friendship to characterize and infuse its life. That life should be a culture quite other than that of the world. It should be a life that is organic, relational, and open-ended rather than technical, rational, and manipulative.

The Believers Church stream within the history of the church can be identified sociologically through reference to the categories created by Ernst Troeltsch (1865-1923) in his influential 1911 book, *Social Teaching of the Christian Churches*. He saw across church history a dualistic tendency in the Christian understanding of the essence of the church. One tendency, drawn from Paul and traced through Augustine, Thomas Aquinas, and the major Reformation bodies to the present day, provides the basis of the inclusive, sacrament-dispensing, institutionalized church. The other provides the basis for the disciplined, obedient "sect" which works as salt to preserve the true in the midst of the institutionally compromised. It was this second tradition, exemplified by the sixteenth-century Anabaptists and transmitted later through the English Puritans, which anticipated and exemplified three principles that would be affirmed on the North American continent as self-evident: the voluntary church; the separation of church and state; and religious liberty.

A key link in this historic chain is the eighteenth-century Methodist revival in England and America. Concludes Howard Snyder: "If Methodism had arisen within the Roman Church, it might have become a recognized order, Wesley perhaps seeking an accommodation with Pope Benedict XIV. Conversely, if Methodism had been born two centuries earlier within Reformation Protestantism, it would likely have been forced to become a separate believers' church."[58]

---

[58]Howard A. Snyder, *The Radical Wesley and Patterns for Church Renewal* (Downers Grove, Ill.: InterVarsity Press, 1980), 151.

Why? The political realities with the established churches were different (Anglicanism at least tolerated the Methodist renewal). What was not very different was Wesley's "radical" vision of serious Christians banding together in countercultural covenant communities that can nurture the growth in grace of all members and speak prophetically to the world and the institutional church.[59] Such radical Protestantism is Christian discipleship within committed community. It is the church prepared to trade all for the privilege of gathering voluntarily around the person and example of Jesus Christ and of giving all for the present cause of Christ's mission in the world.

Such voluntary gatherings came to comprise a whole tradition of Christian faith, the Believers Church tradition with its numerous expressions that have evolved in later centuries and in many cultural settings. Despite the many surface diversities, these expressions reflect a discernible pattern of commonality regarding how Christian faith is to be viewed theologically and lived out in obedient discipleship. This pattern is explored in chapters four and five, first with a theological and then with a discipleship focus.

---

[59]See D. Michael Henderson, *John Wesley's Class Meeting: A Model for Making Disciples* (Nappanee, Ind.: Evangel Publishing House, 1997).

4

Identifying the Faith:
Theology

According to the ancient prophet, God has made this very clear: "For my thoughts are not your thoughts, neither are your ways my ways, says the Lord. For as the heavens are higher than the earth, so are my ways higher than your ways and my thoughts than your thoughts." (Isa. 55:8-9)

First, it is important to note that the Anabaptist community was formed by reading the Bible from the perspective of a persecuted, suffering people. Given our contemporary "sociology of knowledge" understandings, we are now able to see that Anabaptists read the Bible through a different lens than did the Catholic or established Protestant churches. Since almost all the New Testament literature was preserved during the first three centuries by a persecuted, suffering church that kept only those writings that were worth dying for, i.e., those that empowered them in their suffering, it is no wonder that the suffering Anabaptists found Scripture to be so powerful in sustaining them in their experience.[1]

---

[1]Willard Swartley, "The Anabaptist Use of Scripture," in C. Bowman and S. Longenecker, *Anabaptist Currents* (Penobscot Press, 1995), 69-70. See also the essays by H. Zorrilla, R. Padilla, L. Rutschman, W. Swartley, R. Sider, and J. Driver in D. Schipani, ed., *Freedom and Discipleship: Liberation Theology in an Anabaptist Perspective* (Maryknoll, N.Y.: Orbis Books, 1989), 17-75, 85-111.

The Believers Church tradition begins its theological work with awareness that God's thoughts are higher than those of humans (Isa. 55:8-9) and that theological establishments often lead away from the Bible and sometimes toward the persecution of faithful Christians. Final answers often are not available; faithful obedience always is necessary to at least approach some adequacy in apprehending an awareness of God's being, will, and ways. This tradition sometimes has had to pursue its theological work in oppressive circumstances, thus requiring of later interpreters an appreciation of the impact of setting on perspective and emphasis.

This tradition does not receive its distinctive teaching flavor from any one particular theological notion or from the teachings of any one reformer or representative denomination. As the Mennonite John Howard Yoder has made clear, the distinctive flavor comes from "a set of shared experiences of grace and a common *stance*." This stance he identifies as the belief that the "Constantinian" commitment to inclusivism in regard to the membership of the visible church is a "root mistake." By inclusivism he means church membership that lacks significant biblical standards, even membership that is virtually automatic because of one's place of residence, parentage, or citizenship in the realm of the prevailing political regime. In direct contrast with accommodationist inclusivism, authentic Christianity "demands the formation of communities based on a common adult confession of faith."[2]

It is assumed that any secular power that imposes its defining will on the church, or any leader within the church who imposes a "system" of structures or beliefs on other believers, is destructive to Christian faith and witness. To be in Christ must be a free choice that leads to voluntary communities of real believers in which room remains for honest searching and total obedience to what comes to be seen as the divine will.[3] Thus, concluded the Believers Church Conference in

---

[2]John Howard Yoder, "Thinking Theologically from a Free-Church Perspective," in John Woodbridge and Thomas McComiskey, eds., *Doing Theology in Today's World* (Grand Rapids: Zondervan, 1991), 252.

[3]See, for instance, William H. Brackney, ed., *The Believers Church: A Voluntary Church* (Kitchener, Ont.: Pandora Press with Herald Press, 1998).

1967, we "reject any pattern of establishment or any church practice …whereby Christian allegiance is affirmed, imposed, or taken for granted without the individual's consent or request."[4] Therefore, one should not expect to find any inclination toward highly intellectualized systematic theologies, especially if they are separated from practical Christian living and set forth as presumably authoritative for believers.

The distinctive theological vision of this tradition roots in biblical revelation and in the centrality of serious discipleship to be realized in covenant community, not in the settledness of church structures, traditions, or systems of theology. Most of its teaching lies well within the "orthodox" faith boundaries established ecumenically over the centuries.[5] Orthodoxy, however, is viewed less as compulsory tradition and more as a Spirit-directed faithfulness in the context of the serving community of true believers in the Jesus of New Testament history—as opposed to the philosophically articulated Jesus of later centuries. The Believers Church tradition tends to approach Christian theology in a way similar to how Alister McGrath defines "spirituality." He says that it "designates the Christian life—not specifically its ideas, but the way in which those ideas make themselves visible in the life of Christian individuals and communities. Spirituality represents the interface between ideas and life, between Christian theology and human existence."[6] In this way, the Believers Church is something of an interfacing tradition, not lacking in strong ideas, but caring deeply about the relation of ideas to life, community, and service.

---

[4]See Appendix B, section 1A.

[5]The 1526 catechism of Balthasar Hubmaier, e.g., focuses on the teaching of the Ten Commandments, the Lord's Prayer, and the Apostles' Creed. For an affirming but cautious and somewhat qualified approach of the Believers Church tradition to the classic ecumenical creeds, see J. Denny Weaver, "A Believers' Church Christology," *Mennonite Quarterly Review* 57 (April 1983), 112-131. Weaver was the key organizing person in the 1980 Believers Church Conference that convened at Bluffton College (Ohio) of the General Conference Mennonites. Its theme was "Is There a Believers' Church Christology?" Also see Weaver's more recent "Christus Victor, Ecclesiology, and Christology," *Mennonite Quarterly Review* 68:3 (July 1994), 277-290.

[6]Alister McGrath, *Spirituality in an Age of Change* (Grand Rapids: Zondervan, 1994), 31-32.

In the 1930s and 1940s Robert Friedmann and Harold Bender focused their understanding of the essential nature of the sixteenth-century Anabaptist movement around the themes of discipleship, nonresistant love, and fellowship.[7] This triad of theological motifs has been a matter of primary consideration since the Schleitheim days of 1527 and the time of the ministry of Menno Simons in the Low Countries (1536 and following). The exact theological meanings and ethical implications of these motifs certainly did vary among the often diverse segments of early Anabaptism, but there is a way to focus the heart of this tradition which appears to represent most of the non-magisterial or Radical Reformation. It is the principle of "solidarity in Christ."

The old triad flows into "the idea of the present body of Christ as an extension of the incarnation of its head.... [This] means that every individual member of the body must visibly resemble and imitate the head."[8] Luther and Calvin taught a similar solidarity, but for them the visibility comes from the offices of the church rather than from the lives of her individual members. The true church, they said, is where the Word is rightly preached and the sacraments properly administered. But the Anabaptists, more radical indeed, expected that every believer should reflect solidarity with Christ in all aspects of life, so that the visibility of this Christlikeness in them and their voluntary gatherings is the witness of the true church to the world. Thus, the true church is where the Word is rightly received and embodied in a faithful fellowship serving as Christ in the midst of the world. Theology and discipleship are to be linked closely, becoming almost one in the same.[9] As the Findings Committee of the 1967 Believers Church

---

[7]See Leonard Gross, "Recasting the Anabaptist Vision: The Longer View," *Mennonite Quarterly Review* 60:3 (July 1986), 352-363.

[8]J. Denny Weaver, "Discipleship Redefined: Four Sixteenth Century Anabaptists," *Mennonite Quarterly Review* 54:4 (October 1980), 256.

[9]Balthasar Hubmaier has been referred to as the most eloquent spokesperson and profound theologian of sixteenth-century Anabaptism. Because of his strong and public reforming convictions, he was burned to death in Vienna in 1528. His theologizing was hardly an exercise in abstract academics in an ivory tower, although he was an educated and articulate man. The 1989 Believers Church Conference held at Southwest Baptist Theological Seminary in Fort Worth, Texas, was devoted wholly to Hubmaier and his

Conference affirmed, there is a Christian norm fixed in the Christ events as reported faithfully by the Apostles. Accordingly, "the church exists where these events are reported and their meaning interpreted by believing witnesses to believing hearers."

Priority of the Lived Faith

There is little tolerance in the Believers Church tradition for theology in isolation—theology for its own sake. The observation of Myron Augsburger is significant. The Anabaptists of the sixteenth century, and most of those who yet share their rich and "radical" Christian tradition, were "theologians of praxis rather than of reflection." Theirs was not "a rationalistic theology conditioned by categories of Greek thought, but an existential biblical theology of relationship."[10] As the Findings Committee of the 1967 Believers Church Conference put it:

> ...the most visible manifestation of the grace of God is His calling together a believing people.... The shorthand label "Believers' Church" therefore points first of all not to the doctrinal content of beliefs held, nor to the subjective believingness of the believer, but more to the constructive character of the commitment in defining the visible community.[11]

One good example is the early "Quaker" movement (Society of Friends) in England. George Fox (1624-1691), after an intense personal struggle, forsook church attendance, dismissed contemporary religious controversies as trivial, and in 1647 began to preach that truth is to be found in God's voice speaking to the soul. By 1650 he was in prison for being a blasphemer and had a judge nickname his

---

thought (see *Mennonite Quarterly Review,* January, 1991, 5-53). A contemporary theologian of the Believers Church tradition, the Baptist James McClendon, Jr., begins his systematic theology with a volume on ethics (*Ethics: Systematic Theology,* vol. 1, Nashville: Abingdon Press, 1986). To him, the life of faith and theological reflections on that life are inseparable.

[10]Myron Augsburger, "Concern for Holiness in the Mennonite Tradition," *The Asbury Seminarian* (October 1981), 32. Also see Robert Friedmann, *Mennonite Piety Through the Centuries* (Goshen, Ind.: Mennonite Historical Society, 1949), 82.

[11]See Appendix B, section 1A.

followers "Quakers" after Fox had exhorted the magistrates to "tremble at the word of the Lord." Robert Barclay (1648-1690) was the Scottish theologian who soon gave important intellectual structure to the pioneering and prophetic ministry of Fox. The central paradox of this structure is that Barclay "sought to reach learned men with something which unlearned men had discovered."[12] That something was the Christ of *experience* placed in careful balance with the Christ of *history*. He sought a means of bringing the whole body of Christian teaching into vital relationship with experimental religion. The result was the emphasis that Christian tradition, especially the Bible, is crucial; but authentic faith must be "religion in the present tense!"[13]

There is an essential paradox to be held in careful tension. For instance, such strategic balancing has been an historic preoccupation of the Brethren in Christ, with its Anabaptist, Pietist, and Wesleyan heritages.[14] It also has been central for the Church of God (Anderson) that has featured the combination of rather conservative biblical preaching and the group slogan, "Where Experience Makes You a Member" (referring to transforming spiritual experience with Jesus Christ). The *historic* Christ is none other than the *Living* Christ. The "Inner Light," absolutely essential, nonetheless must be the "Light of Christ" to be truly Christian.

Discipleship concerns have overshadowed theoretical musings. Holiness has been understood to be essential to authentic Christian life. There has been deep concern about the Protestant teaching that often emphasizes the necessity of the *forgiving* grace of God (presumably mediated in part through the "sacraments") while minimizing the possibility of God's *transforming* grace that is meditated through God's Word and Spirit. There also has been concern that the Christian faith not be seen primarily as a fixed set of ideas, especially abstract and lifeless ideas mandated by some civil or church estab-

---

[12]D. Elton Trueblood, *Robert Barclay* (N.Y.: Harper & Row, 1968), 3.
[13]Ibid., 139.
[14]See Luke Keefer, "Brethren in Christ: Uneasy Synthesis of Heritage Streams," *Wesleyan Theological Journal* 33:1 (Spring 1998), 92-110. He reports a current imbalance within the historic synthesis, largely because of the recent and undue influence of "evangelicalism," a new and awkward partner in the balancing pattern of this denomination.

lishment. The proper theological work of the church is hardly to maintain given belief systems by intellectual combat, a dialectical dueling that the average believer cannot even understand. Rather, it is to encourage and nourish Christian discipleship and evangelism. For Rodney Clapp and the Believers Church tradition generally, "what comes first is lived faith, or actual Christian community."[15] The proper function of Christian theology is to articulate with care the foundations and implications of being committed wholly to the rule of Jesus Christ.

The ecumenical vision that has marked a central goal of the worldwide network of Christian churches across most of the twentieth century rests on a common affirmation of the sovereignty of God. In light of the God who is above all human concepts, institutions, and programs, this vision affirms that all that is human should be relativized, including the incidentals of the life of the church on earth. Human attempts to structure the church, however well-intentioned, always fall short of functional adequacy. Human claims to have fully grasped and rightly worded what is most true, worthy as all such creeds may be, stand under the judgment of the One who alone is holy, wise, adequate, and complete. The first two of the Ten Commandments say it well. Commandment one, "You shall have no other gods before me," calls for faith in the one God of Israel, the "Abba" of Jesus, "the Truth above all truths."[16] The second, "You shall not make for yourself a graven image," reminds constantly that the human hold on the one Truth is always preliminary. To claim otherwise is to engage in idolatry.

To avoid idolatry, including the persistent temptation to absolutize even its own best insights, the theological stance of the Believers

---

[15]Rodney Clapp, *A Peculiar People: The Church as Culture in a Post-Christian Society* (Downers Grove, Ill.: InterVarsity Press, 1996), 12. Captured more by the rationalistic modernism of recent generations is church historian Mark Noll who laments the failure of contemporary "Evangelicalism" to engage intellectually with other Christians and the prevailing culture (*The Scandal of the Evangelical Mind*, Grand Rapids: Eerdmans, 1994).

[16]Michael Kinnamon, *Truth and Community: Diversity and Its Limits in the Ecumenical Movement* (Grand Rapids: Eerdmans, 1988), 20.

Church tradition has tended to highlight only the Bible as authoritative, thus agreeing with the *Sola Scriptura* principle of the Protestant reformers. There has been clear preference for biblical over systematic theology because no *system* is to be a stumbling block to discipleship. Alexander Mack (1679-1735), early leader of the Brethren movement,[17] is a good example. Rather than being a formal theologian, he was a generalist who wrote out of the urgency of his context. Nonetheless, several clear emphases emerged from his work. They are:

1. The church is called into existence by God.
2. Christ is the Lord of the church.
3. Scripture is the church's objective authority.
4. The Spirit leads the church.
5. The life and doctrine of the early church, i.e., the church of the first and second centuries, provide the normative pattern for the church.
6. The church is responsible for shaping the character of its members.[18]

These convictions, an interplay of Pietist, Anabaptist, and Reformed elements, have been focused more recently into three pervasive themes judged to be central characteristics of authentic Christianity by this "radical" or Believers Church tradition.

First, truth is to be defined by the person of Jesus Christ, who is the center of Christian faith.

Second, Jesus brings into existence a new social reality, the church, the community of believers who focus on Christ and together are being formed by Christ through the work of Christ's Spirit.

Last, this new and distinctive body of believers in Jesus, because of its being shaped into the image of Christ, exercises its disci-

---

[17]Organized in 1708, this Brethren movement took the name German Baptist Brethren in 1871. Its largest body today is known as the Church of the Brethren.

[18]As worded by Dale R. Stoffer, *Background and Development of Brethren Doctrines: 1650-1987* (Philadelphia: Brethren Encyclopedia, Inc., 1989), 69.

pleship best by seeking to be on mission in this world in Christ's particular way.

These three assumptions "function as regulative principles, a set of interdependent beliefs which structure a way of life, an alternative society."[19] They once defined common ground for the otherwise diverse Anabaptist movement of the sixteenth century and still can do the same for an equally diverse Believers Church community at the opening of the twenty-first century.

This chapter offers an overview of the first of these three central themes, especially as it informs the belief and theological life of believers. The next chapter addresses the second and third themes, with particular attention directed to the individual and corporate lives of believers. In focusing on the first theme, the defining centrality of Jesus, one discovers a particular approach to and style of doing Christian theological work. Similar to the work of John Wesley in the eighteenth century, himself called a "radical" reformer,[20] Christian theology

> ...remained a practical discipline, ultimately basing the most metaphysical reflections about God on the life of faith and drawing from these reflections ethical and soteriological implications. Thus, as Wesley understood and practiced theology, the defining task of "real" theologians was neither developing an elaborate system of Christian truth-claims nor defending these claims to their "cultured despisers"; it was nurturing and shaping the worldview that frames the temperament and practice of believers' lives in the world.... The quintessential practitioner of theology was not the detached academic theologian; it was the pastor/theologian who was actively shepherding Christian disciples in the world.[21]

---

[19]These three pervasive themes are those identified by J. Denny Weaver in *Becoming Anabaptist: The Origin and Significance of Sixteenth-Century Anabaptism* (Scottdale, Pa.: Herald Press, 1987), 120-121.

[20]Howard Snyder, *The Radical Wesley* (Downers Grove, Ill.: InterVarsity Press, 1980).

[21]Randy L. Maddox, *Responsible Grace: John Wesley's Practical Theology* (Nashville: Kingswood Books, Abingdon Press, 1994), 17.

This Wesleyan focus on the "practical" resonates through the history of the theological tradition of the Believers Church.

Jesus: The Standard of Truth

The inspired plot of the whole biblical story focuses on Jesus Christ, in whom all things are said to be made new for believers. The biblically-based insights into the salvation and discipleship meanings of Jesus as the Christ soon would be analyzed, theorized, and philosophized in attempts by many generations of Christians to explain and defend their faith and life to multiple non-Christian circles. First, however, the faith was not a *proposition* but a *Person*, not a complex creed but a living Christ. According to Myron Augsburger:

> While accepting the *Sola Scriptura* of the [Protestant] Reformers, it may be said that their [Anabaptist] emphasis was *Sola Christus*, for Jesus as the Christ is the center of faith. For the Anabaptists, the Christian life meant discipleship in the freedom of Christ, an identification of the total life with Jesus Christ, and a commitment to walk in the Spirit [of Christ].[22]

The Christian confession concerning the Christ initially was derived from historical narrative, autobiographical testimony, the story of divine reality as experienced in the life, teachings, death, and resurrection of Jesus. Explaining this incarnation reality philosophically and theologically would come later in the process of struggle with competing claims and the challenges involved in engaging in world mission.[23] But first came the foundational witness of the New Testament to the joy of the living reality of Jesus the Christ. The conviction of the Believers Church tradition is that all christological formulating should remain in close touch with the biblical witness to and the living reality of Jesus Christ.

---

[22]Myron Augsburger, op. cit., 28.

[23]The Believers Church tradition joins John Wesley in having limited interest in *explaining* Christ's nature as God-incarnate, a process often speculative, politically influenced (see the discussion later in this chapter), and an "unwarranted imposition of philosophical conceptions on the simply-expressed teachings of Scripture and the earliest Church" (Randy Maddox, *Responsible Grace: John Wesley's Practical Theology*, 1994, 94-95).

Good perspective is available in the analysis of C. Norman Kraus. Anabaptism as a whole, he reports, was Jesus-centered. For those radical Christians of the sixteenth century, the Bible was important as a sacred instrument, not an end in itself. It was received as the authentic and indispensable witness to Jesus. Theories of inspiration, like the modern debate over "inerrancy," were not emphasized because the concern was not technical analysis, but practical obedience and real relationship. Theologians in the Believers Church tradition tend to hesitate in the face of any attempt to intellectualize Christian faith in ways sometimes done in twentieth-century evangelicalism. Nonetheless, they often are inclined to appreciate, at least in general, Alister McGrath's current agenda.

McGrath is pursuing "the intellectual coherence of evangelicalism" with the intention of "laying foundations for the emergence of a distinctively evangelical worldview." He has tired of the anti-intellectualism which often obstructs the engagement of evangelicals in serious theological dialogue among themselves and with others.[24] His key affirmation is that the evangelical passion for truth should focus on the person of Jesus Christ who *is the truth* (an affirmation shared strongly by the Believers Church tradition). Christianity is the religion of Jesus, not of a book. McGrath cautions that even so, "there is an inextricable and intimate connection between the word of God incarnate and the word of God in Scripture in that Jesus Christ is made known to us through the witness of Scripture, which in turn centers on his person and work."[25] Centering on the biblical witness is critical, of course, but for the purpose of centering on Jesus the Christ.

Beyond the rational dimension of belief should be the crucial considerations of practical obedience. Believers are to resist attributing to

---

[24]Note the similar agenda of Mark A. Noll, expressed in *The Scandal of the Evangelical Mind* (Grand Rapids: Eerdmans, 1994). For critiques of this book from scholars representing less of an establishment evangelicalism than Noll, see David Bundy, Henry Knight, and William Kostlevy in the *Wesleyan Theological Journal* (32:1, Spring 1997), 157-192.

[25]Alister McGrath, *A Passion For Truth: The Intellectual Coherence of Evangelicalism* (Downers Grove, Ill.: InterVarsity Press, 1996), 53-54.

any creedal statement the status of absolute word, the final way of conceiving and saying something best for all time. The historic fourth and fifth century creedal statements about Christ, for instance, are pivotal theological milestones of the Christian tradition. Even so, they are the "end product of one kind of translation of the Jesus narratives into another worldview [and thus]...should not be awarded the status of an absolute norm to which all other statements must conform."[26] One thing the statements from the Councils of Nicea (325) and Chalcedon (451) lack, for instance, is any specific focus on the life and teachings of Jesus. That focus would tie theology to ethics, doctrine to discipleship—key links for the Believers Church tradition.

One certainly should go back to the Bible to recover the narrative foundation for any truly Christian christology since the heart of the Christian faith itself is defined by who Jesus is and what he taught and did while in the flesh. Jesus is the norm, the core context for all fresh theological reflection. Dedicated Christian discipleship is always to be directed by the historical life of Jesus.[27] Given the priority of this historical life, it is inevitable that incarnation-oriented believers would address three of the bigger questions of all. Who was Jesus? What did Jesus teach and do in relation to human salvation? What are the present practical implications of such salvation?

---

[26]J. Denny Weaver, "Perspectives on a Mennonite Theology," *Conrad Grebel Review* (Fall 1984), 200.

[27]A clear example of tying together the historical Jesus, a contemporary setting, and the call to practical discipleship is set forth in Howard Thurman's *Jesus and the Disinherited* (Abingdon Press, 1949). As an African-American seeking to shape christology in a way relevant to the experience of his people, Thurman recalls that the biblical narrative identifies Jesus as a poor Jew, a member of an oppressed minority. Who, then, is Jesus for today's downtrodden? Thurman sees Jesus avoiding the options of active violence and passive withdrawal and instead offering to the Jews of his day a form of resistance based on the Kingdom of God understood as an internal reality that nonetheless is relevant to outward circumstances. James Evans (*We Have Been Believers*, Fortress Press, 1992) notes two biblical references of Thurman that became "central motifs in the subsequent development of christology in black theology" (85). They are: "the Kingdom of God is in us"; and "the Spirit of the Lord is upon me [Jesus], because he hath anointed me to preach the gospel to the poor." These themes emerge directly from the biblical narrative about Jesus and lead to the demand for current and costly discipleship.

Interpreting the Jesus Story

A return to the Gospels and the earthly life of Jesus opens the right door for understanding the special way of life to be lived under the reign of Christ, the way that was inaugurated among us with the coming of Jesus. The elements of all resulting theology should become thoughtful motives for mission. They enable fresh ways of conceptualizing the person and work of Jesus without a loss of the biblical foundation. The goal is never merely to get just right an abstract doctrine about Jesus as the Christ (although some doctrines clearly are more faithful to the biblical witness than others!). God wants disciples of Jesus to get just right a *special way of life*, the Jesus way, modeled in Galilee and Jerusalem before it was expressed in classic creeds. To avoid the heresy of excessive abstraction which can undermine rather than inspire serious Christ-like discipleship, C. Norman Kraus insists on the

> ...firm conviction that this messianic image must be understood in light of the fact that the Christ is none other than Jesus of Nazareth. Christology moves beyond the biographical categories of a historical Jesus in its attempt to assess his significance, but it must never abandon its historical referent. The historical revelation in Jesus remains the norm for defining the authentic Christ image and the Christian's experience of God.[28]

Clearly, any Christian believer's experience of God should center in the presence of God in Jesus, the understanding of which depends in large part on the nature of the Bible's witness to Jesus as the Christ of God. What does Christology have to do with practical Christianity? Theological theory is intended to function in the service of Christian practice and mission.

Within the New Testament itself one sees several interpretations of the Jesus story made by early Christians in relation to differing worldviews already being faced. In chapter one of Colossians, for example,

---

[28]C. Norman Kraus, *Jesus Christ Our Lord: Christology from a Disciple's Perspective* (Scottdale, Pa.: Herald Press, rev. ed. 1990), 25.

Jesus is presented as superior to the presumed network of supernatural powers. In chapter one of John, Jesus is said to be prior to a kind of gnostic hierarchy. The book of Hebrews views Jesus in relation to an elaborate Jewish sacrificial system. These three worldviews tend not to be our own today. Therefore, it follows that contemporary theologians can and should exercise the same kind of discretion in christological interpretation exercised by the biblical theologians and those of the following centuries. Seeking culturally sensitive ways of expressing Christian views is appropriate if, in the concern to be relevant, the expressions remain rooted to the real Jesus as biblically presented.

Appropriate discretion in developing new ways of expressing the enduring meaning of the person and work of Jesus begins by reestablishing the uniqueness of Jesus and his visible representation of the presence and reign of God on earth, based mostly on the Gospel accounts. Theologians develop christologies which must account both for the biblical materials and the modern cosmology. Biblical materials remain basic. All language about God is to be recognized as metaphorical. Theological language, to be helpful, should be shaped to the times. Always, discipleship in the context of the present time is to be the immediate, practical goal. Therefore, the task is to make a faithful and fresh translation of the meaning and implications of the affirmation "Jesus is Lord." The translation should draw directly from the biblical narratives about Jesus and then relate them to the contemporary cultural circumstances.[29]

To illustrate, John Howard Yoder surveys the christologies found in John 1, Hebrews, Colossians 1, and Revelation 5.[30] They are diverse in

---

[29]For instance, "process" philosophy is one shaping worldview common in our times. Every human system of thought, certainly including this one, is limited, and no such system should replace Jesus Christ as the central paradigm within which all Christian believing and living is to occur. Even so, as evangelical theologians like Clark Pinnock have shown, a dialogue between biblical foundations and process insights can yield some productive results. See Clark Pinnock and Delwin Brown, *Theological Crossfire: An Evangelical/Liberal Dialogue* (Grand Rapids: Zondervan, 1990).

[30]John Howard Yoder's presentation was at the Believers Church conference at Bluffton College (Ohio), October 1980. A revised version is found in his *The Priestly Kingdom: Social Ethics as Gospel* (University of Notre Dame Press, 1984, rev. ed., 1994).

circumstance and expression. Each was an affirmation of Jesus the Christ in response to a prevailing thought system seeking to absorb Jesus as a new footnote to itself. Each of these New Testament christologies brings the story of Jesus to a competing system and demonstrates in that system's thought environment that Jesus is both relevant and superior to the limits of that worldview. Each New Testament christology, observes Yoder, shares a common "deep structure" as it faces a given challenge in its distinctive way. That structure: (1) places Jesus above and in charge of the cosmos; (2) identifies the lordship of Christ by focus on the rejection and suffering of Jesus in human form; (3) affirms the pre-existence of Christ, co-essential with the Father and participating in creation and providence; and (4) teaches that writer and readers can share by faith in the victory of Jesus. Christologies will vary in expression because of varying cultural environments, but they must at least be faithful to these four elements of the New Testament's "deep structure."

No one New Testament christology, then, is the ultimate or exclusive one, although they all share a common historical base, set of themes, and discipleship implications. So, when developing christology in a worldview setting different from those faced in the New Testament, one should not simply repeat one of these christologies, but rather should return to Jesus and the deep-root biblical affirmations about him and, on that primary base, make a fresh and faithful translation of his person and work for today. The Nicene, Chalcedonian, and other classic Christian creeds are such translations, very important and instructive ones for the thought worlds of their times and the Christian's thought heritage of all time. But they are not the last word, the ultimate translation for all settings and times. The work of Christian theology has its anchors and ongoing challenges.

Were theological thieves encountered by the Christian community as it traveled the road from Bethlehem and Jerusalem and on to the famous church councils at Nicea (325), Constantinople (381), and Chalcedon (451)? That is, was something of the New Testament's narrative witness to God's action in Jesus lost or inappropriately added by the time the church formalized its classic christological statements in the fourth and fifth centuries? Was the Jesus of history unjustifiably transformed by zealous followers into the Christ of faith? Was the adoption of the church by the establishment of the Roman Empire[31] in effect a domestication of the church by the political interests of the world? Were the church's creeds about the nature of Jesus Christ, emerging after the "Constantinian shift," a worldly as much as a churchly product? Is classic christology only dated abstraction fitted to the philosophic environment of another time—and thus archaic in ours? Within today's Believers Church community, such questions spawn lively debate. This is a particular Christian tradition in which the actual person of Christ rather than establishment theological positions about Christ is central (at some "deep structure" points, of course, there is no difference). The concern is to minimize abstractions, stay with the basics of the biblical revelation about Jesus, and maximize current discipleship. There is special sensitivity to the importance of the separation of church and political establishments and the necessity of a distinctive, Christ-like lifestyle in contrast to the world.

One contemporary representative of the Believers Church tradition concludes: "Our current efforts to write a Mennonite theology become a continuation of the task of reinterpretation visible already in the Bible. It is yet another attempt to restate what it means to be God's people in one more context and cosmology."[32] The theological process involves the Bible as base and the church as context. Favored is an honoring of the historical life and teachings of Jesus rather than being controlled by some alternate philosophic world and agenda. In special focus are the practical demands of serious discipleship—"just as you did it to one of the least of these who are members of my family, you did it to me" (Matt. 25:40). While usually affirming what the classic creeds generally consider "orthodox" belief about Jesus as the

---

[31]Note, e.g., Emperor Constantine, Edict of Milan, 313, as one of the key steps in this process of the Empire adopting the Christian faith and the church excessively accommodating itself to the social surroundings.

[32]J. Denny Weaver, "Perspectives on a Mennonite Theology," *The Conrad Grebel Review* (Fall 1984), 193.

Christ, the Believers Church "has an inherent proclivity toward discovering and discerning Jesus in his human particularity rather than in knowing him through his ontological deity."[33] Jesus frequently deflected his disciples from fruitless speculation and challenged them, "Follow me!" In other words, "Do as I say and you will come to know who I am." Failure to *do* will always end in failure to *be* or *know*.

Victory of Jesus Over the Powers

A clear example of various theological expressions arising in changing cultural contexts is the range of Christian understandings of what Jesus Christ accomplished that now enables human salvation. Among many conservative Christians in recent centuries, the accomplished work of Jesus Christ on behalf of human salvation has been understood primarily by use of the concept of "substitution." That is, Jesus is viewed as having become the substitute for sinful humanity, absorbing the wrath of God toward sin and paying the price required for redemption from sin. Jesus was the perfect sacrifice, the slaughtered lamb by whose shed blood comes the full satisfaction of divine justice. Numerous Believers Church theologians in recent decades, however, have both affirmed some elements of such a substitution model of the atonement and been critical of others. John Howard Yoder, for example, sees in such a model the danger of abandoning the central New Testament affirmation that "God is the agent, not the object of reconciliation." C. Norman Kraus agrees and adds:

> ...a theory which implies that God is bound by a law of justice to demand violent retributive penalty in order to "satisfy" his own moral nature has simply failed to reckon with the radical nature of agape as displayed in the cross. The cross is the victory of agape over penal vengeance, and not the admission that in the end love must recognize the moral right of such vengeance as "justice".... Therefore, the cross cannot be understood as an act of penal sacrifice which reconciles conflicting dimensions of

---

[33]J. Denny Weaver, "A Believers' Church Christology," *Mennonite Quarterly Review* (April 1983), 114.

God's character, but the agapeic sacrifice which reconciles self-alienated humanity to God and itself.[34]

The Christus Victor (Christ As Victor) model of the meaning of the reconciliation accomplished in Jesus is in some ways more compatible with the general theological stance of the Believers Church tradition. Its focus is not deliverance from God's wrath by satisfaction of divine honor and justice (the substitutionary atonement model), but deliverance of humans by Christ from the bondage of evil powers.[35] This model was common in the early Christian community (when the church was a persecuted minority) until Anselm (c.1033-1109),[36] whose substitutionary thinking about Christ's atonement work reflected the ethos of medieval feudalism. Anselm's approach of God's honor satisfied and justice done then was common Christian thinking until the popularity of the "moral influence" model rose in the very different setting of the nineteenth century. In the face of the dramatic evils of the twentieth century, many Christian theologians now have begun taking with renewed seriousness the demonic dimension of life, something prominent in the thought and actions of Jesus and not to be dismissed lightly as mere "mythology" of biblical times.[37] This has brought back an appreciation for the Christus Victor approach to the work of Christ.

Swedish theologian Gustav Aulén (1879-1977) revived the Christus Victor model.[38] Aulén's view of Christ's work emphasizes the mil-

---

[34]C. Norman Kraus, "Interpreting the Atonement in the Anabaptist-Mennonite Tradition," *Mennonite Quarterly Review* (July 1992), 308, 310.

[35]For a review and explanation of the several classic atonement models, see Barry L. Callen, *God As Loving Grace* (Nappanee, Ind.: Evangel Publishing House, 1996), chapter 5.

[36]Anselm was Italian born, became a monk, and later was the Archbishop of Canterbury in England from 1093 until his death in 1109.

[37]The Enlightenment mentality tended to regard the "Christus Victor" view of Christ's work as primitive. Dismissed as premodern superstition was all belief in a personal devil and the domination of human existence by satanic forces of sin and evil.

[38]Gustav Aulén, *Christus Victor*, Eng. trans. 1931 (reprinted by Macmillan, 1969, with a foreword by Jaroslav Pelikan). See also Aulén's *The Faith of the Christian Church*, 2nd Eng. ed. (Philadelphia: Fortress, 1960), 196-213. Several contemporary Mennonite theologians champion this atonement model as biblically faithful and directly compatible with traditional concerns of the Believers Church tradition (e.g., John Howard Yoder, J. Denny Weaver, John Driver, Thomas Finger, and C. Norman Kraus).

itary metaphor (e.g., Col. 2:15).[39] Christ liberates humanity from binding powers and himself emerges victorious in the resurrection. The issue highlighted is not only an individual's release from the guilt of sin by some process of justification before God. Human sin is recognized as having resulted in humans being released by God into the control of satanic forces, working in personal and institutionalized forms. While the substitutionary model tends to focus on the death of Jesus and the moral influence model on the life and death of Jesus, the Christus Victor model calls special attention also to the resurrection, that glorious event that completed Jesus' triumph over the powers, rescuing believers from the *control* of sin.[40] It views Christ's achievement in relation to evil (or its personified head, the devil).[41] It appears best suited to the Believers Church concepts of salvation and the church, in part because it assumes a social component to both evil and salvation and stresses victory through love, sacrifice, and the faithfulness of God in the face of human sin.[42]

According to most traditions of the Western church, the atonement that releases from sin is grounded exclusively in the death of Jesus and not in his resurrection. The resurrection, while crucial, is understood only as divine authentication of the work of Christ. But Christ both died and rose for us (Rom. 5:10). Beyond forgiveness for past guilt, the goal of God in Jesus is to create anew in place of the "old that has passed away" (2 Cor. 5:17). The resurrection of Christ from the dead is the beginning of the new creation. This is why the Orthodox

---

[39]Given the nonviolent views of most leaders in the Believers Church tradition, it should be emphasized that the military metaphor, while stressing the victory of Christ over a very real enemy, does not imply that the victory came by violence on God's part. In fact, it came by faithfulness, love, and tremendous sacrifice—a truly amazing way for an omnipotent and sovereign God to function. Here lies the Believers Church view that Christians should function in the world like God chose to function in Christ.

[40]Release from the controlling power of sin ("sanctification") was a central concern of John Wesley.

[41]See James McClendon, *Systematic Theology: Doctrine* (Nashville: Abingdon Press, 1994), 208-209. He refers to the Christus Victor approach as Christ's achievement aimed at evil, Christ's saving work defeating the devil. In contrast, Anselm was less oriented toward evil and more toward God, Christ's work satisfying God's honor or justice.

[42]J. Denny Weaver, "Atonement for the Non-Constantinian Church," in *Modern Theology* 6:4 (July 1990), 315, 319.

Church of the East has proclaimed forgiveness at the Easter festival and celebrated Easter as the feast of atonement.

The triumph over sinful forces featured in the Christus Victor view is intended to be seen eschatologically. That is, the war with sin and evil already is won in principle, but with real battles still going on and yet to be fought—although there is a liberating present awareness of future victory. The evil powers are still active and very influential. Paul says that we are enslaved to the "elemental spirits of the universe" (Gal. 4:3, 9; Col. 2:8, 20). These spirits apparently include the law (can become deceiving and enslaving) and sin that takes us captive (Rom. 7:11, 23). While the moral influence model of Christ's atonement sees the church on the frontier of social changes that are to be reducing the rule of evil, the Christus Victor model recognizes that the church still is engaged in a hostile conflict and assumes no early and easy victory. This conflict may persist stubbornly, probably until the end of time. Even so, eventual victory is already to be known. Christ's grave is empty (!) and his resurrection power should be evidenced now in a renewed body of Christ, the church. Suggests James McClendon, "in resurrection light, apostolic Christianity can be construed as the continuation of the Jesus story already begun."[43]

The New Testament teaches that Jesus struggled constantly to overcome Satan (Matt. 4:1-11, 12:22-32, 27:37-44). Liberation from evil powers is a pervasive theme (Gal. 1:3; Acts 10:38), with all powers finally to be subordinated to Christ (1 Pet. 3:22; 1 Tim. 3:16). A classic statement of the Christus Victor atonement model is Hebrews 2:14-15: "Since, therefore, the children share flesh and blood, he himself likewise shared the same things, so that through death he might destroy the one who has the power of death, that is, the devil, and free those who all their lives were held in slavery by the fear of death." Early Christians rejoiced that, in the cross and resurrection of Jesus, God somehow "disarmed the rulers and authorities…triumphing over them in it" (Col. 2:15). The victory motif captures well the biblical story of God's long conflict with enslaving evil powers, beginning with

---

[43]McClendon, op. cit., 272.

the dramatic exodus from Egypt, a primary paradigm of faith and salvation throughout the Hebrew Scriptures. Christ's victory over the rulers and authorities is at the heart of one of the earliest Christian confessions of faith (Phil. 2:9-11).

The battle goes on and is not limited to "otherworldly" evil powers that function only in the spiritual realm. The crucifixion death and resurrection victory of Jesus occurred in the physical, historical world in which we live. God's victorious reign continues to have both reality and visibility wherever and whenever God's people live according to the example of Jesus, giving present visibility and reality to the reign of God. The biblical revelation views the work of Christ as establishing "a new social order which stands over against—in confrontation with—the structures of the world."[44] Such standing against is possible only because of the liberating victory of Christ on our behalf.

This view of Christ's work probably was so popular in the postapostolic period because it spoke forcefully to Christians of both Jewish and Gentile origin, many of whom knew much about oppressive military and spiritual powers. Justo González calls this the "classic" atonement model. He judges that the human problem is not fundamentally that we owe a debt to God (satisfaction) or lack necessary knowledge or inspiration to love God (moral influence), theories related closely to socio-political issues prominent in church life long after biblical times.[45] Such theories often have functioned to support the control of ruling classes in many cultures. Rather, the primary human problem is enslavement to evil "and it is no coinci-

---

[44]J. Denny Weaver, "Atonement for the Non-Constantinian Church," in *Modern Theology* 6:4 (July, 1990), 309. This new social order is the church, the minority ecclesiology as emphasized in the Believers Church tradition. Note that this atonement model has been subjectivized in ways that Weaver finds abortive of the full biblical intent for a visible, social demonstration of the victory of God. Rudolf Bultmann and Paul Tillich used the theme of victory by focusing on existential forces that deprive modern humans of "authentic existence." Valid as far as it goes, this view reduces the atonement of Christ to a subjective victory only within human consciousness. American revivalism often has encouraged a similar reductionism. The biblical narrative is far more outward and historical than this.

[45]See Justo González, *Christian Thought Revisited: Three Types of Theology* (Nashville: Abingdon Press, 1989).

dence that the 'classical' view of atonement began to recede into the background when the church became powerful."[46] No one atonement theory is wholly adequate and each can claim some biblical support.[47] Even so, as the twenty-first century opens and the mass inhumanity so common in the twentieth century lingers as a troubling truth, the divine victory over all evil through the loving and lowly Christ is a compelling way to conceive the wonderful truth of God in Christ for our salvation.

Being Resurrected with Christ

The Believers Church in the sixteenth-century was part of the larger Protestant Reformation's search for a biblically acceptable adjustment to the typical theology of human salvation taught by the medieval Roman Catholic Church. A key difference between the adjustment made by the "magisterial" reformers (Martin Luther, John Calvin, etc.) and those more "radical" was the understood meaning and effect of divine grace in human and church life. The difference usually was the Anabaptist emphasis on the divinely intended significant effects of the atonement on believers and the Christian community (the themes of holiness and ethics). The focus was on Christ as redeemer, example, and enabler, with relatively little concern for the abstractions of elaborate atonement theories. Luther, for instance, focused on the role of faith in the justifying work accomplished on the cross.

Anabaptists often repeated this fresh focus on forensic justification, but were quick to add an ethically sensitive recreative or holiness aspect to the understanding of Christ's atonement. Christ had righted the broken divine/human relationship, thus reopening the possibility and obligation of a solidarity between God and the justified believer. The believer, now justified by grace through faith, can and

---

[46]Justo González, *Mañana: Christian Theology from a Hispanic Perspective* (Nashville: Abingdon Press, 1990), 154.

[47]See Barry L. Callen, *God As Loving Grace* (Nappanee, Ind.: Evangel Publishing House, 1996), 234ff.

should participate in the divine nature.[48] Legal justification alone could tempt a believer to be grateful for relief from sin's penalty without significantly altering prevailing values and behaviors not consistent with Christ. That potential abortion of the full intent of Christ's atonement was not viewed as acceptable. Christ's self-giving on our behalf was to engage us in his own life and mission (as well as free us from the guilt and penalty of past sin). We are freed *from* so that we can be free *to*—to be Christ-like in the church and in the world. All grace that truly saves will be responded to, and appropriated, gratefully and responsibly.[49]

A New Testament verse crucial for defining the heart of the Christian life ties the crucifixion of Jesus to the intended transformation of his disciples. The Apostle Paul testified: "I have been crucified with Christ and I no longer live, but Christ lives in me. The life I live in the body, I live by faith in the Son of God, who loved me and gave himself for me" (Gal. 2:20). Beyond the crucifixion, in view here is resurrection life, both Christ's and, through him, ours. If death, the final evil, already has been conquered in Christ, and if the resurrection power exhibited in Jesus now abides in those who believe in him (cf. Eph. 1:19-21), then nothing, including death, can defeat the life and love now flowing through the ministry of Christ's Spirit. The earliest Christians were filled with a hope through which they freshly viewed all reality—past, present, and future. They—and we—are now enabled to view the *not yet* of God's redemptive intentions in light of the *already* which has been accomplished in Jesus Christ. A proper eschatological perspective is what enlivens the church's vision for mission in the present. It allows the faithful church to minister in the present in light of God's past and out of the resources of God's future.

---

[48]The "can" is significant. The insistence on freedom of the human will to choose reappeared in Anabaptism and then again in the work of John Wesley in the eighteenth century. Believers are responsible for the lives they lead after being justified by Christ. The Spirit of Christ is available to cleanse, comfort, gift, and guide.

[49]A similar emphasis on holiness and ethics, participation in the life of God and responsibility related to the reception and employment of divine grace, is characteristic of the theology of John Wesley. See Randy Maddox, *Responsible Grace: John Wesley's Practical Grace* (Nashville: Kingswood Books, Abingdon Press, 1994).

In fact, one Mennonite theologian has developed an entire systematic theology with eschatology as its integrating focus.[50]

If justifying grace is what rights the gone-wrong relationship between humans and God, sanctifying grace is the culminating phase of the Christian teaching of present salvation. Jesus prayed that those justified persons who already were his disciples might also be sanctified by God's presence and truth (John 17:17). The church's task is to teach and live "so that we may present everyone mature [*teleion*] in Christ" (Col. 1:28).[51] The purpose of the work of the Holy Spirit is to enable believers to become "holy" (mature in Christ-likeness) by their loving, serving, and reflecting God's nature as they were originally intended to do. The Spirit's goal is that the life of the believer become united with Christ's life so much so that, by faith and over time, Christ's life and the believer's life become one.

Some historical perspective is helpful. The Brethren in Christ and Church of God (Anderson) movements, for instance, have sought to be "sects" in the sense defined by Ernst Troeltsch. He defined a sect sociologically as a voluntary society composed of Christians who have been born anew and are committed to living a distinctive life separate from the sordidness of this world.[52] In this sense the Free (Anabaptist) or Believers Church tradition has been sectarian, stressing the central place of holiness. Through spiritual rebirth and discipline within their ranks, such Christians have sought to keep the church pure and unblemished from the world. This is the way and work of the Spirit.

---

[50]Thomas N. Finger, *Christian Theology: An Eschatological Approach* (Scottdale, Pa.: Herald Press), 2 vols., 1985, 1989.

[51]The concept of "perfect," often used to describe holiness, is misleading today since it often is taken to mean flawless being and performance. John Wesley spoke often of "perfect love" (see Mildred Wynkoop, *A Theology of Love: The Dynamic of Wesleyanism*, Kansas City: Beacon Hill Press, 1972, 294-301). See Gene Miller, "*Teleios* as 'Mature,' 'Complete,' or 'Brought to Completion' in the Pauline Writings," in Barry Callen, ed., *Listening to the Word of God* (Anderson, Ind.: Anderson University and Warner Press, 1990), 121-130.

[52]Ernst Troeltsch, *The Social Teachings of the Christian Churches and Groups* (London: Allen and Unwin, 1931), 2:993.

In America, the Baptists, Methodists, and "Christians" (Stone-Campbell movement) often led the way. The age-old paradox prevailed. How can the church be *in* but not *of* the world, serving the world without sharing its perverted values? How can holiness be a practical reality, a real separation from the world, without leading to social irrelevance? The New Testament, especially the parts written by Paul, argue that the answer lies with the church living in the power of the Spirit, the present power of the messianic age now dawned in Jesus Christ. To be "holy" is to be truly "in Christ" through the Spirit and thus increasingly like Christ on God's mission to the world.

The work of Christ on the cross addresses more than humanity's juridical (legal) status before God, justifying past sin by divine grace in response to faith and true repentance. It also intends a re-creation of fallen and now forgiven humanity. The already justified are to be filled with the Spirit of love (Rom. 5:5) so that they can give thanks always (Eph. 5:18-21) and grow up into the likeness of Christ (Eph. 4:15). Justifying grace "works *for* the sinner; sanctifying grace works *in* the pentitent faithful.... Justifying grace is juridically a *finished* work of the Son on the cross, while sanctifying grace is actively a *continuing* and current work of the Spirit in our hearts and social processes."[53] The former brings change in a person's relative position before God; the latter effects a real change in the believer's actual being in relation to God.[54]

To be holy is costly to self-centered egos and middle-class lifestyles in prosperous societies. To walk the path of holiness is necessarily to break with the habits of comfortable religion. It is to renounce the "cheap grace" that only gives a religious sugar-coating to our world-

---

[53]Thomas Oden, *Life in the Spirit* (Harper SanFrancisco, 1992), 218.

[54]Real change is regeneration, actual new life. Justification, the forgiveness of sin, is the necessary preface to or first stage of actual rebirth. Regeneration involves reorganization of a believer's motive life by the work of the Spirit so that the prevailing motive becomes love for God and loyalty to Jesus Christ. Such reorganization is sanctification begun, the larger outworking of justification. John Wesley insisted that God graciously has provided both pardon for sin and an empowering, "perfecting" Presence, the Holy Spirit in the lives of believers and in the church.

liness and instead embrace the grace that will cost our lives and give deliverance not only from the *guilt* but also from the *power* of sin. Holiness also entails "a turn toward the despised, the forsaken, the marginalized, the poor, the least of these."[55] It is to follow humbly the God of the cross into the sordidness of a lost world as new creations in the Christ of the cross. Fruit is inevitable if faith is authentic. In fact, the fruit that flows from faith is an essential part of what "salvation" means. Claiming to be "saved" without exhibiting the Christ-life is to profess a lie (1 John 2:9-11). From the "Radical" (Anabaptist) Christian tradition comes the view that salvation is "to walk in the resurrection" (Schleitheim, 1527). Christian conduct, rather than merely a consequence of salvation, is itself basic to the very meaning of salvation. The "salvific gift of God and its human answer in following Jesus were [are] two sides of one reality."[56]

What God has accomplished in the past, especially in the work of Christ, is intended to send believers on a journey outward to others and forward to the completion of God's redemptive work in the world. Christian life is "more than acceptance of the forgiveness of sins and personal transformation. It also is the vocation to participate in the preparation of all creation for the coming of a new community of justice, freedom, and peace in partnership with the Triune God."[57] To be walking by Christ's Spirit is to have enhanced the capacity for truly loving others in the full range of their lives. Faithful believers become a reflection of the God of loving grace.[58] Anything less is not worthy of the vision of the Christian life characteristic of the Believers Church tradition.

---

[55]Theodore W. Jennings, Jr., "The Meaning of Discipleship in Wesley and the New Testament," *Quarterly Review: A Journal of Theological Resources for Ministry* (Spring 1993), 18.

[56]James McClendon, Jr., *Systematic Theology: Doctrine* (Nashville: Abingdon Press, 1994), 118.

[57]Daniel Migliore, *Faith Seeking Understanding* (Grand Rapids: Eerdmans, 1991), 184.

[58]Laurence Wood defines love as "our capacity to reach beyond ourselves to penetrate the lives of others and embrace them as part of our own reality" (*Truly Ourselves: Truly the Spirit's*, Grand Rapids: Francis Asbury Press, 1989, 75).

This vision of holy lives joined in a holy community, the church, is derived from Scripture. In the Believers Church tradition, one finds a distinctive pattern of biblical interpretation that consistently highlights this vision.

Distinctive Biblical Interpretation

A commonly heard assertion among "free" churches is that "the Bible is our only creed." It is, after all, from the Bible that believers in all times and places receive their primary witness to the life, death, and resurrection of Jesus. Since the Bible requires interpretation, however, the real issue turns out to be one of hermeneutics—the pattern and standards by which one interprets the biblical text.

The more fundamentalistic elements of modern conservative Christianity tend to search the Bible for propositional truths or revealed doctrines that are insured to be trustworthy by the reader's pre-commitment to "inerrancy," the presumed fully and factually accurate inspiration of the original biblical text. But the Believers Church tradition has been convinced over the centuries that "truth" in a Christian sense is far more than correct religious information. Further, the Bible is always read in communities of interpretation that are highly influential on what readers understand the Bible to be saying, whether this influence is recognized or not. The Roman Catholic Church of the early sixteenth century certainly was a prominent interpretative community. Soon various "Protestant" communities would emerge with similar community characteristics, despite their protesting agendas against the claimed perversions of established Catholicism. There also were the more "radical" Christians who reacted to all state-oriented and power-controlled faith communities and evolved their own distinctive perspective, consciously choosing the kind of community in which they would read the Bible and thereby understand and practice the faith.[59]

---

[59]It is important to recognize the considerable diversity in the Believers Church tradition, both among the Anabaptists of the sixteenth century and those of this general heritage now entering the twenty-first century. Cautions C. Arnold Snyder (*Anabaptist History and Theology*, 382): "A particular tradition of biblical interpretation has been part

Highlighting the Bible over all human traditions, these "radicals" placed the emphasis on salvation received and lived out in the context of the new people of God. In addition to the concern for doctrinal orthodoxy, the Believers Church "placed a strong emphasis upon lifestyle and discipleship." It was a "hermeneutics of obedience" in which the "goal was not to gain abstract knowledge, but to find the wisdom and courage we need to follow Jesus."[60] As Franklin Littell summarizes:

> Both the "Keys of Peter," to loose and to bind (church disci-pline), and the "Key of David," which unlocked Scripture, belong to the congregation. They were not only protected there-by from the errors of the Reformed, with their ahistorical con-ception of Scripture as a monolithic body of authoritative rev-elation. They were also protected from the error of the Spiritu-alizers, who reduced both Scriptures and sacramental order to a minor rank after individual insight and conscience.[61]

Christ was judged central to understanding Scripture. Pivotal understanding of the sacred text is mediated by the Spirit as the Bible is opened in the fellowship and obedient life of the church. It is not that the church is lord of Scripture, the virtual claim of Roman Catholicism, but the church is the vital context that is a shaping force, even while it is in the process of being shaped and disciplined by the Spirit. Thus, when the church is faithful, it is the best context in which to perceive the Spirit's wisdom being conveyed through Scripture. As the early Quaker Robert Barclay said: The Scriptures "are only a dec-laration of the fountain, and not the fountain itself; therefore they are not esteemed the principal ground of all truth and knowledge...[but]

---

of the Believers Church inheritance.... To be part of the Believers Church tradition has meant to have received a well-established 'canon within the canon' that already provides the answers to what a 'pure and simple' reading of Scripture should conclude. These interpretations have been passed on as traditional (self-evidently true) teachings. Part of the conscious reappropriation of the Believers Church tradition must be ready to include a fresh reading of Scripture that is prepared to test the received tradition not only against Scripture, but also against other theological traditions."

[60]Clark Pinnock, "Catholic, Protestant, and Anabaptist," *Brethren In Christ History and Life* (December 1986), 267.

[61]Franklin Littell, *A Tribute To Menno Simons* (Scottdale, Pa.: Herald Press, 1961), 21.

they are and may be esteemed a secondary rule subordinate to the Spirit...."[62] Barclay was clear that the Bible provides essential tests for judging and verifying any presumed leadings of the Spirit in the present time.

Nadine Pence Frantz notes six hermeneutical marks generally characteristic of the Believers Church tradition.[63] In brief, they are:

1. There is a key correlation between *epistemology* and *obedience*. Knowing and practicing the faith are crucially interrelated. Each step of a believer's obedience increases knowledge of Scripture's meaning, a meaning that will be largely unknown apart from committed participation in the life that the Christian gospel requires and enables.

2. There is a key *location* for adequate biblical interpretation. It is the gathered community, the local congregation of believers. The Spirit of God will guide an obedient congregation to a common understanding of what is currently vital to its Christian life and witness.[64]

3. There is a key *distinction* between levels of revelation. Divine revelation is *progressive* in nature and understood best in the contexts of its original historical appearance, canonical position, and current mission.

---

[62]Robert Barclay, as quoted by Wilmer A. Cooper, *A Living Faith: An Historical Study of Quaker Beliefs* (Richmond, Ind.: Friends United Press, 1990), 20. Comments Cooper (23): "Evangelical Friends rely primarily on Scripture coupled with the interpretive role of the Holy Spirit, while liberal Friends rely on the "'Light Within,'" with occasional support from the Bible."

[63]Nadine Pence Frantz, "Theological Hermeneutics: Christian Feminist Biblical Interpretation and the Believers' Church Tradition," doctoral dissertation, Divinity School, University of Chicago, 1992, 148-174.

[64]Dale W. Brown adds: "In hermeneutics the locus of infallibility shifted from the [biblical] text itself, to the technically qualified theological experts, or official interpreters of the church to the committed and listening congregation gathered around the word" ("Communal Ecclesiology," *Theology Today*, April, 1979, 25-26). John Howard Yoder helped popularize the concept of the "hermeneutical community" as a distinctively Anabaptist approach to Scripture. Interpreting Scripture is a communal exercise in denial of a prior authority being granted to tradition, formal creedal statements, or the political interests of the state (see Yoder's "The Hermeneutics of Peoplehood" in Michael Cartwright, ed., *The Priestly Kingdom*, South Bend: Notre Dame University Press, 1984, 15-45).

4. There is a key *interpretive focus* for understanding biblical revelation. As the gathered community of Christ seeks to be obedient in its time, what it seeks primarily is the mind of Christ—known historically in the teachings, actions, death, and resurrection of Jesus. According to John Howard Yoder: "The writers of the New Testament text are best understood when we perceive them to be aiding their readers to be more faithful to the meaning of Jesus for their time."[65]

5. There is a key correlation between the *Outer* and *Inner* Word, between the written word of Scripture and the conviction inspired by the *illuminating Spirit of God*. The Spirit is a present, active, and essential power who enables the ancient text to become a living letter in the reader's heart and congregation's life.

6. There is a key presupposition that the gathered Christ community, illumined by the Spirit and obedient to Scripture's meaning and mission for the present, will be perceived as a *peculiar people*.[66] A correct reading of the Bible will always challenge the dominant culture.[67] The Bible's voice is heard best by those not part of the powerful majority and leads to sacrificial service to the oppressed. This is a *minority hermeneutic*.

The process for discerning truth that is implied in these six interpretive characteristics places much responsibility on the body of believers for reading the Bible rightly, knowing the essential content of the faith, critiquing appropriately current forms of Christian life, and being open individually and corporately to the current direction of the Spirit of God.[68] The Bible is to be accepted as a book of the Spirit,

---

[65]John Howard Yoder, "The Authority of the Canon," in Willard Swartley, ed., *Essays On Biblical Interpretation: Anabaptist-Mennonite Perspectives* (Elkhart, Ind.: Institute of Mennonite Studies, 1984), 277.

[66]See Rodney Clapp, *A Peculiar People: The Church As Culture in a Post-Christian Society* (Downers Grove, Ill.: InterVarsity Press, 1996).

[67]Prominent in exploring this theme in the Bible is Walter Brueggemann. See, e.g., his *Hope Within History* (John Knox Press, 1987) and *Interpretation and Obedience: From Faithful Reading to Faithful Living* (Fortress Press, 1991).

[68]An excellent presentation of the agreements and points of diversity on the issues of biblical inspiration and authority that are resident in the contemporary Church of the Brethren (and elsewhere in the Believers Church tradition) is found in Joan Deeter, *Biblical Inspiration and Authority* (Elgin, Ill.: The Brethren Press, 1980), 26-29.

interpreted best in the light of God's self-revelation in Jesus Christ. Disciplined and informed interpretation is required and should proceed within the community of faith and with openness to the current work of the same Spirit who originally inspired the biblical text. The Bible is the primary source for defining perspective on the essence of Christian faith. The continuing process of interpreting the Bible happens best within the truth-questing, obedience-minded, and Spirit-sensitive community of sincere believers. The biblical material "is not primarily a collection of self-evidently comprehensible propositions nor a divinely-validated rulebook.... It is a record of and also a product of the reflections and analyses and interactions of the people of God with each other and with God in their attempts to understand the events around them in light of belief in Yahweh's control of history."[69] The Bible is foundational to authentic Christianity. In fact, "no creed but the Bible" is a rallying slogan heard often in many sectors of the Believers Church tradition. The slogan is deceptive if it means either that Christians can get along without post-apostolic creedal formulations of the faith or that any reading of the Bible can avoid some pre-set grid through which the reading tends to be filtered. Recognizing that all such creedal formulations and tradition-informed interpretive grids are both inevitable and fragile, the Believers Church seeks to keep testing all of them, including one's own, in an ongoing process of new learnings, new Spirit leadings, and constant self-correction.

Convictional Non-Creedalism

Conviction has been strong in the Believers Church tradition, but there has been a basic aversion to formalized theology, especially of the systematic and speculative kinds. With the early German Brethren of the eighteenth century, for instance, there was the assumption of an intimate connection between doctrine and life, so that proper theological method is biblically centered in content and devotional and

---

[69]J. Denny Weaver, "Perspectives on a Mennonite Theology," *The Conrad Grebel Review* (Fall 1984), 193.

existential in style. This was reflective of the Pietist influence on the early Brethren that rejected entirely the theological method of Protestant Scholasticism. Thus, Alexander Mack of the Brethren worked with the assumption that

> ...contemporary expressions of the faith need to be assessed continually for their faithfulness to the Word of God. No theological tradition—Anabaptist, Radical Pietist, or Reformed—was above scrutiny by Scripture. He therefore criticized the deterioration in life and doctrine of the Mennonites, the private inspiration and asceticism of the Radical Pietists, and the scholasticism and rigid orthodoxy of the Reformed.[70]

The theological method of John Wesley is similar to that of Alexander Mack and continues to be instructive for today's believers. His is a perspective on authority in Christian faith that is particularly sensitive to central Believers Church concerns—without being overly vulnerable to typical Believers Church weaknesses. Wesley was very much a product of both the Reformation and the Enlightenment. From the former he inherited a high view of Scripture which grounds revelation in objective reality. From the latter he gained an appreciation for human reason as an alternative to primitive superstitions and vain imaginations.[71] Although not a "systematic" theologian in the usual sense, Wesley was interested in providing coherent doctrinal norms that give needed guidance without having to be defined too narrowly or separated from the vibrancy of direct spiritual experience.

---

[70]Dale R. Stoffer, *Background and Development of Brethren Doctrines: 1650-1987*, 84.

[71]Randy Maddox notes a fact crucial for the self-understanding of all believers: "Our earliest patterns of preunderstandings are conveyed to us socially long before we begin conscious evaluation of them. As such, few of Wesley's theological convictions were initially 'chosen' in an unbiased conscious manner; they were imbibed with his familial and ecclesial nurture. In other words, 'tradition' (socio-culturally defined) was the initial source of much of Wesley's theology. When experience called some aspect of this assumed theology into question, he then had to decide whether to retain, revise, or reject the conviction at issue. The mature Wesley consciously sought to guide such decisions by Scripture—as enlightened by reason, experience, and 'tradition'" (*Responsible Grace: John Wesley's Practical Theology*, Nashville: Kingswood Books, Abingdon Press, 47).

Wesley's working concepts of doctrinal authority were "dynamically balanced," just what is required to enable the needed gaining of "studied insight and divine guidance."[72]

In Wesley we see a theological method, the so-called Wesleyan "quadrilateral," featuring Scripture as the pre-eminent norm. Scripture, however, necessarily is to be interfaced with tradition, reason, and Christian experience, three interactive aids in the interpretation of the Word of God in Scripture.[73] Accordingly, God's revelation includes a written witness (the Scriptures), a remembering community (the traditions), a process of existential appropriation (experience), and a way to test for internal consistency (reason).[74] Wesley was comfortable with some variation in theological formulation if there was consensus at least on essential Christian doctrine (biblically normed and Christ-centered). After all, Christians are called beyond "orthodoxy" to authentic spiritual experience, from the *form* to the *power* of religion, from the *status*-changing before God of our justification to the *character*-changing of our sanctification by God. The Bible is the *fount* of revelation, while Christian *experience* energizes the heart, empowers truth's fullest discernment, and enables the believer to speak and do the truth in love.[75] In fact, Wesley so valued the fruit of

---

[72]Albert Outler, "The Wesleyan Quadrilateral in John Wesley," in T. Oden and L. Longden, eds., *The Wesleyan Theological Heritage* (Grand Rapids: Zondervan, 1991), 24.

[73]This interactive role is explained well in Donald Thorsen, *The Wesleyan Quadrilateral: Scripture, Tradition, Reason and Experience as a Model of Evangelical Theology* (Grand Rapids: Zondervan, 1990). Thorsen sees this quadrilateral as integrating all historic authority claimants. It involves an affirmation of (1) biblical authority as primary, although not exclusive, (2) tradition that extends to classical orthodoxy in Christian antiquity, (3) rational methods of inquiry, viewing theology more as an ongoing process than a completed system, and (4) experience as a genuine source of religious authority (251). He sees in this quadrilateral "invaluable insights for developing a more thoroughly catholic model of evangelical theology" (251).

[74]Wesley's "quadrilateral" of theological authorities may be described best as "a unilateral rule of Scripture within a trilateral *hermeneutic* of reason, tradition, and experience" (Randy Maddox, *Responsible Grace*, 46).

[75]Note the disturbing observation of Justo González: "The Bible has traditionally been interpreted in ways that are oppressive to minorities and to powerless groups, and that serve to justify the actions and values of the oppressors" (*Out of Every Tribe and Nation*, Nashville: Abingdon Press, 1992, 38). He sees this fact requiring a broadened understanding of the components of the Wesleyan quadrilateral. For example, "experience"

faith that he even measured truth by the moral test of love.[76] As awareness of divine truth emerges from actual participation in the life of God, so the present integrity of that truth can be tested in part by the evidence of the fruit of God's love reflected in the believer's life. This is a classic emphasis of the Believers Church tradition.

Convictions are to be strong, but not coerced. Discipline and commitment are to be central, but they are to function in contexts where it is assumed that the institutional expressions of the faith are not themselves the heart of the faith. Doctrines are understood as interpretations of the meaning and implications of the biblical revelation of God, first in Israel and then in Christ. The biblical narrative is primary, while doctrines are judgments about proper ways to read and freshly express the narrative. For Christians, affirming that "Jesus is the Christ" is the proper way to read the story of Jesus of Nazareth. Read this way, Jesus gives (is!) guidance on what to believe about God, humanity, creation, destiny, etc. Doctrines, while arising from and interpreting the biblical story, are a secondary language of faith never independent of the biblical revelation itself.[77] Christians, then, should unite around biblical authority, not divide over differences in doctrinal formulations. For this to be possible, all Bible reading and theological work must proceed under the guidance of the Spirit of God and in the love which should unite humble believers.

Here is a "radical" addition to what often passes as adequate orthodoxy. Just as we fallen humans are "dead" in our sins until enabled by

---

should be more than "religious" experience since the African-American community inevitably brings to the interpretive process the experience of slavery, and other groups bring their various backgrounds of oppression (as did the ancient Israelites who worked from their memory of slavery and divine rescue from Egypt). This inclusion of personal and communal stories need not undermine biblical authority. What it does is expose false and self-serving interpretations, thereby enriching the process of interpretation.

[76]David Cubie, "The Theology of Love in Wesley," *Wesleyan Theological Journal* (Spring 1985), 122-154.

[77]See the analysis of Roger Olson in *Christianity Today* (Feb. 9, 1998, 40-50). He sees two contrasting theological mindsets among evangelicals who otherwise share much in common. A key difference between the "traditionalists" and "reformists" is highlighted by their viewing doctrine as either first-order or second-order language. The Believers Church tradition inclines toward the latter.

God's prevenient grace to respond to the offer of forgiveness, the written Word of God also lies dormant until enlivened by the Spirit for present readers. In the words on the Bible's pages lie the essential records, the crucial salvation story, and normative interpretations of the meaning of God's pivotal acts in human history. But proper perception, existential power, and contemporary cultural relevance rely on the present work of the Spirit in conjunction with the fresh theological effort of dedicated disciples. God's Spirit, who first inspired the Word, now chooses to dwell within the searching heart and the faithful community to inspire again, witnessing afresh to the truth in Scripture. Always, the Spirit is God, not the book. The book, clearly essential as an instrument of revelation, does not supplant the Spirit who remains the inspirer, the One revealed and the One revealing.

Theologically speaking, what is the life of the church to be like as conceived by the Believers Church tradition? As in the past, there will continue to be commonality and diversity, commitment and dialogue. There was, for instance, obvious diversity and yet also considerable teaching commonality shared by the Swiss, South German/Austrian, and Lowlands Anabaptists of the sixteenth century. Their shared teaching was represented well by Balthasar Hubmaier's 1526 catechism that is written in dialogue form between a "Leonhart" and a "Hans." C. Arnold Snyder concludes:

> Perhaps in light of the evolutionary historical development of Anabaptism it would be best to say that what is needed is a "recovery of Anabaptist conversations," rather than a "recovery of the Anabaptist Vision." ...My proposal as a Believers' Church historian is simply to suggest that the dialogue that shaped this faith tradition be allowed to inform contemporary Believers' Church conversations.[78]

In the spirit of Snyder's proposal, Merle Strege has set forth the ideal of a "dialogical church" where traditionalism, the dead faith of the living, is replaced with a healthy tradition which is the living faith of the

---

[78]C. Arnold Snyder, *Anabaptist History and Theology* (Kitchener, Ontario: Pandora Press, 1995), 97.

dead in active conversation with the insights and challenges of today's church.[79] His view is based in part on a pivotal essay by John Howard Yoder that views the church as a community that "can affirm individual dignity…without enshrining individualism. They can likewise realize community without authorizing lordship or establishment."[80] Enhanced is the authority of being and gifting more than the authority of office and power.

---

[79]Merle Strege, *Tell Me The Tale: Historical Reflections on the Church of God* (Anderson, Ind.: Warner Press, 1991), chapter six.

[80]John Howard Yoder, "The Hermeneutics of Peoplehood," in *The Priestly Kingdom: Social Ethics as Gospel* (Notre Dame, Ind.: University of Notre Dame Press, 1984), 24.

5

Living the Faith:
Christian Discipleship

A new kind of Christian had emerged in the course of the Radical Reformation, a composite of the medieval pilgrim to Jerusalem, the ancient martyr of the heavenly Jerusalem, and the emissary of the neo-apostolic Jerusalem. This new kind of Christian was not a reformer but a converter, not a parishioner but a sojourner in this world whose true citizenship was in heaven.[1]

The value of structure of Amish life rests on *Gelassenheit*—the cornerstone of Amish values. Roughly translated, the German word means submission—yielding to a higher authority. It entails self-surrender, resignation to God's will, yielding to others, self-denial, contentment, and a quiet spirit. For early Anabaptists, *Gelassenheit* meant forsaking all ambition and yielding fully to God's will—even unto death. Christ called them to abandon self and follow his example of humility, service, and suffering.[2]

As the previous chapter seeks to demonstrate, the Believers Church tradition provides a distinctive lens through which all Christian believing becomes understood in a particular perspective. This

---

[1]George Williams, *The Radical Reformation* (Philadelphia: Westminster Press, 1962), 844.

[2]Donald Kraybill, in Kraybill and Lucian Niemeyer, *Old Order Amish* (Baltimore and London: Johns Hopkins Press, 1993), 3.

perspective usually concurs with most of the classic beliefs of Christians, but with some cautions insisted on and certain emphases highlighted. A key emphasis is the need *to live* that which is believed. Doctrine is not to be separated from discipleship. To be a disciple of Jesus means that "a person's heart was 'strangely warmed' in his presence…that one's mind was engaged with his teachings, that one's whole life was oriented around his power, and that one accepted his way of life and was willing to be engaged in his mission."[3]

The Believers Church tradition has been formed around a vision calling for believers in Jesus Christ to be, first and foremost, committed to the realm and reign of God, not to the power arrangements and perverted values of this world. Such a vision has significant implications for how the church-in-the-world is to be understood and what it means to be a true and faithful disciple of Christ. Admittedly, talk of humility, submission, and obedience fly in the face of the cherished individualism and aggressive achievement mentality that characterize the culture of the West today. That, however, is hardly the point. The point for Christians is being loyal disciples of God's will and way regardless of the cultural surroundings or personal costs. The proper metaphor for the Christian life intended by God is that of pilgrim, emmisary, even martyr if necessary.

Two modern exponents of this Believers Church vision have expressed their desire that today there might be

> …a church that again asserts that God, not nations, rules the world, that the boundaries of God's kingdom transcend those of Caesar, and that the main political task of the church is the formation of people who see clearly the cost of discipleship and are willing to pay the price…. The church exists today as resident aliens, an adventurous colony in a society of unbelief.[4]

The appropriate image for today's church may well be pilgrim, emissary, resident alien, even martyr. Hopefully a new kind of Chris-

---

[3]Gilbert W. Stafford, *Theology for Disciples* (Anderson, Ind.: Warner Press, 1996), 425.
[4]Stanley Hauerwas and William Willimon, *Resident Aliens: Life in the Christian Colony* (Nashville: Abingdon Press, 1989), 48-49.

tian is emerging in the West's now secularized societies, a kind that is rediscovering humility, committed community, service, and, when necessary, a kind that is prepared to endure suffering for the faith.

Consequently, the church today needs to review its apostolic heritage and its renewed role as a minority body in the modern marketplace of faith options. The church never was supposed to be seen primarily as an institution or merely a place for receiving personal inspiration and finding a welcome network of supportive friendships. The church is to be that community of God's Spirit which is comprised of believers who know and are savingly related to the God of loving grace and are prepared to live out the gospel of Christ in an intentional community of the Spirit.[5] A Christian convert is saved by Christ into the midst of the life of Christ's body, the church. Salvation is not to be defined as a spiritual relation to Christ apart from a social relation to the church. Baptism in the Believers Church tradition is seen simultaneously as entrance into Christ and into the church, making the candidacy of infants unacceptable since such entrance is to be a voluntary act. The Christian by definition is a willing and committed part of the body of Christ that is to be nurturing, discipling, witnessing, and serving in the world.

An attempt at good balance is seen in the early German Brethren who were influenced both by Pietism and Anabaptism. It was recognized that the inwardness of Pietism can easily lead to a separatist subjectivism,[6] while the corporate outworking of Anabaptism can degenerate into harsh legalism. The Brethren, therefore, sought to *inspire* its

---

[5]See C. Norman Kraus, *The Community of the Spirit* (Scottdale, Pa.: Herald Press, rev. ed., 1993).

[6]See Dale W. Brown, *Understanding Pietism* (Nappanee, Ind.: Evangel Publishing House, rev. ed., 1996). Pietism often has been identified negatively as emotionalism, mysticism, and otherworldliness. Brown argues that this negativism is overdrawn and concludes: "Anabaptism and Pietism shared the desire to carry the [sixteenth century] Reformation to its logical conclusion. They held in common a belief in the guidance of the Holy Spirit, who taught correct understanding of the Scriptures; the idea of the restoration of the primitive church; the centrality of *Wiedergeburt* ('new birth'); and the ethical motifs of *Nachfolge Christi* ('imitation of Christ'), the Sermon on the Mount, and the Christian life as a fruit of faith" (17).

Anabaptism and *discipline* its Pietism. For Alexander Mack, inward devotion to the Christ of faith and outward obedience to the Jesus of history were equal necessities. For instance, full obedience to the ordinances believed to have been instituted by Jesus requires the functioning reality of communities of faith. Further, for many Anabaptists, full obedience to Christ's great commission soon suggested a church model of mobility for the sake of widespread evangelism. Early leaders, sometimes of necessity, wandered as pilgrims seeking relief from persecution. They opposed in principle the settled and territorial restrictions of state-established Lutheranism. Many contacted with appreciation the Moravian communities, pilgrim believers who spread the gospel with great intentionality and had the disciplined community structure to sustain such an evangelistic enterprise. Living the faith, submitting to the discipline of a community of faith, and spreading the faith are Christian interlocking privileges and responsibilities. Adequacy lies only in the fullness of the balance of true inwardness and outwardness. Salvation is by faith alone, but saving faith is never alone. It is in company with other believers. The one who believes also chooses to belong. Whatever else it is, Christian discipleship is first Christian fellowship.

The Body—Church

Sixteenth-century pioneers of the Believers Church tradition were "radical" at least in the sense that their intent was to go well beyond a marginal critique of the standing order in Christendom.[7] Some "Protestant" reformers hoped to bring helpful changes in the "system" by their reforming activity within the system, what Franklin Littell once called a "conventicle program for the enrichment of the established churches." Instead, Littell continued, the larger vision of these more radical pioneers included this: "They counted themselves spiritual children of the Covenant of Abraham, with the very meaning of history itself embodied in their congregations. Their view of the

---

[7]The word "radical" in this context is intended to mean going to the very root of the matter rather than merely being extreme.

Church was a 'high' view; their understanding of its universality was rich and full."[8] The Believers Church tradition, consequently, has been based on the concept of a "gathered" as opposed to a "given" church. Being *gathered* intends to be dynamic and voluntary, while being *given* speaks of the church as established and settled in its accumulated order, formalized wisdom, and standardized sacramental practices. Being *gathered* highlights the responsiveness of faith in relation to the ongoing work of God's gracious Spirit; being *given* easily degenerates into merely the inevitability of institutional legitimacy and dominance.

The gathered church stance hopes to be free enough from worldly ties and human conventions to be authentically itself under the immediate reign of God. It usually views givenness as overly compromised and in need of renewal by the dynamic of Christ's gospel. Rather than any such compromise, the volunteeristic view especially values the quest for holiness—which in turn often leads Believers Churches to be "leavers" churches, communities of "come-outers" in the heritage of Israel's leaving the bondage of Egypt and hoping to remain God's special people amid all the trials of the wilderness and the temptations in Canaan. Typically they have become "free churches" who are accused of being "sectarian" because of their determination to be freshly authentic and largely disconnected from dictating establishments in either the religious or secular arenas. They usually avoid heavy stress on officially mandated beliefs in isolation from obedience, purity, simplicity, discipleship, and covenantal accountability to the law of love and to others in the household of faith. They think of the church as a pilgrim community journeying together with the very present guidance of God's Spirit.

Three classic options of the nature and work of the church were highlighted in the range of reformation efforts in sixteenth-century Europe and have appeared often in other contexts, even to the present time. John Howard Yoder calls them "theocratic," "spiritualist," and

---

[8]Franklin Littell, *The Free Church* (Boston: Starr King Press, 1957), 135.

"Believers Church." He urges believers today to stop oscillating between the first two and move with courage to the third option. The theocratic is "that vision of the renewal of the church which hopes to reform society at large in the same blow." The spiritualist "moves the locus of meaning from society to the spirit [and by default] leaves the established church in place."

The Believers Church, a genuinely third option according to Yoder, joins spiritualism in resisting the compromised formalism of "official theocratic churchdom," but goes well beyond merely resisting it by a spiritual retreating inwardly to private religion nurtured by parachurch groupings. Rather, it dares to develop "those forms which are according to Scripture and which are expressive of the character of the disciples' fellowship."[9] In other words, the tradition of the Believers Church seeks to encourage the body of believers in Jesus Christ to *be the church*, actually, visibly, a gathering of God's people who are necessarily *in* but also are intentionally *over against* the world, for the sake both of the integrity of the church and the potential salvation of the world. The church's primary reality, then, rests in local congregations that are covenant communities of the Spirit, countercultural seedbeds of maturing believers who are helping each other to come to know who they are in Christ and what they are to be doing as Christ's people and for Christ's agenda in the world.

This third of Yoder's options is radical indeed. It dares to declare that at the door of the true church there is an end of the world's claims of privilege based on gender, class, and race. There is only one privileged position in the church and it is the fact that the grace of God is available equally to all ("for all of you are one in Christ Jesus," Gal. 3:28). Yoder insists that "the message is the medium," that is, "the distinctness of the church of believers is prerequisite to the meaningfulness of the gospel message." The biblical call to holiness and mission requires "the separateness of a called people and the *distinctiveness*

---

[9]John Howard Yoder, "A People in the World: Theological Interpretation," in James Garrett, ed., *The Concept of the Believers' Church* (Scottdale, Pa.: Herald Press, 1969), 256-257.

of their social existence." The church is to be understood as a special "political" reality. Yoder concludes:

> The political novelty which God brings into the world is a community of those who serve instead of ruling, who suffer instead of inflicting suffering, whose fellowship crosses social lines instead of reinforcing them. This new Christian community, in which the walls are broken down not by human idealism or democratic legalism but by the work of Christ, is not only a vehicle of the gospel or fruit of the gospel; it *is* the good news. It is not merely the agent of mission or the constituency of a mission agency. This *is* the mission.[10]

The church, therefore, serves the gospel of Christ and a lost world best when it derives its life and legitimacy, its vision and standards, from the Christian gospel. The church becomes good news for the world only when its own unique existence emerges from the gospel and becomes the Christ community living visibly in and for the world.

The pivotal task of the church is to be people who together are really living in light of God's reign, living by the Spirit's grace and power in the *now* of Christ's mission in the world. Being the church is a powerful political act. All pleas to the world on behalf of justice, for instance, remain hollow until those Christians issuing the pleas are themselves participating visibly in faith communities that are actually experiencing and practicing the first fruits of love and justice. Yoder identifies five New Testament links between the worship life of the early Christian communities and their social vision and moral practices. There was reconciliation, universal giftedness by the Spirit, decision-making by open dialogue and consensus, a sharing of the basics of life, and rejecting the discriminatory impact of social differences.

---

[10]Ibid., 274. One "working agreement" that emerged from the 1970 Believers Church Conference in Chicago was: "Society is changed not only by direct actions, but also by new options in life styles and institutions offered by changed persons. Fellowships are created which shatter societal distinctions and categories. Those groups concerned for the kingdom of God and fostering structures harmonious with it thus find social relevance" (The Chicago Theological Seminary *Register*, September, 1970, 59).

Each of these functioned then and should function now as distinctive corporate implications of the redemption found in Christ. They are to be central features of Christian "body life." Such life is to constitute a distinctive Christian culture called the church. While individuals are made new creations in Christ,

> ...no trust is placed in the individual's changed insights (as liberalism does) or on the believer's changed insides (as does pietism) to change the world. The fulcrum for change and the forum for decision is the moral independence of the believing community as social body. The dignity of the individual is his or her uniqueness as a specific member of that body.[11]

In other words, for the church to impact the world in Christ's way, it must function within its own life in ways consistent with the dramatic social implications of the transforming presence of the Spirit of the Christ.

As Franklin Littell once put it, the issue comes down to an "irreducible struggle between two mutually exclusive concepts of the church." Luther and Zwingli, for instance, with all their sincere reforming work, finally were committed to the state church and the parish system with its territorialism and hierarchical control. On the other hand, the Anabaptists were "out to restore apostolic Christianity."[12] In so doing, restoration tends to return Christians to the Pentecost event, that marvelous work of God's Spirit that first formed a new community, the Spirit community, an extension of the incarnation in Christ. The Spirit empowers as *present reality* what Jesus was historically in the flesh. The presence of the Spirit of Christ is the dynamic that makes possible the ever-new community of the Christ, the church. This church was born at Pentecost as a mission to the world. It was "apostolic," that is, sent to the world with a commission to proclaim

---

[11]John Howard Yoder, "Sacrament As Social Process: Christ the Transformer of Culture," *Theology Today* 48:1 (April 1991), 42.

[12]Franklin Littell, *The Anabaptist View of the Church*, rev. ed. (Boston: Starr King Press, 1958), 14.

Christ's lordship over all things. This lordship is first to be seen most clearly in the church itself. The church is called to be a resurrection community which itself becomes an essential part of the proclamation of good news to the world. If those renewed in and sent by Christ are not like Christ, their message will lack credibility. The life and character of the church is essential to its witness.

The Believers Church tradition has been uncomfortable with justifying the obvious imperfections of the visible church by retreating to a concept of the true church as "invisible" in this world.[13] Is not God's church on earth to be very visible, actual Christ-like believers worshipping and serving together in actual Christ-like communities of faith? To be the church in a "radical" way is to live communally from a vision that prevailing political and even church establishments rarely will tolerate. Christians prepared to live out of such a vision must be willing to be at risk, daring to bridge the worldly barriers of class, race, gender, culture, and ethnicity. They must be prepared to be faithful to a higher vision than the one currently established by the local powers and principalities of the church and world. Rosemary Ruether has said it well. The Believers Church vision centers in "the community of those who are willing to put their lives on the line to venture a new possibility for human existence, and to run the risks of ostracism and persecution that this may raise in their relation with the dominant structures of society which do not allow for such a possibility."[14]

God called a special people into being and gave the early promise to Abraham that this new nation would somehow be the means of

---

[13]Traditionally the Believers Church tradition has understood "salvation" as necessarily including an active relationship with the visible body of God's people, the church. To be "saved" means that an individual has freely repented of sin, received new life in Christ, and voluntarily entered the fellowship and disciplines of the church. The view that the church is not essential to the salvation of the individual was the position of the major (magisterial) Protestant reformers in their reaction to the medieval Roman Catholic position. This was a key reason why they did not feel the need to take the visible church with the same seriousness as did the Anabaptists.

[14]Rosemary Ruether, "The Believers' Church and Catholicity in the World Today," *The Chicago Theological Seminary Register* (September 1970), 6.

blessing the entire world (Gen. 12:1-3). This people of Israel struggled and often failed in the turmoil of its own history, but God remained intent on restoring true community among humans and between creation and Creator. It is in this light that the New Testament views the body of believers in Jesus, the fulfillment of the ancient promise. It presents the church as an eschatological event, a creation of the Spirit, a new people of God founded on the fulfilling event of salvation: the living, serving, suffering, dying, and rising of Jesus Christ. The church has an eschatological mission, embodying and proclaiming the coming of God's kingdom in its own life and in the yet-unfilled future. The church is not yet the fully-realized reign of God on earth,[15] but it is to be the firstfruits of God's rule, a provisional form of the divine realm manifest already and visibly in human history.

Christian theology today should champion the gospel's potential for impacting the *present* time of believers. Rather than being shackled by fixed formulations from the past or being immobilized by any speculative anticipation of the second coming of Christ that renders the church passive in the meantime,[16] it should be a theology of the future that both appreciates its historic roots and focuses on present realization. The incarnational God cares about concrete existence now, placing "political" responsibility on Christians. Theology should address the big public issues of our time, offering a unique hope and an alternative for change. God's intended reign on earth is not primarily about the future in any way that writes off the present as hopeless in God's eyes. The church is to be the future revealed in Christ and now really present in human history. It is to be the body in which the Word of God is preached, honored, and lived faithfully in a Christ-like community. The good news of the reign of God, already come in Jesus and still coming in the Spirit, "can create, will create, perhaps even now is creating a movement of new vitalities coursing

---

[15]See George Eldon Ladd, *The Presence of the Future* (Grand Rapids: Eerdmans, 1974), chap. 11, and John Bright, *The Kingdom of God* (Nashville: Abingdon Press, 1953), chap. 8.

[16]See Barry Callen, *Faithful in the Meantime: A Biblical View of Final Things and Present Responsibilities* (Nappanee, Ind.: Evangel Publishing House, 1997).

through the varicose veins of a church with tired blood."[17] The faithful church is the future reign of God already operative under the limiting conditions of this present and sinful age.

The church is called to be the Body of Christ expressing now within its own life the characteristics of the coming reign of God—peace, love, joy, freedom, equality, and unity. The church is "like an arrow sent out into the world to point to the future."[18] It is a new community of hope founded by the impact of the future of God in the history of the cross and resurrection of Jesus. It is on the way. It has not yet reached the goal of hope, but it knows the way and is deliberately moving that way under the guidance of the Spirit. The church "exists to exhibit through its life *in* the world a living hope *for* the world."[19] The church is intended to be a community where people of faith experience continuous collisions with the future, where the coming of God is recognized, celebrated, and then embodied in witness for the sake of a world groping for any credible glimpse of God's future. To be a true Christian disciple is voluntarily and gratefully to be part of this colliding, celebrating, and embodying community of Christ.

At the heart of the Believers Church vision lies the corporate reality of God's people being faithfully together under the rule of God. The church is to be a sabbath people conducting periodic sabbath services that demonstrate and nurture rest and hope. Israel's expectation of the future, in which "the whole earth will be full of God's glory" (Isa. 6), was to be experienced in the weekly sabbath observance. The rhythm of the sabbath is to interrupt the flow of ordinary time with the rest of God, a rest which is the goal of creation and one day will be the end of human history. Likewise, the Sunday worship of Christians should be an eschatological interlude, a resting in God, a celebration of Christ's resurrection, an in-streaming of the power of

---

[17]Carl Braaten, *Eschatology and Ethics* (Minneapolis: Augsburg Publishing House, 1974), 84.

[18]Jürgen Moltmann, *Theology of Hope* (SCM Press, 1967), 328.

[19]Carl Braaten, *The Future of God: The Revolutionary Dynamics of Hope* (New York: Harper & Row, 1969), 111, 117.

God's reign yet to come in its fullness, but already present to make God-like life possible.

Jesus' concern with social justice and human need also falls within the historic Jewish tradition and the Believers Church vision. It serves as a corrective "against the temptation to be carried away by dreams of an apocalyptic glory" and reminds Christians that "we are to live the life of faith under the conditions of this world."[20] Jesus brought salvation down to earth. Christian faith is an incarnation faith. Note these prophetic insights of Michael Kinnamon:

> In a world seemingly bent on self-destruction, in a world where empathy seems so often confined to members of like-minded enclaves, in a world that appears to live more by fear than by hope, the ecumenical vision of Christ's one body, living as sign and foretaste of God's *shalom*, is not an optional commitment, not a luxury that is conveniently demoted on our ecclesiastical lists of priorities, not something best left to experts on the nuances of theological debate. It is an inescapable and indispensable part of what it means to be the church God wills.[21]

Featuring the New Testament Greek word *koinonia*, Harold Bender helpfully saw as the very essence of the church a "fellowship community."[22] The idea of fellowship is not to be trivialized into merely a supposedly sacred setting where people have many friends and much fun. It necessarily involves coming together in worship of God and being obedient together in the service of others on behalf of Christ. Beyond the issue of warm feelings, there is to be a profound Spirit-life which arises from shared spiritual experience and results in serious engagement with each other and joint action in Christian mission. Not surprisingly, Bender saw the enemies of such genuine *koinonia* in the contemporary Mennonite church as individualism and institutionalism.

---

[20]Otto A. Piper, "Church and Judaism in Holy History," *Theology Today* 18(1961), 68.

[21]Michael Kinnamon, *Truth and Community: Diversity and Its Limits in the Ecumenical Movement* (Grand Rapids: Eerdmans, 1988), 118.

[22]Albert N. Keim, *Harold S. Bender, 1897-1962* (Scottdale, Pa.: Herald Press, 1998), 501.

The first undermines the very presence of real relationships; the second perverts the relationships by focusing power in the hands of a few. The church of God is the resurrection people who are inspired by the resurrection of Jesus and now anticipate their own. John Howard Yoder has called for the church to understand herself and her role while in this world as a renewal people on their way to a better place— and always on alert in the meantime. He said:

> We are not marching to Zion because we think that by our own momentum we can get there. But that is still where we are going. We are marching to Zion because, when God lets down from heaven the new Jerusalem prepared for us, we want to be the kind of people and the kind of community that will not feel strange there.[23]

The church is not the fully realized reign of God, but in present history it is to be an active participant in resurrection realities, a sign of the coming reign of God, a "between the times" agent of God's will and way. While not yet the ideal, the church is called to begin representing the ideal as it receives the promise of the coming fulfillment of God's reign and learns to live out of the assurance of that final victory. Like her Lord, the church is to be *incarnational*, being truly *in* but clearly not *of* the world (John 17:13-15). The church is to be purified by the Spirit so that it can play a prophetic function in present society.[24] Accordingly, even though the church is to be decidedly different from the world, it is a grave error to think of the church in terms of withdrawal from the world. The church must not abandon its "worldly" mission because it sees itself as weak, or fears persecution, or chooses not to risk contamination by a "dirty" world. To the contrary, the church's mission is to be an eschatological community both because it witnesses to God's future victory and because it is to display the actual life of God's reign in the present evil age. The very existence

---

[23]John Howard Yoder, in Michael Cartwright, ed., *The Royal Priesthood* (Grand Rapids: Eerdmans, 1994), 207.

[24]An excellent study of how the church is to be prophetic is Howard Snyder, *The Community of the King* (Downers Grove, Ill.: InterVarsity Press, 1977), 106-116.

of the church is intended to be a witness to the world of the triumph of God's reign accomplished in Jesus and initially being embodied in the church.

One good definition of the church can be constructed from unusual uses of the verb *to be*. The church is that body of believers in Jesus Christ who are dedicated to being a body of God's people, an advancing actualization of the *is-ness* of the *shall-be* of God's reign. The reign of God is realized *already* and is clearly *not yet*. It is that for which the church now lives and for which it yet waits. It is the Christian task and hope. It is an accomplishment, but even more a divine gift. Believers work. They wait. They live between the times and find themselves caught up in a tension between the age to come and this present evil age. Such is the nature of the history that follows the first-century coming of Christ and precedes his eventual and possibly imminent coming again.

The Ban—Discipline

Living what is believed is not an option. Fulfilling in life what is proclaimed in word, and doing so gratefully and voluntarily within the community of believers, is the way God would have it. Christian discipleship exceeds the limits of individualism. To mature and serve as every disciple of Jesus should requires the gifts of other believers and the nurture and discipline found only within the body of Christ. Christian discipleship also gives proper focus to theology. Since Gilbert Stafford, for instance, writes his systematic theology from a discipleship perspective, he naturally places strong emphasis on spiritual formation, prayer, holiness, and service.[25] Such themes are crucial in the Believers Church tradition. They require discipline and reach toward the faith's maturity and relevancy.

In advance of a season of professional baseball, there comes what is called "spring training." An athlete wishing to excel in the sport during the season first finds it necessary to train in the required skills, engage in discipline of the mind and body, and blend constructively

---

[25]Gilbert Stafford, op. cit., 2.

with teammates who, although different in some ways, are prepared to focus together on a common goal. The demands of the many games that lay just ahead become a primary life consideration. This necessity of serious preparation is hardly new. The Greek word for "training" (e.g., athletes) was *askesis* from which comes the English word *asceticism*. This word quickly came into the Christian tradition since it turns out that there are disciplines required in order for committed disciples to be ready for the "race" of the life of faith, to be prepared to walk the special way of Jesus Christ in this world. Paul, who evidently knew the world of athletic competition of his day, spoke of competitive running and boxing:

> Do you not know that in a race the runners compete, but only one receives the prize? Run in such a way that you may win it. Athletes exercise self-control in all things; they do it to receive a perishable wreath, but we an imperishable one. So I do not run aimlessly, nor do I box as though beating the air; but I punish my body and enslave it, so that after proclaiming to others I myself should not be disqualified. (1 Cor. 9:24-27).

Robert Barclay, the early intellectual of English Quakerism, maintained that there is no real church without a serious expectation of moral difference. He was unwilling to settle for a merely forensic doctrine of justification.[26] The danger of resting complacently in the assurance of forgiveness is the unacceptable temptation to make no progress in holiness. In this regard, it was the genius of the later John Wesley to join the doctrine of salvation to the subsequent necessity of disciplined discipleship in pursuit of holiness. He offered this perspective of "the primitive church": "The soul and the body make a man; the spirit and discipline make a Christian."[27] The implication? No believer can be a real Christian without willing participation in church discipline. The relationship of church discipline and the current ministry of the Spirit of God, inseparably joined as a soul to the body, was critical not only for Wesley's conception of Methodism as

---

[26]D. Elton Trueblood, *Robert Barclay* (N.Y.: Harper & Row, 1968), 179.
[27]John Wesley, "Causes of the Inefficacy of Christianity," *Works*, IV, 90.

a reform movement within the Church of England of the eighteenth century, but also for his assessment of world Christianity. Wesley concluded the following in light of the inherent relationship between discipline and the present ministry of the Spirit:

> But if this be so, is it any wonder that we find so few Christians; for where is Christian discipline? In what part of England (to go no farther) is Christian discipline added to Christian doctrine? Now, wherever doctrine is preached, where there is no discipline it cannot have its full effect upon the hearers.[28]

Humility and sacrifice for the sake of the pearl of greatest price is at the heart of the Christian spiritual life. Often it is called asceticism. Admittedly, the history of Christian asceticism is filled with abuse. The very mention of it today usually brings to the popular mind some sad picture of isolated monks hating the world or hermits punishing their bodies out in the desert. Occasionally it was said with a touch of cynicism that Puritans lived in fear that somewhere, sometime, someone was having a good time! But asceticism cannot be dismissed as only and always a deadening and legalistic thing. Jesus himself fasted and recommended it; he held out the ideal of voluntary poverty and even celibacy for the sake of nurturing the reign of God within. He demanded that his disciples give up everything for the high purpose of following him as committed disciples.

Thus, the ascetic life, whatever its particular forms in given cultural settings, is a means to Christian growth in holiness. It is part of spiritual "spring training" so that a follower of Jesus can assimilate into life a responsiveness to the divine grace necessary to really be a disciple.[29] It is the self-denial that allows a believer to say "no" to some ways of thinking, acting, and being, thus opening the door wider for the saying of "yes" to another, to God, and to the call of God's grace for sacrificial ministry in the world. Asceticism either leads to greater love and thus service to others or, as Paul once said, if "I have pro-

---

[28]Ibid.
[29]See Lawrence Cunningham and Keith Egan, *Christian Spirituality: Themes from the Tradition* (N. Y.: Paulist Press, 1996), chapter six, "Asceticism."

phetic powers and understand all mysteries and all knowledge and have faith to move mountains but have no love, I am nothing" (1 Cor. 13:2).

When spring training is over, its purpose is complete if the team is now *focused*. The players need adequate separation from the distractions of the off-season and a coming together as a working unit. To achieve together the winning goal of the coming season, the team needs a direction and resolve that launches it into the rigors of the many games ahead. A vision of the task will keep the players on track, measure their progress, and fire their wills. For Christians in the Believers Church tradition, the locus of authority is the Holy Spirit in the midst of those faithful believers who are in active covenant with Christ and each other. The point of discipline is not to enthrone prohibitions against petty cultural negatives, but to build up spiritual health and strength for being God's people and doing the work of Christ in the world.

"Piety" in the spiritual realm, like jazz as a musical form, tends to resist precise definition. It has to do with a believer's personal relationship to God; it thus tends to be significantly subjective and easily degenerates into an individualistic rejection of any authority. Although intense piety and the church as a committed community of Christ need not function as opposing forces, unfortunately there is such a recurring historical pattern. However, the Believers Church tradition (especially its Anabaptist stream) has long taught that the most legitimate and fulfilling form of Christian pietism occurs *among the body of believers* as each believer willingly accepts a yieldedness, a submission to the wisdom and discipline of the gathered community of the faithful.

Seen especially beginning in the sixteenth century was a "free-church" phenomenon that rejected the whole complex of structures and values called "Christendom," what Franklin Littell once called "the immobility and ethnicity of culture-religion."[30] Instead there was

---

[30]Franklin Littell, "The Contribution of the Free Churches," The Chicago Theological Seminary *Register* (September, 1970), 53-54.

raised again the biblical standard of a pilgrim, covenant people of God on earth. Littell reported that "when churches relax their church discipline and accommodate to prevailing cultural norms and ethnic values, they are vulnerable to the outward attacks and inward infiltrations of those serving another lord and obedient to another discipline."[31] The free-church response featured an obvious concern for the spiritual well-being of each member and the related well-being of the church itself. Church discipline was thought to be essential and have integrity only when grounded in the assumption of volunteerism. That is, prior to any discipline being employed, there must be the expressed willingness of each member to accept admonition and correction from the body. Rightly understood, discipline amounts to members of the body helping other members to be more fully what each is to be within the gifting and calling of God.

The church, then, is the fellowship of Christ that supports, nurtures, and sometimes admonishes in a context of freedom and mutual commitment. Anabaptist historiography argues that the church was corrupted when, once official in the old Roman Empire, it took in masses of people who had little or no understanding of or commitment to the faith. Later, through the practice of infant baptism, it continued this damaging pattern, completing the compromise process. In fact, the church is not "child's play," but a way of life requiring voluntary commitment, openness to discipline, and vigorous dedication to corporate and ethical living according to the way of Christ. Wrote Charles Wesley, and prays the serious Christian:

> To serve the present age, My calling to fulfill,
> O may it all my pow'rs engage, To do my Master's will![32]

The early Anabaptists were especially offended by the masses of nominal Christians whose concept of fellowship in the church hardly went beyond a shallow socializing and a scandalous self-interest.

---

[31]Ibid., 51.
[32]Verse two of Charles Wesley's hymn, "A Charge to Keep I Have," as in *Hymns for Praise and Worship* (Nappanee, Ind.: Evangel Press, 1984), 509.

Summarizes Franklin Littell:

> The idea of a covenantal relation to God and one's fellows became the foundation of the Anabaptist community, and through it came the use of the Ban (spiritual government). The Anabaptists said repeatedly that true baptism was that submission to the divine authority described in 1 Peter 3:18-22, the responsibility of a good conscience toward God. They saw that this couldn't be done easily in this kind of a world, but required brotherly admonition and exhortation, the practice of intentional fellowship.[33]

The "free" churches intended to be free in the sense that participation in them was a voluntary matter; they surely were not free in the sense that members were given freedom to think and act as they pleased. Anabaptist leaders were convinced that a spiritual separation from the world was essential to accomplish rigorous internal discipline in an intentional community seeking to restore the New Testament faith and life. When sin entered the faith community, action was required. If the sin was against one of the members, the discipline likely would be according to Jesus' teaching in Matthew 18.[34] No separation needed to take place unless the offender rejected the counsel of the Spirit of God through arrogance. If the sin was gross (see Galatians 5:19) or rejection of counsel continued, the offender could be expelled from the church, according to 1 Corinthians 5:13. There might first be a barring from the Lord's Table and then, if absolutely necessary, the ban—expulsion from the fellowship. Discipline, however, was meant to be positive and purposeful, a process of redemption, even an intentional arming of the church for her mission in the world. Like the sports team, it was the church consciously staying focused, enhancing its divine giftedness, maximizing its maturity potential, being faithful.

---

[33]Franklin Littell, *The Anabaptist View of the Church* (Boston: Starr King Press, Beacon Hill, 1958, 2nd ed.), 85.

[34]The 1526 catechism of Balthasar Hubmaier states that by baptism one publicly vows to God and agrees in the strength of God the Father, Son, and Holy Spirit to henceforth believe and live according to God's divine Word. If the baptized believer breaks this agreement, brotherly admonition, according to Christ's order (Matt. 18:15ff) will be accepted.

Being a citizen of any realm, including God's, carries a loyalty price. Members of Christ's body should be ready to "put on the whole armor of God" before they go forth as representatives of the church in the world. The Society of Friends, for instance, is indebted to their Puritan forebears for the belief that this world is ultimately accountable to God's order and design. In the meantime, faithful Christians are immediately accountable to function as reflections of the present reign of Christ. According to Quaker theologian Wilmer Cooper:

> Since the time of George Fox, Friends have had a deep sense that one ought to be able to live as if the kingdom of God were a reality here and now and not some golden age of the past or some blessed event of the future. Along with a drive for Christian perfection in one's personal life, there must be a corresponding drive for Christian perfection in the corporate, social, and political world.[35]

By the middle of the twentieth century, even among "free churches," there had developed a significant acculturation of Christianity in both Europe and North America. As Franklin Littell put it, there was "a growing promiscuity of membership standards and frivolity of preaching and practice."[36] In response, a Believers Church Conference convened at Goshen College in 1992 and focused on "The Rule of Christ" (Matt. 18:15-20) and how the churches might gain fresh appreciation for "a rightly conceived moral authority of the church and recover a ministry of dealing redemptively with believers in spiritual or moral difficulty."[37] There were presentations on how the Society of Friends (Quakers) evolved a "gospel order" in the England of the seventeenth century and how John Wesley in the eighteenth cen-

---

[35]Wilmer A. Cooper, *A Living Faith: An Historical Study of Quaker Beliefs* (Richmond, Ind.: Friends United Press, 1990), 102. Cooper refers to a set of "social testimonies" highlighted among Friends, including integrity, simplicity, peace, and equality. He concludes: "The bottom line of the testimonies is consistency: a consistent correspondence between what we believe and how our beliefs get translated into action, which carries us back full circle to the testimony of integrity" (110).

[36]Franklin Littell, *The Free Church* (Boston: Starr King Press, Beacon Hill, 1957), 116.

[37]Unpublished "Findings Committtee Report," May 23, 1992, 1.

tury placed the "Rule of Christ" within the responsibilities of bands and class meetings where full sharing was expected and even demanded. This Wesleyan revival involved a key emphasis on personal discipline and spiritual submission within the new Methodist societies. These were essential components of John Wesley's educational strategy. The device of the "class meeting" in particular "was the instrument by which preaching and doctrine were harnessed into spiritual renewal. It carried the revolution."[38]

The 1992 conference Findings Committee observed: "We need to acknowledge hesitation to submit our own individual rights to the definitions and discipline of the group." Even in a conservative tradition like the Church of God (Anderson) one encounters such a strong hesitation. For instance, after a national Task Force on Governance and Polity had studied from 1987 to 1992 a range of related issues in this movement's life in North America, it identified as a basic issue "the tension between authority and autonomy." "Free" churches who wish the liberty of functioning within the dynamic of the Spirit (who might blow unpredictably as does the wind) often struggle with the coordinate need to be genuinely accountable within the wisdom and discipline of the body of believers.[39]

Increasingly, secular structures supplant or unduly influence not only traditional church structures, but also the values and disciplines that they have sought to uphold. In awkward contrast to the communal and disciplined nature of the Believers Church tradition, modern Western society is characterized by a rampant individualism that wants little if anything banned from the realm of personal choice. The very integrity of the church, therefore, is at stake. The following observations and questions posed by a modern Believers Church leader are worthy of careful note:

> ...while the conception and practice of the ban was, on the whole, literalistic and legalistic in the sixteenth century, and

---

[38]D. Michael Henderson, *John Wesley's Class Meeting: A Model for Making Disciples* (Nappanee, Ind.: Evangel Publishing House, 1997), 31.

[39]See Barry Callen, *Journeying Together* (Anderson, Ind.: Leadership Council of the Church of God and Warner Press, 1996), 144.

became even more so as the century proceeded, there are dimensions of the ban that call for thoughtful reconsideration. The linking of the ban to believers' baptism cemented an important factor of accountability between church members that emphasized the communal nature of the fellowship. The inner spiritual change led not only to individual water baptism, but led necessarily to community and to a mutual accountability within that community. Can there be "Believers' Churches" in the absence of such accountability? How might this dimension be recovered in a secular and individualistic age such as our own?[40]

Observed David Elton Trueblood of the Quaker tradition: "We shall not be saved by anything less than commitment, and the commitment will not be effective unless it finds expression in a committed fellowship. If we have any knowledge of human nature, we begin by rejecting the arrogance of self-sufficiency."[41] Franklin Littell adds this about "integral" Christianity:

Integral Christianity implies above all that the People of God shall not pretend to a program of action which is beyond its disciplined capacities, that it shall not declare any new idea or plan to the world until it has made incarnate the consequences thereof within its own ranks. A Church of integrity, in short, will not moralize to the world about the evils of discrimination and racialism until it admits to membership and the communion table all qualified persons regardless of race or color; it will not talk about a materialistic success philosophy in the world while it allows a callow type of careerism in its pulpits; it will not prate about corruption in politics at the time it holds its membership open to those same corrupt politicians. It will begin and carry through its renewing and redeeming mission with self-examination, internal discipline, and obedience to the governance of the Ruler of the Church.[42]

---

[40]C. Arnold Snyder, *Anabaptist History and Theology* (Kitchener, Ont.: Pandora Press, 1995), 393.

[41]D. Elton Trueblood, *The Company of the Committed* (N.Y.: Harper and Row, 1961), 22-23.

[42]Littell, *The Free Church*, 141.

An undisciplined Christian life insures immature believers and ineffective communities of faith. Group discipline, admittedly, suggests the danger of coercive churches. Thus the dilemma—or at least the paradox. Volunteerism must be joined to a sincere commitment that is free of arrogance and open to correction and growth. In the Christian setting, to be appropriately free is to be disciplined. Included in the discipline is regular and informed participation in the worship life of the church. The needed growth among Christians involves certain worship practices that instruct memory, enhance identity, and stimulate growth.

The Bond—Rituals

Since the Fourth Lateran Council in 1215, official Roman Catholic dogma has included the language of "transubstantiation" to define the "substance" of Christ's flesh and blood that is said to be literally present in the "accidents" of the bread and wine. Here is an example of a high level of mandated creedal formulation tied to a central worship practice of the church, the Lord's supper. The earliest Anabaptist leaders like Andreas Karlstadt and Conrad Grebel rejected such dogma, including the larger concept of the Roman mass as a sacrifice and means of grace. Rather, the Lord's supper was to be seen as a memorial to the death and resurrection of Christ, a sign of loving and often suffering fellowship among Christians.

The general focus of the Believers Church has been more on the real presence of the Spirit of the Christ in his visible body, the people who are his disciples. The church is the fellowship of believers who are to be sharing by grace in the current life of the Spirit. This is true whether they are baptizing, partaking of the Lord's supper, or ministering to the poor. The disciplined covenant communities of the early Anabaptists reflected their concern for commitment and unity in various ways, including "closed" or "close" communion. Those approved for participation in the Lord's supper were to be living as one with the local church body. Menno Simons taught that participants were to be the "penitent," those who "walk with their brethren in love, peace, and unity, who are led by the Spirit of the Lord into all truth and righteousness, and who prove by their fruits that they are the church and people of God."[43] Michael Sattler, who likely authored the articles on the Lord's supper in the 1527 Schleitheim Confession, understood the suffering Christ to be the same as the ascended Christ. This Christ is "really present" in the visible congregation that is disciplined and separated from the world. For Sattler and most early Anabaptists,

> ...the Lord's Supper confronted Christians with a bond of love that compelled them to offer their lives for each other, in the way Christ's life had been offered for the forgiveness of sins. The Lord's Supper tied Christ's redemptive suffering to their bodily suffering for each other in the genesis and maintenance of an egalitarian community.... All Anabaptists rejected the mass, a theology of bodily presence of Christ in the elements, and denied the sacrificial character of the mass as a means of grace. All rejected the *ex opera operato* understanding of a sacrament. Similarly they all rejected the mediation of the ritual through a sacredotal priesthood....[44]

A prominent characteristic of the Anabaptist approach to the Lord's supper was the "horizontal" understanding of sacrificial love. In light of the suffering and sacrifice of Christ, participation in the supper was to be a dramatized sign of obligation and commitment to suffer as necessary for Christ and for brothers and sisters in the church. Said Balthasar Hubmaier in his 1526 catechism, the Lord's supper is "a public sign and testimonial of the love in which one brother obligates himself to another before the congregation, that just as they now break and eat the bread with each other and share and drink the cup, likewise they wish now to sacrifice and shed their body and blood for one another...."[45]

---

[43]As quoted in John C. Wenger, ed., *The Complete Writings of Menno Simons*, trans. Leonard Verduin (Scottdale, Pa.: Herald Press, 1956), 740.

[44]Jeff Bach, "Incorporation into Christ and the Brethren: The Lord's Supper and Feet-washing in Anabaptist Groups," in Carl Bowman and Stephen Longenecker, eds., *Anabaptist Currents* (Camden, Maine: Penobscot Press, 1995), 136, 146.

[45]As in C. Arnold Snyder, *Anabaptist History and Theology* (Kitchener, Ontario: Pandora Press, 1995), 92.

With the Bible assumed as foundational, the Spirit's ongoing illumination of the Bible's present significance as essential, and the context of the church and its discipline as vital, how then are such practices as baptism and the Lord's supper to be understood within church life? Hubmaier responded: "These are only outward symbols. They are nothing other than water, bread, and wine [as opposed to the Roman claim of the actual body and blood of Jesus].... The end is the gathering of a church, the covenanting publicly to live according to Christ's word in faith and brotherly love, and the submitting...to a brotherly discipline and the Christian ban because of their sins.... This is the important thing...and not the water, bread, or wine."[46]

Clearly the early Anabaptists flatly rejected the medieval sacramental understanding of the Lord's supper. They wished instead to remember Christ with gratitude and symbolize in their covenant communities the commitment, love, and unity suggested by this common meal. Even so, as the Believers Church tradition has evolved since, there has come to be more "sacramental" variety than often is recognized. It usually features a Zwinglian memorial/remembrance view of the supper, but not always this view exclusively.[47] The range now stretches from a strict memorial-only view common among many Baptist bodies to the "means of grace" perspective of the Wesleyan tradition (nurturing, not saving grace). There is also the continuum from the Christian Church (Disciples of Christ) that centers weekly worship around the Lord's supper to the Society of Friends (Quakers) that typically avoids any formalized liturgical practice in favor of worshipping God "in spirit and truth."[48]

The Believers Church approach to liturgical practices is seen clearly in its historic witness to Christian baptism. This witness can be traced back at least to the sixteenth century. The Schleitheim Articles

---

[46]As quoted by Donald Durnbaugh, in Dale Stoffer, ed., *The Lord's Supper: Believers' Church Perspectives* (Scottdale, Pa.: Herald Press, 1997), 73.

[47]For a helpful study, see John D. Rempel, *The Lord's Supper in Anabaptism* (Scottdale, Pa.: Herald Press, 1994).

[48]See Dale Stoffer, ed., *The Lord's Supper: Believers' Church Perspectives* (Scottdale, Pa.: Herald Press, 1997).

(1527) is a theological declaration that played a significant role in consolidating the Swiss and South German streams of the early Anabaptist movement. The first article of this statement of faith freshly addressed baptism at a time when witness was needed to counter an institutionally entrenched and clergy-controlled view of baptism as a central and essential means of grace.[49] Soon Menno Simons (1496-1561) spoke about baptism in a way similar to the Articles, with a confessional form of his view appearing in the 1632 Dordrecht Articles. In his 1539 essay "Christian Baptism," Menno said that baptism is a sign of obedience that proceeds from faith. Regeneration (new birth in Christ) comes by faith in God's Word rather than by receiving the sacrament at the hands of established clergy. Baptism follows regeneration instead of effecting it. More recently, Russell Byrum (1889-1980) identified the church as "the aggregate of those who have been regenerated."[50] Regeneration and not "sacraments" as such were said to be God's criterion for placing members in the church through the work of saving grace. Baptism is the resulting witness, not the instrument of salvation.[51]

The church is "where Christian experience makes you a member."[52] The central question is not whether baptism makes one a

---

[49]The Schleitheim Articles stress that baptism is for those who understand the gospel's demands (thus no infants), witness to sins forgiven through Christ, and express desire to follow Christ in a life of dedicated discipleship (see Marlin Miller, "The Mennonites" in Merle Strege, ed., *Baptism and Church*, Grand Rapids: Sagamore Books, 1986, 16-17).

[50]Russell Byrum, *Christian Theology* (Anderson, Ind.: Warner Press, 1925, rev. ed. 1982), 424.

[51]Following extensive dialogue over the issue of baptism, representatives of the Church of God (Anderson) and the Christian Churches/Churches of Christ stated the following: "We are agreed that baptism is commanded by the Lord Jesus to be practiced by all of His followers. This baptism is to be by the immersion in water of penitent believers. Baptism is symbolic of the atoning death, burial, and resurrection of Christ. By its nature as well as by biblical teaching, baptism is involved with forgiveness of sin. We take pains, however, to repudiate any doctrine of baptismal regeneration, holding that forgiveness is wholly a matter of God's grace" (as in Barry Callen and James North, *Coming Together In Christ*, Joplin, Mo.: College Press, 1997), 214.

[52]The intent of this slogan, commonly used in the Church of God (Anderson), is to oppose a view like Walter Scott's "five finger exercise" made famous during his evangelistic preaching on the Western Reserve (northeast Ohio, 1827-1830). With the sequence

Christian instead of repentance and actual regeneration, but whether there is a crucial link between baptism and church membership. Responding affirmatively, the Believers Church tradition sees a corporate dimension of the baptismal meaning.[53] Beyond confession of personal faith and a promise to answer the call to discipleship, in some settings the candidate for baptism is asked: "Will you be loyal to the church, upholding her by your prayers and your presence, your substance and your service?" Insisting that "the covenant with God through Christ cannot be separated from the covenant with brothers and sisters," there is the Brethren practice of laying on of hands immediately following baptism, symbolizing the truth that "the Spirit comes to us through the lives of others in the body of Christ."[54] Baptism, among other things, is the believer's ordination to ministry, a highlighting of the priesthood of all believers, and an unmistakable commitment to belonging responsibly to Christ's body, the church.

---

significant, Scott taught faith, repentance, baptism, remission of sins, and the gift of the Holy Spirit (counted on five fingers). The Church of God movement and many other Wesleyan and Anabaptist bodies have understood, to the contrary, that the remission of sins necessarily precedes baptism. Alexander Campbell, famous associate of Scott, held a complex and often misunderstood view of this subject. He complained that "some of my brethren...have given to baptism an undue eminence—a sort of pardon-procuring, rather than pardon-certifying and enjoying efficacy" (*Millennial Harbinger*, 1840, 544-45). But he also wrote that, as long as previous faith and repentance are present so that salvation is by faith and not by any merit-producing work, baptism "is the means of receiving a formal, distinct, and specific absolution, or release from guilt" (*The Christian System*, 1839, 61-62). Rather than merely a *sign*, baptism was seen by Campbell as a *step* in the saving process, the time when sins are remitted and the gift of the Spirit given (see: *Christian Baptist*, April 7, 1828, 82). Baptism was said to complete one's adoption into the family of God. It is "a sign of God's grace toward us and a way of our saying 'yes!' to that grace" (Clark Williamson, *Baptism: Embodiment of the Gospel*, St. Louis: Christian Board of Education, 1987, 37).

[53]Note: "The influences of pietist, revivalist and charismatic renewal movements...have frequently contributed to what sometimes amounts to an overemphasis on the subjective and individual dimensions of Christian baptism in Mennonite teaching and practice" (Marlin Miller, "Baptism in the Mennonite Tradition," *Mennonite Quarterly Review*, July, 1990, 236). The same could be said about many similar bodies. While personal experience with the Spirit is essential, it does not replace the need for the communal context, discipline, and practices through which the Spirit often chooses to work.

[54]Dale Brown, "The Brethren," in Merle Strege, ed., *Baptism and Church* (Grand Rapids: Sagamore Books, 1986), 33.

Most participants in the Believers Church tradition, then, have chosen to continue certain "rituals" in church life, although they tend to be viewed as responses, signs, and commitments rather than mere formalities or themselves the substance or direct cause of spiritual realities. Instead of automatic conveyors of divine grace through the controlling hands of a clergy that can be corrupted and coercive, they are voluntary acts of the faithful church community. Beyond this, however, something more is to be learned from Pilgram Marpeck, one of the few early Anabaptists to think systematically about "sacramental" issues. He was not comfortable with the view that outward ceremonies are nothing more than reflections of inner spiritual conditions and thus are of no necessary significance. To the contrary, he argued that they can and should be vehicles within church life that point toward divine reality and lead believers to deeper levels of love, gratitude, yieldedness, and obedience. This view reflects many Believers Churches today that are beginning cautiously to recognize again the spiritual power of visible symbols and rituals that both reflect and can enhance the believer's appropriation of the gospel of Jesus Christ.[55]

M. Robert Mulholland, Jr., speaks of "the rhythm of community, the rhythm of life together in Christ." This rhythm sometimes is called "liturgy" or an intentional patterning of worship life that itself can become "a means of grace in which God more fully speaks forth into being the human community, binds them more closely to himself in love, bonds them more closely to one another in love, and thrusts them into the world as agents of God's love."[56] Biblical teach-

---

[55]Beyond baptism and the Lord's supper, footwashing has been another sacred ritual frequently practiced in the Believers Church tradition. Gilbert Stafford (*Theology for Disciples*, Warner Press, 1996, chapter 23) argues that "footwashing has as much basis for being a liturgical act with spiritual significance for disciples as does baptism and the Lord's supper" (590). He adds: "John 13:1-20 tells about Jesus washing the feet of his disciples—an enacted condemnation of Judas' mode of life, a dramatic lesson for Jesus' disciples about the divine approach to life, and the establishment of a liturgical observance for spiritual renewal" (571).

[56]M. Robert Mulholland, Jr., *Shaped by the Word* (Nashville: The Upper Room, 1985), 78-79.

ing appears to call for a believer, having repented and been justified before God, to take full advantage of the continuing ordinances (sacraments) of the Christian faith as established by Jesus (adopting a classic Wesleyan view, but under the cautious eye of Believers Church concerns). One should appreciate John Wesley's emphasis on "means of grace" for spiritual growth, even in the midst of the effort to avoid the all-too-common institutional distortion of church power and practices. The purposes of baptism, the Lord's supper, and foot-washing, while not themselves the means for accomplishing initial or final salvation, nonetheless are significant to the health and fruitfulness of that salvation. They are means of graphic remembrance, public witness, corporate identity building, and ongoing personal sanctification. They may not be basic to the *being* of the church, but they are crucial to its *well-being* as a growing and distinctive body of God's people in a sinful world. They are frameworks in which the rhythm of church life can proceed properly.[57]

The Battle—Peace

The Believers Church tradition tends to resist any disconnection of ends and means.[58] If Christ has brought into being a distinctive Christ community, the church, he surely also intends that this community function in the world in a Christ-like way. Through obedience to its own divine calling as the church, nothing other than the living body of Christ in the world, the church's very faithfulness becomes its primary evangelistic and social strategy. The *what* and the *how* of its faithfulness are to be closely linked. One key issue of how best to be in the world involves whether or not the church should endorse the use of violence in some circumstances.

---

[57]For an elaboration of this line of thought, see Barry L. Callen, *God As Loving Grace* (Nappanee, Ind.: Evangel Publishing House, 1996), 331-341.

[58]Similarly, see Randy Maddox, "Reconnecting the Means to the End," *Wesleyan Theological Journal* 33:2 (Fall 1998), 29-66. Maddox speaks of the goal of Christian "holiness" in this life and its realistic potential only when a believer actively pursues the full range of the graciously-provided divine means for nurturing true holiness of heart and life. The Believers Church would concur generally with this sentiment and apply it also to the social life and mission of the church.

The Bible is full of the concept of the realm and reign of God. Related themes that unpack their meanings are land, house, city, justice, Sabbath, Jubilee, and peace. The last, *shalom*, is a comprehensive vision of God's intent to bring into human life right relationships, harmony, and the proper functioning of all aspects of the creation. Tied directly to the kingly rule of the Messiah (Isa. 9:6-7) is the "Prince of Peace" role of reintroducing things in God's way and toward God's original purpose. Peace is at the heart of God's reign. To know true citizenship in God's kingdom is to participate by grace in "righteousness, peace, and joy in the Holy Spirit (Rom. 14:17). Jesus is God's shalom, "making peace through his blood, shed on the cross" (Col. 1:20). Jesus creates a reconciled and reconciling community where there no longer is a "dividing wall of hostility" between Jew and Gentile, slave and free, male and female (Eph. 2). Thus, "in God's kingdom plan, peace is both the final goal of the kingdom and the present experience of the community of Jesus' disciples."[59]

In the sixteenth century there were differences among the Anabaptist groups about how to apply the New Testament aversion to violence. The generally accepted rule among them seems to have been that the civil magistrate played a divinely-given and essential role in relation to the evils of society and, with at least passive obedience, should be obeyed except in matters of Christian conscience. The Swiss Brethren refused to bear arms, but were criticized by the Hutterites because they did pay war taxes. Others would not fight or pay, often bringing on their heads more than mere criticism. Determining how to best live out the expected way of Christ in the surrounding evil of the world has never been easy.

Franklin Littell sees three accents in the Anabaptist view of the magistrate: their opposition to compulsion in religion; their opposition to revolution;[60] and their sense of destiny as the Church of the

---

[59]Howard A. Synder, *A Kingdom Manifesto: Calling the Church to Live Under God's Reign* (Downers Grove, Ill.: InterVarsity Press, 1985), 22.

[60]After the Münster tragedy (1535), there was widespread opposition among Anabaptists to aggressive and even violent civil disobedience as a means to social betterment in this world. The result was the tendency to assert the authority of the magistrate, at least within its proper sphere.

Martyrs. The early Anabaptists "were a disciplined lay community with a vivid eschatology."[61] Faithfulness in a fallen world brought suffering because the obedient church understood itself to be a countercultural movement which, by its very faithfulness to its Christlike nature, points by its word and deed to the coming reign of Christ's righteousness. Concludes Dale W. Brown in a contemporary setting: "A community which cares and shares with one another and which is hospitable to the stranger and enemy possesses more real evangelistic power than those which adopt the media and manipulative techniques of Madison Avenue." Further, "in a world in which weapons in the hands of any may trigger a holocaust, the option of prophetic, witnessing, suffering, supporting communities may become more necessary and viable."[62]

Characteristic of Jesus' life was the sympathetic attention he paid to widows, orphans, outcasts, and strangers. Argues J. Denny Weaver, "as important as *who* Jesus identified with is *how* he identified with them.... Jesus rejected violence as a way to help the powerless and alleviate their suffering."[63] Christians today still face the decision of whether the way of non-violence is fundamental to the way followers of Jesus are to be in the world, or whether it is an admirable ideal that can be abandoned in the name of supposed higher goods like national pride, or the survival of a political system like democracy, or an economic system like capitalism.

There is obvious danger in identifying any nationalist goal with the Christian faith. On the other hand, one must consider the perspective of a man like Andy Rooney. Rooney, the resident curmudgeon of television's *60 Minutes*, was a young journalist in Europe in the 1940s. He went to Buchenwald after it was liberated to see if the rumors of genocide were true. He was stunned by a reality as bad as any rumor. Then he wrote: "For the first time I knew that any peace is not better

---

[61]Franklin Littell, *The Anabaptist View of the Church*, rev. ed. (Boston: Starr King Press, 1958), 106-107.

[62]Dale W. Brown, "Communal Ecclesiology: The Power of the Anabaptist Vision," *Theology Today* 36:1 (April 1979), 28-29.

[63]J. Denny Weaver, *Becoming Anabaptist* (Scottdale, Pa.: Herald Press, 1987), 134.

than any war."[64] There is the difficult tension between the ways of peace and the evils of the world.

The Christian belongs to a higher order than national citizenship, ethnic background, or any "tribal" tradition. American Christians face the challenge of living today in the world's only remaining "super power" and doing so in a way that honors a sovereign God. This God is the One who chose to save the world through the coming of a vulnerable baby and then through a crucified man who could have avoided or destroyed his enemies, but would not. Those who now would take up their own crosses to follow this Jesus are to have the attitude that is the same as that of Christ Jesus (Phil. 2:5), not the mind and means of the world.

While the Wesleyan tradition is not one of the historical "peace" traditions, a stance of the United Methodist Church in the United States speaks from their central convictions:

> *War and Peace.* We believe war is incompatible with the teachings and example of Christ. We therefore reject war as an instrument of national foreign policy and insist that the first moral duty of all nations is to resolve by peaceful means every dispute that arises between or among them; that human values must outweigh military claims as governments determine their priorities; that the militarization of society must be challenged and stopped; that the manufacture, sale, and deployment of armaments must be reduced and controlled.[65]

Governments are self-serving, almost by definition, and find it easy to resort to violence when their self-interests are perceived to be threatened. Christians, however, are not to be self-serving. The church is to exist by the persuasiveness of love.

Surely the Christian who is devoted first to God's reign in all things should be committed to any distinctive *means* that is appropriate to

---

[64]As quoted by Tom Brokaw, *The Greatest Generation* (N.Y.: Random House, 1998), 296.

[65]As of the General Conference of 1992 this statement remained the basic position of the United Methodist Church on war and peace.

the *nature* and *ends* of the ministry of Jesus. The Believers Church tradition typically has judged this assumption to imply at least giving serious consideration to the following thesis. The social-ethical task of the church is to really *be* the church, Christ's servant community in the world. What makes the church the church is its faithful embodiment in the world of the peaceable reign of God that was inaugurated by the sacrificial ministry of Jesus. Further, to the extent that such embodiment implies the peaceful means of pursuing Christlike ends, "nonviolence is not just one implication among others that can be drawn from our Christian beliefs; it is at the very heart of our understanding of God."[66]

Many Christians, even some in today's Believers Church tradition, do not accept "pacifist" as an appropriate or at least not as a necessary characterization of the Christian faith and social ethic.[67] The Church of the Brethren, for instance, represented a traditional pacifist position at least through World War I. But by World War II more than eighty percent of Brethren young men joined the army, either as noncombatants or regular troops.[68] Even so, nearly all Christians have an aversion to violence, are ashamed of the bloody Christian crusades of past centuries, and support either a pacifist or at least a "just war" stance. The latter tends to put the burden of proof on any call to violence in a given set of crisis circumstances. Is war really justified? Have all of the alternatives been explored and exhausted? This common stance might be called "selective pacifism," a preference for peace whenever judged possible and a commitment to confronting and resolving differences without injuring, forcing, or even killing.

---

[66]Stanley Hauerwas, *The Peaceable Kingdom* (Notre Dame, Ind.: University of Notre Dame Press, 1983), xvii. One and possibly the best way of understanding the God revealed in the Bible is "loving grace" (see Barry Callen, *God As Loving Grace*, Nappanee, Ind.: Evangel Publishing House, 1996).

[67]See, e.g., the mixed circumstance of the Church of God (Anderson) as explained by its current historian Merle Strege in his "The Demise (?) of a Peace Church: The Church of God (Anderson), Pacifism and Civil Religion," *Mennonite Quarterly Review* 45:2 (April 1991), 128-140.

[68]Donald Durnbaugh, *A History of the Brethren 1708-1995* (Elgin, Ill.: Brethren Press, 1997), 474.

In the face of injustice and hatred, Christians are to remember that "peacemaking is that quality of life and practices engendered by a community that knows it lives as a forgiven people."[69] Rodney Clapp puts it plainly: "In a warring world we [Christians] are indeed a peculiar people, a people called to survive by worship rather than weapons."[70] The central point is that believers are to be disciples of the Prince of Peace, disciples who are devoted to the mission and means of Jesus and not to the values and ways of the world. In our time of so much hatred and brutality, much of it romanticized on television, it is crucial that Christians live out the Spirit-provided fruit of their salvation: "love, joy, peace, patience, kindness, generosity, faithfulness, gentleness, and self-control" (Gal. 5:22). As Virginia Wiles rightly concludes: "It is only a strong people who can live such gentle lives. And such strength can only be a reality among those who have experienced the grace of God that is in Christ Jesus our Lord."[71]

The Bottom Line—Discipleship

The Believers Church tradition highlights a central perspective of Christianity's Hebrew heritage. Authentic religion is far more than a system of ethics, a code of conduct, or a creed—"orthodox" as they may be. Instead, the Hebrews understood faith in terms of a journey, the way a person of faith actually walks daily in light of belief in the ever-present God. No creedalism or ceremonialism alone will ever meet God's requirement for the good life (Isa. 1:11-14; Amos 5:21-23). Those who please God are only those who act justly and love mercy and walk humbly with God (Mic. 6:8). Therefore, "the essence of religion is relationship; it is walking with God in his path of wisdom

---

[69]Stanley Hauerwas, *Christian Existence Today* (Durham, N.C.: Labyrinth, 1988), 91.

[70]Rodney Clapp, *A Peculiar People: The Church as Culture in a Post-Christian Society* (Downers Grove, Ill.: InterVarsity Press, 1996), 110.

[71]Virginia Wiles, "Gentle Strength: Contemporary Prospects for an Understanding of Salvation," in C. Bowman and S. Longenecker, eds., *Anabaptist Currents: History in Conversation with the Present* (Penobscot Press, 1995), 46.

and righteousness and in his way of service to others."[72] Every day is to be a day of dedicated and sometimes dangerous discipleship.

What is "the way," the bottom line of Christian discipleship? Jesus identified himself as the way (John 14:6), making relationship with him and faithfulness to him central for the Christian life. The way is to be faithful to Christ in the midst of life and in a voluntary covenant community, the church, where the Christ has promised to be. This way is the willing acceptance of a biblically-rooted discipline within the church's life. It is the celebration of the Christ who really does remain present in the visible life of the church. It is the disciple's determination to be faithful and the necessary empowerment by Christ's Spirit that enables the believing church to be in the world in a Christ-like way.

One day all people will give an account and be judged according to their responses to the love of God in Jesus Christ. Has there been faithfulness and thus a truly saving relationship to the person and way of Christ? Was the choice made to be responsible in the loving ways that a saving relationship implies (Matt. 12:36; 2 Cor. 5:10)? Is there evidence of the lived-out fruit of the Spirit? Judgment on this basis is both a present reality (John 3:18; Rom. 1:18-32) and an unavoidable fact of the last day (Rev. 20:11-15). We who are made new in Jesus Christ by faith are expected to be faithful to the implications of that newness until he comes again.

---

[72]Marvin Wilson, *Our Father Abraham: Jewish Roots of the Christian Faith* (Grand Rapids: Eerdmans, 1989), 159.

6

Fulfilling The Vision: Christian Mission Today

Prior to the beginning of the [twentieth] century, Brethren held a vision of the church as a unified body of believers having a common mission which they had gained through radical obedience to the New Testament, through a consistent pattern of church discipline, and through a pattern of separation from and non-conformity to the world. At the end of the present century, a new vision has emerged, one that is more compatible with contemporary cultural and demographic settings. Today many call for the church to view itself as including a world community of believers. Such a church will be characterized by diversity rather than ethnic unity and by contrasting beliefs and life styles rather than uniformity in outward expressions.[1]

In the Holy Spirit, and in the body of Christ anointed by the Spirit, the church has the resources and the power to bring the revolution and produce the firstfruits of the Kingdom. The question is faith and faithfulness to God's economy for the church. Hans Küng has said, "The Kingdom of God is creation healed." Given our faith and obedience, God can liberate the church to heal the world.[2]

In the above quotation of Emmert Bittinger we encounter a provocative perspective regarding the body of believers worldwide

---

[1] Emmert F. Bittinger, in Bittinger, ed., *Brethren In Transition: 20th Century Directions and Dilemmas* (Camden, Maine: Penobscot Press, 1992), 2-3.

[2] Howard A. Snyder, *Liberating the Church: The Ecology of Church and Kingdom* (Downers Grove, Ill.: InterVarsity Press, 1983), 258.

who represent the Believers Church tradition today. Recognizing the contemporary breadth of this particular community of Christians, Bittinger calls for a church that reflects such diversity in its multi-ethnicity and tolerance of "contrasting beliefs and life styles." A key question is: How far can such diversity and tolerance go before there remains no integrity to the Believers Church tradition itself? To put the question in terms of the nature of the church as *gathered* rather than *given* (see chapter five), have Believers Churches at the beginning of the twenty-first century yielded to previously detested forms of givenness, to established and restrictive forms of "worldly" order, wisdom, and practices that do not root in or engender real Christian life in the Spirit of God?

Settings do change, of course, and so do Christian traditions seeking to function, adapt, and minister in them. How can Christians in the Believers Church tradition rediscover and be faithful to the best of their rich heritage in the current context? How can they who know themselves to have been divinely *gathered* in a previous time avoid being essentially *given* churches themselves in this time? This final chapter notes the mainstreaming pattern among Believers Churches, looks for ways to translate its high ideals into contemporary realities, explores some of the obstacles, and concludes that there still remains or can remain something of "the best of the ancient calling."

Historically, the Believers Church tradition has asked pivotal questions and attempted to give them biblical answers to which life itself must be committed. Among the questions have been: What does it mean for Christians to give their lives to Jesus Christ in light of the demands of the gospel? How can the lives of believers be molded on the pattern of Christ's servanthood? What are the concrete implications of loving one's enemies? How is the church to live out its life as a called community of God's people in our kind of world? John Roth is surely correct. The core Believers Church principles of discipleship, community, and nonresistant love, to the degree that they are at the heart of the Christian gospel, have not lost their significance or relevance—and should not be compromised in the name of diversity and tolerance. The pressing questions now are: Do Christians remain committed to these principles? How should these principles of the gospel find their best expressions within the contemporary church?[3] How can the church be an effective instrument on behalf of the goal of God's reign, which is that all of creation be healed of the consequences of its deep sin-wounds?

Answers to such challenging questions must be sought in the midst of the substantial change now being experienced commonly in churches of the Believers Church tradition. A cooling of ardor and at least a measure of negative accommodation with prevailing cultures can and often have taken their toll. The generations following reformers typically temper the tone of the once vigorously voiced ideal and tend to slide slowly toward a more comfortable midstream stance. Note, for example, the personal testimony of theologian Harvey Cox. In the eighteenth century his ancestors fled England for Pennsylvania. Dubbed "Quakers" in England, they had been derided for not respecting the established civil and church authorities and for the "unseemly intensity" of their worship. No hats were removed for bishops or kings and their prayers had a fervor that included some shaking (thus "Quakers"). Ridicule had turned to active persecution and they left for America. By Cox's boyhood some 200 years later, however, this immigrant Quaker community was far less offensive to established authorities and little if anything shook. In fact, they had become "paragons of propriety…[and] pedigreed aristocrats" doing rather well financially in the new world.[4]

A similar transition is chronicled by Richard Hughes in relation to the Christian Churches (Disciples tradition of Thomas and Alexander Campbell). Put in the sociological terms of *sect* and *denomination*, this "Restoration Movement" was a sect initially in the early nineteenth century, standing over against the dominant culture as "the exclusive

---

[3]John Roth, "Living Between the Times: 'The Anabaptist Vision and Mennonite Reality' Revisited," *Mennonite Quarterly Review* (July 1995), 323. Roth is a professor at Goshen College, Director of the Mennonite Historical Library, and Editor of the *Mennonite Quarterly Review*.

[4]Harvey Cox, *Fire from Heaven* (Reading, Mass.: Addison-Wesley Publishing Company, 1995), 7.

domain of both truth and salvation, from which it maintains that other religious bodies and the culture at large have departed." It was a vigorous reforming movement guided by a vision of the true church as a sectarian body restored along the lines of what it saw as the New Testament pattern. However, over time it moved to denominational status, meaning that it

> ...has typically made its peace with the dominant culture, abandoned its exclusivist rhetoric, muted its prophetic voice, and come to behave as a well-mannered, compliant member of the larger culture and of the larger Christian community. Churches of Christ began moving unmistakably toward such a position during the World War I era; now, in the waning years of the twentieth century, they have, with a few notable exceptions, practically completed their sect-to-denomination transition.[5]

Such a mainstreaming evolution is also reported by Donald Fitzkee about a select group of Church of the Brethren congregations. His book *Moving Toward the Mainstream* is "the story of a group of congregations in eastern Pennsylvania who shed many of the peculiar trappings of their plain-sect heritage to plunge into the American Protestant mainstream."[6] Indeed, as he concludes, it may be that "part of the continuing mission of the church today is for the body of believers to discover how the church in its current context can be faithful to the best within its ancient calling."[7] Such a conclusion highlights a central issue that yet lingers. How do we relate best the necessity of a present and vital experience of Christian community and discipleship and at the same time address the claims for the con-

---

[5]Richard T. Hughes, *Reviving the Ancient Faith: The Story of Churches of Christ in America* (Grand Rapids: Eerdmans, 1996), 5. See also Carl Bowman, *Brethren Society: The Cultural Transformation of a "Peculiar People"* (Baltimore: Johns Hopkins University Press, 1995).

[6]Intercourse, Pa.: Good Books, 1995, 9. The Findings Committee of the 1967 Believers Church Conference affirmed that the church is "to work out her being as a covenant community in the midst of the world." However, it registered the concern that "the congregation might misunderstand its proclamation as recruitment of support for its institutional program" (see Appendix B, 4A).

[7]Bittinger, op. cit.

tinuing validity of the church in its more institutional forms? Does the Believers Church tradition, as a continuing stream of Christian renewal movements, *replace* or only *supplement* the institutionalized church with its traditional and formalized structures, teaching, and liturgical practices? J. Denny Weaver (Mennonite) tends to say replace; Rosemary Ruether (Roman Catholic) says supplement; Howard Snyder (United Methodist) offers a "mediating" position.

Snyder argues that both the institutional and "charismatic" approaches are open to criticism and have their strengths. The institutional or traditional church has the tendency to be blind or apathetic to the gulf that too often exists between its profession and its present possession of faith and life. It suffers from self-interest and entrenchment in the status quo. It does, however, represent continuity with the past and carries the core traditions of Scripture, the sacraments, and the deposit of doctrinal truth debated and refined over the centuries. The Believers Church, reacting to the significant weaknesses of the institutional church, tends to lose the significance of history and too easily identifies God's purposes exclusively with its own immediate renewal efforts. Further, such "radicals"

> …are typically naive concerning institutional and sociological realities and blind to the institutional dimensions of their own movement. In their concern with present experience they may fall prey to bizarre apocalyptic, dispensational, or millennial views which are unbiblical and unrealistic and may lead to extreme hopes, claims, or behavior.[8]

Even with these very real weaknesses, the Believers Church persists and often has managed to address directly and wisely its own vulnerabilities.

Renewal clearly is needed in the institutional church today, a renewal that certainly must spring from the real and immediate *experience* of God's transforming grace. For such renewal to be authentic and

---

[8]Howard A. Snyder, *Signs of the Spirit: How God Reshapes the Church* (Grand Rapids: Academie Books, Zondervan, 1989), 273.

constructive, it must come from the Spirit, issue in new life and a disciplined new Spirit community, be an outgrowth and extension of the faith "once delivered to the saints" (thus being tied meaningfully to the long tradition of the church), and be on current mission with the Spirit for the sake of a lost world. The challenge is for the church to be both faithful to its heritage and relevant to its context. The heritage of the Believers Church tradition is filled with high ideals now requiring translation into very less-than-ideal circumstances. The ideals are real and the challenges to their effective translation are as difficult as they are necessary.

Translating High Ideals

In the view of historian Roland Bainton, it was the Anabaptists who, largely by way of the later Puritan revolution, anticipated all other religious bodies in the proclamation and exemplification of three principles which on the North American continent now are among those truths held to be self-evident. They are the voluntary church, the separation of church and state, and religious liberty.[9] Then in 1969 John Howard Yoder laid the groundwork for a soon-to-be influential view which he called the "Anabaptist Vision and Mennonite Reality." To him the Anabaptist vision had been declining ever since the first generations of Anabaptists in the sixteenth century. The culprit was cultural accommodation, the very problem which Anabaptists had opposed in the first place.[10] More recently, John Roth has critiqued Yoder's either/or "pernicious dualism" which implies that, in the Believers Church tradition, "our institutions, congregations, families, ethics are in perfect alignment with the stan-

---

[9]Roland H. Bainton, "The Left Wing of the Reformation," *Journal of Religion* XXI (1941), 125-134.

[10]It often is hard to distinguish between progress and accommodation, genuine faithfulness to tradition and mere pragmatism in the present. In American Mennonite circles, e.g., by 1960 Harold Bender was the middle-ground voice using various church institutions as modernizing agents in the unsettling changes being experienced in the twentieth century. In a sense, Bender was taking a series of progressive steps on behalf of conserving what he understood to be the essence of the tradition now existing in dramatically new circumstances.

dard or we must accept the fact that we are acculturated, middle class, complacent accommodators to the status quo."

Roth insists that "vision" is a misnomer for Anabaptists if it is taken to mean an ideal that never will be actual reality in our kind of compromised world. The ideal is clear enough:

> The heroic disciple of the Anabaptist Vision refuses to think of the ethical imperatives of the Sermon on the Mount as some future hope. Rather, they are historical possibilities, meant to be incarnated in our every thought and deed in *this* life, in *this* aeon. Whereas other "lesser" Protestants find ways around the "hard sayings" of Jesus, we neo-Anabaptists actually, literally, live them out.[11]

The real question, Roth concludes, is not whether there is a gap between vision and reality (there is and always will be). The question is, how will Christians choose to live *within* the gap. The challenge is to journey with the Spirit of God in a way that keeps discovering the enduringly rich substance and the currently relevant forms of Christian community, discipleship, and love.

The year 1970 in the United States was certainly a time when the words "radical" and even "revolution" were heard frequently. The idealistic rhetoric of the young was being tested severely by the growing Vietnam nightmare.[12] Inside traditional church bodies, including those in the Believers Church tradition, there arose assertive denominational minorities with focused and often conflicting and self-serving agendas, some progressive and some conservative in nature. Within the Church of the Brethren, for instance, there evolved the Brethren Revival Fellowship, neo-Pentecostalism, a women's caucus, groups defined by ethnic identity, etc.[13] Convened at Chicago Theological

---

[11]Roth, op. cit., 329.

[12]This story is told in detail by Barry L. Callen in *Seeking the Light: America's Modern Quest for Peace, Justice, Prosperity, and Faith* (Nappanee, Ind.: Evangel Publishing House, 1998), chapter five.

[13]Donald Durnbaugh, *Fruit of the Vine* (1997), devotes considerable space to such developments. In the Church of God (Anderson) at the time, the developments included the new Pastors' Fellowship (hold-the-line conservatives), increasing focusing of the concerns of women and Hispanics, and a high level of sensitivity to the equality concerns

Seminary in volatile Chicago in the summer of 1970 was a Believers Church Conference. The theme was "Is There a Christian Style of Life in Our Age?" Speaker Dale Brown of the Church of the Brethren spoke of "these apocalyptic days" in which the conference was "interested in ministry to a society rent assunder by polarized stances and a world threatened with extinction."

By the grace of God, could something new and constructive emerge? Brown insisted that any authentic witness to meaningful community and genuine justice "must be made in the context of some manifested first fruits of the same." Thus, the Believers Church tradition, featuring separation from the domination of the state and a legacy of religious liberty, potentially was a source of hope "to a generation fighting for the right of conscience and the freedom to oppose the status quo." Brown affirmed that "the principle of voluntarism as a way to join together is relevant to an era which is repudiating authoritarianisms and seeking for new ways to come to community through consensus." In a specifically Christian setting, the purpose of withdrawal from the leveling control of establishment values and institutions is "to make possible the freedom to witness to society concerning the lordship of Christ over all creation."[14]

This witness, hopefully embodied as well as spoken, was elaborated by another of the 1970 speakers, Rosemary Ruether, identified as "a prominent participant in the 'underground' movement in Roman Catholicism."[15] Explained Ruether, the following is the essence of the

---

of African-Americans (a relatively large constituency in the Church of God). Detail is in Barry Callen, *Journeying Together* (Anderson, Ind.: Leadership Council and Warner Press, 1996).

[14]Dale W. Brown, "Tension and Reconciliation in a Split Society or Strategies of Witness for the Believers' Church in a Revolutionary Age," The Chicago Theological Seminary *Register* (September 1970), 31-33.

[15]A few years earlier another Roman Catholic announced that "the Roman Catholic Church is at last following the Free Churches in the rejection of the Constantinian order. For Catholics increasingly appeal to the vision of the Church as the covenanted people of God, and employ the methods of open discussion, lay participation, and consensus as important in the daily life of the Church" (Michael Novak, "The Conception of the Church in Anabaptism and in Roman Catholicism: Past and Present," *Journal of Ecumenical Studies*, Fall 1965, 426).

Believers Church as a gathered community:

> It is a gathered community, not because it consists of people with the same temperament, the same culture, the same ethnic background, or the same style and language in expressing the faith. It is a gathered community because all share the same spirit and the same commitment. That, above all differences in class, culture, race or creed, means they find a brotherhood in a common vision and a willingness to commit themselves to a new radical life style appropriate to this vision; a radical life style which may also put them in many kinds of jeopardy with the powers and principalities of this world.[16]

Ruether went on to speak of the ideal of the Believers Church tradition as "a messianic community in history." It is truly messianic only in a provisional or proleptical sense, itself having only "a tenuous foothold on the new world." Even so, it can and should be "the avant-garde of a new world." "A spark has been lit; a struggle commenced; a liberated zone opened," she announced. This prophetic Christian community should boldly witness that neither it nor any human organization

> ...can fashion institutional guarantees to perpetuate the Spirit through channels of tradition, ordination or succession, for the Spirit can never become the chairman of the board of trustees of anyone's institution. The Spirit is a free spirit; it blows where it wills, and appears wherever it appears, not at the duly appointed times and places, when popes are sitting on the proper chairs, ex cathedra, and everyone is in his Sunday best, but it shows up at all sorts of improper times and unexpected places.[17]

The Spirit's purpose is redemptive mission. Accordingly, the leaders of free churches have been concerned more for effective Christian work and witness than for scholarly debate, institutional mainte-

---

[16]Rosemary Ruether, "The Believers' Church and Catholicity in the World Today," The Chicago Theological Seminary *Register* (September, 1970), 5-6.
[17]Ibid., 8.

nance, and inter-church ecumenical diplomacy.[18] When well-defined church hierarchies engage in extended and complex dialogue, usually Believers Churches hesitate to commit time and resources unless the purpose is perceived to be related directly to addressing the work of Christ in the world. For example, the Believers Church Conference that convened in Chicago in 1970 gathered "to grapple with the nature of life-styles, ecclesiastical structures, and Christian witness for these apocalyptic days."[19] Worthwhile grappling must be no sterile intellectual exercise or organizational adjustment. It must be living evidence of the Spirit's presence and vitality. Concluded Dale Brown: "Our witness is polluted if we do not have in our own life together a foretaste of that which we advocate."[20]

Admittedly, some organizational readjustment is inevitable from time to time, even in church bodies hoping to remain relatively free of such entanglements. The Church of God (Anderson) provides a good example. Its heritage is filled with criticism of the evils of denominationalism and it clearly has intended for itself a "movement" and not a denominational identity. By the 1980s, however, considerable organization had evolved as ministry structures being supported voluntarily by congregations of this movement across North America (with other structures elsewhere in the world). These structures, both affirmed and often criticized, were subjected to intense study under the assumption that the Church of God movement is to be mission- and not structure-driven. A skilled outside consultant was secured and concluded in 1996 that the Church of God "retains few characteristics of a movement and many characteristics of an aging denomination." The consultant found among movement leaders "an intellectual desire for the benefits of centralization which

---

[18]One prominent exception to the usual isolation of Believers Churches from formal ecumenical organizations is the Church of the Brethren. It became involved with the Federal Council of Churches and the World Council of Churches in the middle decades of the twentieth century. See the story of this in Donald Durnbaugh, *Fruit of the Vine* (1997). The typical reasoning in support of isolation is explained in Barry Callen and James North, *Coming Together In Christ* (Joplin, Mo.: College Press, 1997), chapters one and two.

[19]Brown, op. cit., 31.

[20]Ibid., 32.

runs parallel and contrary to an emotional resistance to centraliza-tion."[21] Such a dilemma is reflective of much in the Believers Church tradition, namely substantial reaction to the dominance and often deadness of establishment Christianity and yet a strong desire to be effective and accountable in being and doing what God intends for the church.

The current "postmodernism" trend holds important potential for freshly emphasizing what have been longstanding ideals of the Believers Church tradition. This current thought is that even organi-zational theory has been a creature of modernity, a creature now needing alteration. What might the alternative, a postmodernist orga-nization, look like? It would feature small units that provide infor-mation and service in the context of a flexible labor force and decen-tralized and participative managerial structure. William Brackney envisions for the church a postmodernist pattern that features "a greater application of Free Church polity, especially democratic deci-sion making." This pattern would be based on a voluntarist theology that "must inevitably lead to a reconstruction of the doctrines of the Holy Spirit...that gives continual new life and calls forth unexpected new directions in leadership and mission." Characteristic of this church structure is clear focus on lay empowerment as a central objective of theological education and ministry.[22]

Dale W. Brown is quick to add a caution about the tendency to equate Christianity with American society and thus "wrap both the big gun and the Bible in the Stars and Stripes." The Believers Church stance should not be a purely negative anti-state, but it should issue "the call to love all people, even one's enemies, and to place faithful-ness to the way of Christ above all other allegiances." This challenging of jingoistic attitudes requires "the psychological conversion necessary

---

[21]Leith Anderson, "Movement for the 21st Century," Report to the Leadership Coun-cil of the Church of God, Anderson, Indiana, April 23, 1996, 9-10. For the fuller picture of the organizational development and changes in the Church of God across the twen-tieth century, see Barry Callen, *Journeying Together* (Anderson, Ind.: Leadership Coun-cil of the Church of God and Warner Press, 1996).

[22]William H. Brackney, *Christian Voluntarism: Theology and Praxis* (Grand Rapids: Eerdmans, 1997), 158, 170-171.

to take our [United States] place modestly as one nation in a family of nations" and rests on "the radical commitment which gives priority to the vision of the kingdom [of God] over national or tribal loyalties."[23] This is a difficult assignment for American Christians who identify with the pride of the world's only remaining "super power."

Beyond Brown's caution against an all-too-easy cultural accommodation is the sturdy Anabaptist call for Christians to actively build a new culture according to the standards of God's gracious reign. Life in the church should center around the intentional nurturing into being of a Christ-culture in which believers choose to live as loyal citizens. Paul speaks of Christian conversion and baptism creating a new person, even a new world (2 Cor. 5:17). He further says that when believers truly worship, they "discern the body" (1 Cor. 11:29). They recognize who they are or should be together as the people of Christ, servants who have chosen the rule of God. Summarizes Rodney Clapp:

> This means that in worship we vigorously enflesh a restored and re-created world—a world returned to its genuine normality through holy abnormality—in a civic and cultural form, a public, powerful, visible, political form that challenges and stands in contrast to all other cultures. Worship is not simply world-changing. It is, indeed, world-making.[24]

This surely is the high ideal that yet awaits effective translation into the complex reality of our current day. Attempting this translation means becoming pilgrims who can be patient and faithful in the wilderness.

---

[23]Dale W. Brown, "Communal Ecclesiology: The Power of the Anabaptist Vision," *Theology Today* 36:1 (April 1979), 23-24.

[24]Rodney Clapp, *A Peculiar People: The Church as Culture in a Post-Christian Society* (Downers Grove, Ill.: InterVarsity Press, 1996), 113. Clapp says that "in the work of John Howard Yoder and Stanley Hauerwas I was drawn to and profoundly influenced by Anabaptist theology and social ethics.... It is the neo-Anabaptists and the postliberals who, among contemporary theologians, I think most faithfully and adeptly fit us for the challenges of this day and place" (15).

Impacting the Wilderness

The ancient Hebrew experience of exodus and then wilderness wandering remains instructive. As God's pilgrim people journey today, they face the dangers of distraction and discouragement in the process of their being lured forward by faith. Adherents of the Believers Church tradition can be victimized either by a chosen separation from "the world" that is really self-serving, by a subtle accommodation with the world that retains the heritage's rhetoric while losing much of its reality, or by yielding to disillusionment because of the continuing gap between vision and reality. In North America today, the warning of Philip Kenneson should be heeded:

> I contend that a social/political/economic sphere like the United States, where everyday life is thoroughly shaped and governed by management and market relationships, tends to transform everything (and everyone) into manageable objects and marketable commodities.... When marketing models, marketing values, marketing language, and marketing strategies and tactics are allowed to structure the life of Christian congregations, much that has been previously understood to be central to the Christian faith, and perhaps even the church itself, likewise becomes superfluous.[25]

The church in such a setting easily loses its intended identity. Time moves, cultures shift, and so far Christ has delayed his promised return. So the church struggles in the ongoing interim to be more faithful than frustrated.

Since the earliest generations of Christians, it has been necessary for believers to learn to deal with the delay of Christ's coming again. The problem of delay clearly had a long history in the Hebrew tradition. In the book of Habakkuk, for instance, a prophet surveys the evil and violence that marked his times and asks why God seems so slow to come and correct the situation: "O Lord, how long shall I cry for help, and you will not listen?... Why do you make me see wrongdoing and look at trouble?" (Hab. 1:2-3). The divine answer received

---

[25]Philip D. Kenneson, "Selling [Out] the Church in the Marketplace of Desire," *Modern Theology* 9:4 (October 1993), 319, 343.

was: "There is still a vision for the appointed time; it speaks of the end, and does not lie. If it seems to tarry, wait for it; it will surely come, it will not delay.... The righteous live by their faith" (Hab. 2:3-4). In the early Christian church, the seeming delay of the anticipated soon return of Jesus spawned the fear that believers who died prior to the return would miss out on the chance to experience the new era. Paul addressed this in 1 Thessalonians 4:13-18. But there seems to have developed even more radical questions about the delayed return of the resurrected Christ. So we find this in 2 Peter 3:3-4: "In the last days scoffers will come, scoffing and indulging their own lusts and saying, 'Where is the promise of his coming? For ever since our ancestors died, all things continue as they were from the beginning of creation.'" Peter argues in response (3:8-13) that God's apparent slowness actually represents a merciful extension of the time during which believers can witness to the good news of Christ's first coming and sinners can repent. During the extension, while traveling through the wilderness of this world, it remains the steadfast hope of believers that the dusty trail will one day turn into gold (Rev. 21:18). Meanwhile, brothers and sisters in the faith journey together toward a divine realm whose God has come ahead in the current ministry of the Spirit and has promised to be a constant escort on the way (Matt. 18:20; 28:20).

Beyond the issue of *delay* is the other troubling concern, the crucial issue of *shift*. The United States at the beginning of the twenty-first century is no longer a nation nurtured by or even extensively permeated with the Judeo-Christian tradition. Just a generation or two ago the Christian faith tended to be the only real religious option readily available to most Americans. The society's rhetoric, values, and laws drew heavily on this tradition. But now a major shift has come. Now "few parents, college students, or auto mechanics...believe that one becomes Christian today by simply breathing the air and drinking the water in the generous, hospitable environment of Christendom America.... It is no longer 'our world'—if it ever was."[26]

---

[26]Stanley Hauerwas, William Willimon, *Resident Aliens: Life in the Christian Colony* (Nashville: Abingdon Press, 1989), 16-17.

The demise of a sturdy and singular Christian culture in the United States is not, however, a wholly bad thing. Removing the artificial supports to Christian faith leads increasingly into the wilderness with God—precisely where those early children of Israel found themselves as they moved from slavery to the promised land. Being in the wilderness is hardly comfortable, but it does help people to know who they really are and on what they really can depend. The end of a culture on which Christians can rely to prop them up and help mold their young is an opportunity for the church to find again its own soul. It is a time for the Believers Church to rise again, willingly shun the artificial supports of a presumably Christian culture, and focus on building distinctively Christian communities that witness to the general culture primarily by their very existence and attractive Christ natures.

Free of the temptation to accommodate to a surrounding and supporting ethos, no longer able to rest on the general culture for approval and support, North American and European Christians now "are at last free to be faithful in a way that makes being a Christian today an exciting adventure."[27] To gain the attention of "Generation X" (Baby Busters), the church will have to present a credible alternative to the world, actually and visibly embodying what it hopes the young will take seriously in the church's words of witness. Successful evangelism today will take more than innovative marketing of the church's religious wares. The authors of *Reckless Hope*, for instance, explain well how basic biblical concepts like creation (for a generation concerned about the earth's environment), covenant (for a generation that has grown up with broken promises), and community (for a generation hungry for true family) have power to speak today—especially when the speaker is a credible model of these biblical concepts.[28] If the world today is a wilderness, then the church is to be a living oasis traveling refreshingly in its midst.

One should not romanticize the wilderness adventure. The very idea of "wilderness" suggests the mysterious and unknown. There is

---

[27]Ibid., 18.
[28]Todd Hahn and David Verhaagen, *Reckless Hope* (Grand Rapids: Baker Books, 1996), 113-123.

great distance, danger, dryness, and risk of despair. Thomas Merton once pondered prayerfully the awkward experience of being in the wilderness with God:

> My Lord God, I have no idea where I am going. I do not see the road ahead of me. I cannot know for certain where it will end.... I believe that the desire to please you does in fact please you. And I hope I have that desire in all that I am doing.... And I know that if I do this you will lead me by the right road though I may know nothing about it. Therefore will I trust you always though I may seem to be lost and in the shadow of death. I will not fear, for you are ever with me, and you will never leave me to face my perils alone.[29]

Wilderness is named "Antichrist" in the New Testament. Antichrist is a metaphor for the locus of everything that is not oriented by and to Jesus Christ. There is frightening anti-gospel opposition out there in the untamed wildness of the world. It was clear to the New Testament writers that Antichrist was no distant figure who would appear only once at some isolated end time. John describes this opposer to the Christ in no uncertain terms (1 John 2:18-22; 4:3; 2 John 7) and warns the congregation of his time to be on guard. Paul alerted the Thessalonians about the enemy (2 Thess. 2) who already was at hand. Two important matters appear clear from these texts. The Antichrist is a *present* and a *plural* reality.[30] In all times and circumstances, the church is called to "test the spirits to see if they are of God, since so many deceivers and false prophets exist in the world" (1 John 4:1-3; 2 John 7). That was the case in the first generations of Christians and in all others ever since.

A prominent problem characteristic of the present generation, at least in the developed Western world, is seen in a college student who

---

[29]Thomas Merton, from *Thoughts in Solitude* (N.Y.: Farrar, Straus, and Giroux, 1958). This quotation is featured as a small handout to retreatants at Gethsemane, the longtime Trappist monastery home of Merton in rural Kentucky.

[30]Adrio König, *The Eclipse of Christ in Eschatology* (Grand Rapids: Eerdmans, 1989), 175.

walked across campus wearing a big button that read: "Since I gave up hope, I feel much better." Our time of "downsizing" has taken hope down with it for many people. Suicide is not typically the result, just a quiet resignation that things are not good and probably will not get better. People are left to traveling an empty wilderness with no sure guide, no particular goal, and little if any belief in absolutes of any kind—including God. They are not going anywhere, just surviving the perils of each day. In order to avoid becoming part of this problem themselves, Christian believers always must hope that their own minds are being renewed and that their persons and corporate life as the church are being shaped in ways that will allow them to know and do the will of God (cf. Rom. 12:2). As the Believers Church tradition has always insisted, the first mission of the church is to *be the church*, visibly, sacrificially, intentionally.

The image of a mirage is helpful as Christians seek to be faithful in the meantime (although all images have their limitations). A mirage, as opposed to an hallucination, has a definite relationship to reality. The reality may not be on the immediate horizon as it often seems and as we who gaze longingly hope. Even so, the shape of the mirage relates to coming reality. Christians journey through the present wilderness and may not reach the vaguely visible goal as soon as they think they should. But as the image of Jesus Christ stays before the longing eyes of faith, those eyes know the history of Jesus and by faith the general nature of his coming reality. They know shape and quality if not the exact location and timing of the destiny of faithful believers. The shape of life that is to be lived in the meantime is a servant stance in this world, the Christ life. Having confidence in the coming resurrection of the dead and the life everlasting, it is more possible in the meantime to face with defiance, joy, and confidence the forces that now breed injustice, oppression, and death. We who are drawn forward by the never-fading image of the already come and yet coming Christ discover the courage to die for the sake of life. We will take responsibility for living in the present the implications of "eternal life." Indeed, Christians "will not be allured by the promise of life after death as though this meant the denial of life before death."[31] To be in the wilderness *with* Christ is to impact the wilderness *for* Christ.

Resisting Elements of Evangelicalism

Recent decades have witnessed the dramatic rise to prominence of what is popularly called "evangelicalism." This rise has both supported and threatened the Believers Church tradition that functions in its midst. Stanley Grenz and Roger Olson use for their analysis the term "evangelical." They see fundamentalism as a reactionary response to nineteenth and early twentieth century liberalism. Fundamentalism is pictured as a movement of Bible-believing Christians who tend to abandon the larger intellectual and cultural arena that had become so critical of much of traditional Christian orthodoxy. Those, then, who shared this conservative Protestant heritage but had chosen by the 1950s to re-enter the dialogue in the broad theological arena, and to do so in a less separatistic and combative spirit, came to be known as "evangelicals."[32]

Bernard Ramm's characterization is that fundamentalism "attempts to shield itself from the Enlightenment" whereas evangelicalism "believes that the Enlightenment cannot be undone."[33] He sought to demonstrate in his own numerous writings that Christians still can be intellectually responsible "without either making the concessions characteristic of modern theology or resorting to the blind faith or hyper-rationalism of fundamentalism."[34] Seeking points of unity in the midst of the wide diversity in contemporary evangelicalism, Donald Bloesch argues that "the key to evangelical unity lies in a common commitment to Jesus Christ as the divine Savior from sin, a common purpose to fulfill the great commission, and a common acknowledgment of the absolute normativeness of Holy Scripture."[35] Stanley

---

[31]Theodore Jennings, *Loyalty To God* (Nashville: Abingdon Press, 1992), 224.

[32]Stanley Grenz and Roger Olson, *20th Century Theology* (InterVarsity Press, 1992), 288. For excellent reviews of these developments from the "evangelical" point of view, see Bob Patterson, *Carl F. H. Henry* (Peabody, Mass: Hendrickson, 1983), 13-57, and Carl Henry's autobiography, *Confessions of a Theologian* (Waco, Tex.: Word Books, 1986).

[33]Bernard Ramm, *The Evangelical Heritage* (Waco, Tex.: Word Books, 1973), 70.

[34]Grenz and Olson, op. cit., 300.

[35]Donald Bloesch, *The Future of Evangelical Christianity* (Doubleday, 1983), 5.

Grenz views an "evangelical" as one participating "in a community characterized by a shared narrative concerning a personal encounter with God told in terms of shared theological categories derived from the Bible."[36] This view is less oriented to doctrinal uniformity and more to a common spiritual identity.[37]

Where does the Believers Church fit in? While this tradition is not limited to or fully defined by any one denomination found within its historic stream, two brief case studies help highlight the issues. The first comes from the Church of God movement (Anderson) which is part of the diversity currently constituting evangelicalism. This free-church movement with Wesleyan/Pietist identity has affirmed gladly the points of evangelical unity set forth by Bloesch, especially when the "absolute normativeness of Holy Scripture" is understood in the narrative style of Grenz. Even so, Merle Strege judges it improper either historically or theologically to identify this movement by primary reference to the present evangelical stream. His point is not that there is any significant disagreement about biblical authority, the redemptive role of Christ, or the necessity of sharing the gospel with all the world. There is an important disagreement, however, that tends to affect all of these common affirmations in subtle but significant ways.[38]

Strege's concern is about theological genealogy and focus. Prior to the more recent fundamentalism/liberalism conflict was the seven-

---

[36]Stanley Grenz, *Revisioning Evangelical Theology* (InterVarsity Press, 1993), 17.

[37]Stanley Grenz, himself highlighting the narrative and experiential characteristics of a sound evangelicalism, differs with Bloesch. Bloesch is said to posit for evangelicalism a tension between Reformation theology and Pietism, one he finally resolves by giving priority to the Reformers and doctrine over the Pietists and spiritual experience. Grenz, leaning more toward the Pietists, says that "any revisioning of evangelical theology must begin with a rethinking of the typical 'card-carrying' evangelical understanding of the essence of the [evangelical] movement as a whole with its focus on certain theological commitments.... Evangelicals are pietists," insists Grenz, "in that they...focus on the dynamism of the presence of Christ in the life of the believer" (*Revisioning Evangelical Theology*, 29, 40). An insightful review of the complex relationship between Pentecostalism and Fundamentalism is D. William Faupel, "Whither Pentecostalism?" *Pneuma* 15:1 (Spring 1993), 9-27.

[38]Merle Strege, *Tell Me Another Tale* (Anderson, Ind: Warner Press, 1993), 17-18. Also see Barry Callen, *Contours of a Cause: The Theological Vision of the Church of God Movement* (Anderson, Ind: Anderson University School of Theology, 1995), 193-202.

teenth-century clash between the Pietists, whose assurance lay in the witness of the Spirit, and the "Protestant scholastic dogmatists" whose trademark was "the intellect's assent to sound doctrine." The lineage of the Church of God movement lay more in Pietism, as mediated through the Wesleys by way of American revivalism, and less in Protestant scholasticism and propositional fundamentalism (even as moderated somewhat by Carl Henry, Bernard Ramm, Donald Bloesch, and other neo-evangelicals). A significant epistemological assumption is at stake, according to Strege. The Church of God movement is not comfortable with the inherent limitations of rationalistically derived and formalized creeds that often are used to encourage conformity, foster exclusivism, and breed division (the classic Calvinistic model typical of evangelicalism).[39] Thought more appropriate and constructive in the view of this movement are emphases typical of the Believers Church tradition, including a focus on divine grace received, human lives changed, voluntary and committed community fostered, and church mission fulfilled in the power of the Spirit by Bible-believing and self-sacrificing disciples.

Stanley Grenz sees proper evangelicalism as less a rigid body of beliefs and more a *distinctive spirituality*. His Baptist vision, much like the vision of the Church of God movement, centers in faith's present integrity—not primarily in precise doctrinal formulation, but in the

---

[39]The epistemological question is explored by Douglas Jacobsen through reviewing "The Calvinist-Arminian Dialectic in Evangelical Hermeneutics" (*Christian Scholar's Review* 23:1, September, 1993). He identifies the Calvinistic model illustrated by Francis Turretin (1623-1687) via the later Princeton theology of Hodge and Warfield. Here "hermeneutics and theology in general become largely a matter of maintaining boundaries. Established truths are to be repeated for the instruction of the faithful, and those who differ in theology from the 'orthodox' position are to be cut off from fellowship" (73-77). The Arminian model based on Jacobus Arminius (1559-1609) is much less doctrinaire and more dialogical, less rationalistic and more experientialist. "The hermeneutic of Arminianism recognizes diversity and stresses tolerance; the hermeneutic of Calvinism affirms the singularity of meaning in the text and seeks uniformity" (81). While twentieth century evangelical hermeneutics has seen the rising dominance of Arminianism, evangelicalism maintains a tension between the two. It is still shaped significantly by the Calvinistic model, the one least compatible with the Pietistic-Wesleyan tradition informing the Church of God (Anderson), the Brethren in Christ, and numerous other Holiness and Pentecostal bodies.

radical emphasis on "our shared desire to make the Bible come alive in personal and community life." He speaks of the evangelical vision focusing on "shared stories," testimonial narratives about life-changing transformations. The biblical revelation and traditional theology are, of course, crucial in norming and understanding all spiritual experiences; but at the heart of the "evangelical" vision of the faith is "this experience of being encountered by the living God understood by appeal to categories derived from the biblical drama of salvation."[40] Rodney Clapp readily agrees: "So what God has created in the church is a dynamic, ongoing form of life, a way of being human, which is to say an arena of social interaction that uniquely dwells in relationship with the one and true God...."[41]

A second case study comes from the Brethren in Christ denomination. This body traces its roots to both Anabaptism and Pietism, with Wesleyan revivalism added in the late nineteenth century. The resulting three-part heritage synthesis formed a distinctive and relatively durable denominational identity until about 1950. Then, according to Luke Keefer, a formal relationship with evangelicalism began. The denomination joined the National Association of Evangelicals and soon found that "Pietism is the only aspect of the Brethren in Christ heritage that can mesh significantly with the majority groups of NAE with no doctrinal or ecclesial difficulty." Why the difficulty otherwise? Because North American "Evangelicalism" is characterized predominantly by a "mild Calvinism." The result has been a muting of the Anabaptist heritage by this large new stream of evangelicalism. Keefer notes a current identity crisis being experienced by the Brethren in Christ and similar bodies, a crisis requiring "new and emphatic articulations" of historic elements of Anabaptism and Wesleyanism.[42]

Ronald Sider, associated with the Brethren in Christ, argues somewhat differently. While he admits that contemporary evangelicalism

---

[40]Stanley Grenz, op. cit., 31-35.
[41]Clapp, op. cit., 185.
[42]Luke Keefer, "Brethren in Christ: An Uneasy Synthesis of Heritage Streams," *Wesleyan Theological Journal* 33:1 (Spring 1998), 103, 110.

and the Believers Church tradition have different emphases, they nonetheless are potentially compatible; in fact, they need each other. If each were really consistent with its own heritage, each would mirror the other. The Believers Church historically has been orthodox in theology, Bible believing, and evangelistically-minded—all at the heart of evangelicalism. Conversely:

> Evangelicals, if they were consistent with their own commitment to biblical authority, would affirm emphases frequently associated with Anabaptism—an emphasis on costly discipleship, on living the Christian life, on the church as a new society living the ethics of the kingdom (and therefore living a set of values radically different from the world), on the way of the cross as the Christian approach to violence.[43]

Further, since both traditions affirm as central a personal, living relationship with Jesus Christ, they need each other to avoid distortions of this core necessity, distortions to which each is subject. Evangelicals tend toward an unbiblical individualism and social passivity, a less than wholistic evangelism and a public stance that too often lacks costly discipleship. Some in the Believers Church tradition tend to substitute ethnic identity, pacifism, or concern about social justice for the living relationship with Christ, even at times dispensing with key doctrinal stances of the classical Christian community in favor of the almost doctrinally-disconnected ethical life of following Jesus. Sider concludes: "Now neither of these distortions will do!"[44]

While appreciative of this analysis and prescription by Sider, the Mennonite C. Norman Kraus emphasizes the considerable diversity within both contemporary evangelicalism and the Believers Church, which means that all comparisons of them swing on which model of each is assumed. He offers what he judges fair descriptions of each that allow comparison and evaluation. Anabaptism, he says, is a "radical, Jesus-centered, martyr movement." Thus, it calls for fundamental

---

[43]Ronald J. Sider, "Evangelicalism and the Mennonite Tradition," in C. Norman Kraus, ed., *Evangelicalism and Anabaptism* (Scottdale, Pa.: Herald Press, 1979), 150.
[44]Ibid., 154.

change in the individual and social order, including bold witness and obedient lifestyle modeled on the will and way of Jesus. Contemporary evangelicalism is "a revival of classical Protestant theology freed from the negativism and defensiveness of earlier Fundamentalism,"[45] yet still holding to some theological views in sharp contrast to the Believers Church tradition. These include: a spiritualized or "invisible" view of the true church based on presuppositions and definitions of a Calvinistic understanding of divine election; the church as an instrument of grace; salvation as transformation of the individual spiritually, often conceived in separation from discipling; a social vision lacking a clear critique of American culture—and thus "oriented to and supportive of the established government and economic elite." Further,

> Evangelicalism continues its verbal and rationalistic concept of the Word of God as contained in Scripture, and accordingly it views theological orthodoxy rather than authenticity of the church's life as the criterion of continuity with Christ. Evangelicalism is not overly concerned with the question of authentic community because the continuing witness to the kingdom of God is identified with the written Word and not with the witnessing church. The concern is for a correct inerrant Word.[46]

In recent decades, "liberation" theologies have focused on the power of God and the potential of the transformation of this present world by concerted Christian action. They tend to reflect an optimistic world view like the older postmillennialism of the nineteenth century (characteristic of the optimism-of-grace Wesleyans of that time). Much less centered in the calls for dramatic social action, contemporary evangelicalism by contrast has tended to be "patriotic" and work through public institutions to implement key elements of Christian mission. The Believers Church offers a third way for our time. It calls for rigorous discipleship, experience with the Holy Spirit's power,

---

[45]C. Norman Kraus, in Kraus, ed., *Evangelicalism and Anabaptism* (Scottdale, Pa.: Herald Press, 1979), 173, 177.
[46]Ibid., 178-179.

biblical critique of contemporary culture, and the strategy of a new-community model of the church as a fundamental aspect of a holistic witness to Christ in the world. This model affirms some aspects of current evangelicalism and actively resists others. The resistance roots in part in the Believers Church being an eschatological people, a people keenly aware of the nearness and intended *present reality* of God's promised future.

Living Between the Times

A study of the goal of the biblical revelation concerning human history's process, meaning, current status, and coming climax is called *eschatology*. In Christian perspective, eschatology is a focused assessment of the movement of cosmic and human history in the special light of the advent of Jesus Christ. Eschatological reasoning "inquires into how creatures who, having their beginning in God, and having fallen and received redemption in God, have their final destiny and end in God."[47] Biblically speaking, the key concept is the realm and reign of God. For the Believers Church to fulfill today the vision of its heritage, the biblical perspectives and present implications of the Christian hope and Christ's lordship over time and eternity must be clear.

Jesus proclaimed the imminent coming of the reign of God, even in his own person and ministry. His message had two important emphases. First, the messianic salvation anticipated by the Hebrew prophets was being fulfilled in his own person and ministry; second, there yet remains a later consummation when this salvation will be perfectly accomplished in an age yet to come. The "kingdom of God" (Greek *basileia*, Hebrew *malkuth*) at least means the active reign or rule of God as opposed to the concrete idea of a specific realm being ruled. God's rule, of course, exists universally by virtue of who God is; but functionally, by God's choosing to grant human freedom and human choosing to sin with this freedom, God's active reign exists in

---

[47]Thomas Oden, *Life in the Spirit: Systematic Theology*, vol. 3 (San Francisco: Harper, 1992), 369.

this evil age only when people voluntarily submit themselves to it. The reign of God actually has come in Jesus, in whom full submission to God was present. The announcement to Mary was that God would give to Jesus the throne of David and Jesus would reign forever (Lk. 1:32-33). That is, "before the eschatological appearance of God's Kingdom at the end of the age, God's Kingdom has become dynamically active among men in Jesus' person and mission."[48] To understand the Kingdom's present meaning and future nature requires understanding the person and work of Jesus. He should be the defining meaning of Christian eschatology as well as all of Christian life.

The Gospel of Mark presents Jesus as the definitive interpreter and fulfillment of Israel's prophetic tradition. God continues to contend with humans, although they often choose to remain in active opposition to God's will and reign. While God's full sovereignty and final judgment are never in question, neither God nor humanity is locked in any fatalism or fixed cosmic calendar. History is a dynamic arena of the relationship between God's reign and the resisting human will. Indeed, the future is as secure as God's faithfulness, but exactly how the future develops depends in part on the repentance and faith of humanity in relation to the current reign of the Lord Jesus Christ (Acts 28:23-31).[49]

How near is this end? The New Testament materials suggest an ambiguous answer. The two letters addressed to the Thessalonians, for example, seem to have somewhat different emphases in this regard. First Thessalonians 5 follows the common apocalyptic motif that the end will come "like a thief in the night," so that there always should be a sense of urgency and a need to be ready for what could come at any moment. But in 2 Thessalonians we find a scheme of final events, implying that the end is not necessarily near. While this scheme does

---

[48]George Eldon Ladd, *The Presence of the Future: The Eschatology of Biblical Realism* (Grand Rapids: Eerdmans, 1974), 139.

[49]See Barry Callen, *God As Loving Grace* (Nappanee, Ind.: Evangel Publishing House, 1996), 73-80 and 114-121, for discussions of the particular way God has chosen to work in the world and the possible effectiveness of prayer in actually changing what God does in given instances. For extensive discussion of Christian eschatology in general, see Barry Callen, *Faithful in the Meantime* (Evangel Publishing House, 1997).

not lessen the need for believers always to be ready, it does suggest a longer timetable before the end actually will come.

Beyond the question of the timing is the equally crucial question about the nature of Christ's eventual coming again. Biblical scholarship has made considerable advance over the intensely rationalistic atmosphere of the Enlightenment mentality that encouraged criticism of any focus on "last things" as more superstition than revelation. In recent centuries, eschatology for many believers became only a theological curiosity, or merely a realm of moral values toward which society is advancing (Albrecht Ritschl), or nothing more than a network of symbols ("myths") to be interpreted existentially (Rudolf Bultmann). But Johannes Weiss and Albert Schweitzer rediscovered the apocalyptic character of the preaching of Jesus and argued that the kingdom of God is primarily an eschatological vision.

One cannot escape a serious dealing with apocalyptic eschatology by engaging in modern "historical" reconstructions of the life and thought of Jesus. Those who do so inadvertently attribute to Jesus their own assumptions and social visions.[50] For instance, Jesus was more than the moral educator of people and their fumbling human societies (as he often was depicted in the nineteenth century). The New Testament presents him as nothing less than the inaugurator of a new age. The reign of God was fully present in Jesus at his first coming and now remains active in human history, especially in the church, although its full realization still lies in the future. John Wesley's view often is commended for the creative tension it seeks to hold between the present and future dimensions of the Christian hope. For Wesley's eschatology, Randy Maddox prefers the designation "processive." This adjective highlights the present significance and dynamic nature of God's ongoing work of transforming grace.[51] The full and very present reign of God has been inaugurated in this evil world.

God is the Alpha and the Omega, both the Creator and Consummator of all history. Rather than being the last in a series of theolog-

---

[50]See Albert Schweitzer (1875-1965), *The Quest of the Historical Jesus* (1906).

[51]Randy Maddox, *Responsible Grace: John Wesley's Practical Theology* (Nashville: Abingdon Press, Kingswood Books, 1994, 235-236).

ical topics, Christian eschatology highlights the final hope that frames and radically contextualizes all temporal things, including political bodies and institutions of the church. Such an assessment of history provides a vision of hope that saves sinful and oppressed people from being overwhelmed by historical disillusionment. Jesus believed firmly that God's gracious reign would ultimately triumph. When proclaiming the nearness of the kingdom of God, he probably was not declaring the soon end of the world so much as that, in his own ministry, God's promises to Israel were coming to fulfillment. The words and works of Jesus were evidence of God's reign already being at hand (Isa. 35:1-10; Matt. 11:1-15)—without, of course, exhausting the future implications of this reign for all creation and for the "time" beyond human history. Several difficult New Testament texts are made clearer when it is understood that the reign of God is "the dynamic working of God's rule in the world in advance of the eschatological consummation."[52]

God's reign in its fullest reality and final consummation awaits the second advent of Christ. That is not yet. In the meantime, as the result of Christ's first advent, the divine reign now is an inaugurated reality that people are called to enter (Mark 9:47; Matt. 21:31-32). God extends an invitation for all who will to live in the power of this divine presence, consciously deciding for this reign (Matt. 13:44-46) and doing God's will (Matt. 6:10, 7:21-23). God's kingdom will be fully understood and realized only at the eschaton, the very end of time itself. Nevertheless, already the reality of the divine reign is at work, breaking into the human present from God's future. It is this present reality that warms the heart and fires the will of the Believers Church heritage.

The Gospel of John emphasizes that new existence in Christ by the Spirit is to be a *present reality*. Life under God's loving rule is to function now, not merely be a hope reserved for the future. The believer already has made the transition out of death into life (John 5:24). Said Jesus, "Now the judgment of this world takes place, now the prince of

---

[52]George Eldon Ladd, *The Presence of the Future* (Grand Rapids: Eerdmans, 1974), 158.

this world will be thrown out; and I, if I am lifted up from the earth, will draw to myself all people" (John 12:31). The believer knows resurrection in and through Christ in the present time (John 5:21, 24 and 11:25). Rudolf Bultmann concludes that this focus on presentness precludes a future fulfillment also, but his exclusion fails to do justice to the biblical evidence. John takes seriously both the consequences for present time of the work of Jesus and affirms that the present action of the risen Lord extends to future horizons (John 5:17, 11:25). The Johannine eschatology is understood best through its central insight that eschatology for Christians is *Christology*. That is, "to the Son is committed the carrying out of the eternal purpose of the Father; this he has achieved, he is achieving, and he shall achieve *eis telos*"[53] (toward and until the end). To remain true to its own heritage, the Believers Church must hold to this Christ-centeredness and its many present implications for believers and the church.

The church of the Christ, the body of the newly created in Christ, is called to live the new life now, and live it in hope as it continues to remember and embody the crucified and resurrected Christ by the ministry of the Spirit of God. The reign of God, yet to come in its fullness, is now present "as the new redemptive order established by the Christ and Pentecost events that inaugurated the eschatological last days promised in the Old Testament and consummated when Christ returns."[54] This order is the church and its life is the current working of God's Spirit. Summarizes Jürgen Moltmann:

> The present power of this remembrance and this hope is called "the power of the Spirit," for it is not of their own strength, reason, and will that people believe in Jesus as the Christ and hope for the future as God's future.... Faith in Christ and hope for the kingdom are due to the presence of God in the Spirit.[55]

---

[53]George Beasley-Murray, *Word Biblical Commentary*: John, vol. 36 (Waco, Tex.: Word Books, 1987), lxxxvii.

[54]Boyd Hunt, *Redeemed!: Eschatological Redemption and the Kingdom of God* (Nashville: Broadman & Holman Publishers, 1993), 68.

[55]Jürgen Moltmann, *The Church in the Power of the Spirit* (New York: Harper & Row, 1977), 197.

Paul refers to the Spirit of God as the "first fruits" or "downpayment" of the final resurrection (Rom. 8:23; 2 Cor. 1:22; 5:5; Eph. 1:13-14). Into our troubled human present has broken God's future! What then of the resurrection of Jesus Christ? It was more than an isolated event in which one individual overcame death by the re-creating action of God. It was "the death of the old aeon and the birth of the new aeon. Hence to be in Christ or in the Spirit (which we have seen to be synonymous) is to be in the age to come and to participate in its power."[56] Chapter two of this book focuses on starting with the Spirit. New life begins with the Spirit, is to be focused on present possibilities and responsibilities enabled by the Spirit, and is founded in the hope of the full and final realization of the reign of the Spirit of God in a time of God's choosing.

The present experience of the Spirit of God features the resurrection power of Jesus, the risen Christ. Jesus' disciples, once aware of his resurrection, knew that it was really just the beginning of God's coming future for all who believe. Given the richness of their Jewish heritage and now the dramatic saving events of God in Christ, God was propelling the faithful into the future. They were learning that "to be a Christian was [is] to be a risk-taker. Every day they could expect that God's Spirit would do creative things in making Jesus' presence real."[57] To live in Christ is to live by God's loving grace, through the Spirit of God, as an extension of the emerging post-resurrection life of Jesus. To do so together as the body of Christ is to be the church, the community of the Spirit on mission in the present. This is the enduring teaching of the New Testament and the vision of the Believers Church tradition.

The prayer that Jesus taught his disciples (Luke 11:2-4), the "Lord's Prayer," has as its whole thrust a petitioning for God's future reign to be *present reality* in very practical ways—Thy Kingdom come now, on earth, bringing forgiveness, daily bread, and the ability for believers

---

[56]H. Ray Dunning, *Grace, Faith and Holiness: A Wesleyan Systematic Theology* (Kansas City, Mo.: Beacon Hill Press of Kansas City, 1988), 476.

[57]Alan Kreider, *Journey Towards Holiness: A Way of Living for God's Nation* (Scottdale, Pa.: Herald Press, 1987), 204.

to survive temptation, all because believers recognize God as Loving Father and hallow the divine name. Jesus accepted the conviction of Israel that God's reign would be fully evident one day, with all divine promises finally fulfilled. This future and its security, however, are not centered in a complex pattern of predictions about specific future events, but focus on faith in the God of Israel, now come in Christ, the God who keeps divine promises and offers the future and its security as gifts of faith that center on Jesus and allow forgiven and fruitful living, Christ-like living *now*.

In concluding his masterful study of Mark 13, George Beasley-Murray chooses an excellent quotation to summarize Mark's recounting of the early church's expectation of the nearness of Christ's return and its relation to their present discipleship responsibilities in the meantime. The early disciples had

> ...the eschatological attitude of those who stake their all on the sovereignty of God in the sovereignty of Jesus Christ and, like Jesus himself, in his Spirit, enable the power of God's sovereignty to be perceived, and cause God's sovereignty to reach human beings in its healing power—and at the same time to await its fulfillment from God through Jesus Christ.... It is realized and concretized on the way by following in cross bearing (Mark 8:34-38), on the path that is free from anxiety because it is radical trust in God and his Son Jesus Christ in the power of the Holy Spirit (13:9-11), a way which leads to death and to the hoped-for resurrection promised in Jesus Christ.[58]

Having such an eschatological attitude empowers the church to resist all principalities and powers and be her resurrected self living redemptively "between the times" of Christ's first and final coming.

The Best of the Ancient Calling

It began with the earliest apostolic church and was relived dramatically by the Anabaptists of the sixteenth century and many who

---

[58]R. Pesch, *Naherwartungen* (1968), quoted by George Beasley-Murray, *Jesus and the Last Days* (Peabody, Mass.: Hendrickson Publishers, 1993), 475.

have followed in this train since. The church knew herself in this world as a radical, Jesus-centered, martyr movement. The message of good news was wonderful, obstacles from the surrounding world were great, and the need to nurture a strong Christ-community was essential for the faith's survival and its mission's success. As the twenty-first century begins, numerous settings around the world are forcing on the faithful church similar negative environments. The Christian community needs to recover the best of its ancient calling to be the authentic people of God in the midst of our kind of world.

The proper concern of today's church is, of course, the present and future, not any glorifying of the past. A Christian tradition like that of the Believers Church must find the heart of its enduring identity, that around which its diverse members can rally in unity. The Findings Committee of the 1967 Believers Church Conference addressed this need helpfully. It recognized that the Believers Church now has many confessions of faith, but no official creeds. At times representatives of this tradition have talked past each other, in part because of a lack of common terminology. Nevertheless, there was discerned "a commonality of stance which underlies the profusion of formulations.... [Thus] the gift of unity is prior to our discovery and articulation of it.... If we acknowledge the gift, we must as well accept the challenge to manifest it in future brotherly relationships."

This 1967 Believers Church Conference had convened at Southern Baptist Theological Seminary in Louisville, Kentucky, in search of the tradition's essential unity and on behalf of "future brotherly relationships" among Believers Church bodies. Unfortunately, in the decades to follow there would evolve substantial conflict in the Southern Baptist Convention itself, including a virtual fundamentalist capturing of the SBC in the 1980s.[59] One resisting organization was the Southern Baptist Alliance which issued a declaration of principles in 1987. The Alliance affirmed the freedom of the believer and the local church in the face of what it judged a newly "given" church, the cap-

---

[59]See, e.g., Nancy Tatom Ammerman, *Baptist Battles: Social Change and Religious Conflict in the Southern Baptist Convention* (New Brunswick: Rutgers University Press, 1990).

tured SBC. A decade later a group of young Baptist scholars in the southern United States drafted "Re-Envisioning Baptist Identity: A Manifesto for Baptist Communities in North America."[60] It warned that there were two abortive paths, each imperiling authentic Baptist life. They were the two now-hardened sides in the SBC controversy, one that would in effect "shackle God's freedom to a narrow biblical interpretation" and one that would "sever freedom from…the community's legitimate authority." Both lean toward an idolatry, one a biblicism and the other an individualism. A constructive alternative is offered, centering in a series of Baptist practices (shared Bible study, evangelism that calls for a new shared life, the church as a divine fellowship, the church as a counter-cultural and counter-political reality, and shared church celebration in baptism, preaching, and the Lord's table).[61] This approach focuses on the *practice of church*, the functioning of lives voluntarily bound together in Christ, as opposed to control by secured institutions or official faith formulations.[62]

Although speaking specifically of the contemporary Church of the Brethren, Melanie May's comments relate well to the Believers Church tradition generally. One great gift that the Believers Church has available for giving

> …is our sensibility for the sacredness of all life, the traditional Brethren sense that there is no sacred sphere or space separate from the world of daily life.… To live life as sacred, as sacrament,

---

[60]Published in *Baptists Today* (June 1997).

[61]Each of these Baptist practices is interpreted briefly by James McClendon, Jr., in William Brackney, ed., *The Believers Church: A Voluntary Church* (Kitchener, Ont.: Pandora Press, and Scottdale, Pa.: Herald Press, 1998), 190-192. The earlier writings of McClendon had been influential on the drafters of "Re-Envisioning Baptist Identity."

[62]McClendon, op. cit., 192, asks some hard questions and then points to a key answer. "If 'come out from among them' is thus always the path of the voluntary church, if we always say no to some given ecclesial home in order to say yes to a gathered church, will the voluntary church not repeatedly fall into heresy and schism?… Protestants have their *sola gratia* and Catholics their *magisterium*; what have we radicals to keep us integral and true?… For answer, consider Ephesians 4:1-16, that I believe points to our Christian future. This paragraph speaks of the unity of the church, and indeed of the great confessional unities that Ephesians says should bind all together: one body, one Spirit, one hope, one Lord, one faith, one baptism. It concludes with appeal for growth 'completely into Christ, who is the head' (4:15)."

is an act of resistance that reveals the reality of God's reign redeeming the whole creation that makes manifest an alternative to the ways in which present powers and principalities are determined to desecrate and destroy life.[63]

A key reason why this gift fails to be given effectively is that on occasion, even in a free-church setting, focus gets confused and power abused. While thinking itself a peculiar and persecuted people, marginalized by the world's powerful, the Believers Church sometimes fails to admit that it has power, at least among its own, and has not always been responsible in its use. Further, this heritage of resistance to the intrusions on the faith of all principalities and powers of this world has evolved its own institutions and traditions which now have a tendency to call for loyalty to themselves. That which once was reformed and renewed can itself easily drift into a state of being established to the point of seriously diminishing returns. To be true to the burden of the Believers Church tradition, there must be recognition that "as long as we are preoccupied with the work of our hands lest it perish…our hands will not be open to receive God's gift of new creation in Christ, a promise whose fulfillment we await."[64]

So the central question lingers. What is the contemporary relevance of a "free church" tradition? Thinking biblically, which this tradition always encourages, it is clear that God's present reign implies "the glorious freedom of the children of God" (Rom. 8:21). The challenge facing God's people is to stand firm in the freedom Christ has provided, avoiding the constant twin dangers of legalism and self-indulgence. The church is the community of the Spirit, and wherever the Spirit is and is honored, there is freedom that truly liberates toward the life that God intends (2 Cor. 3:17). This Spirit-community, the church, is to be an alternative to the communities and ways of the world, a new-creation community that shares and celebrates Christ's view of reality.

---

[63]Melanie A. May, "Now Is the Time So Urgent: Called Into God's Future," in Emmert Bittinger, ed., *Brethren In Transition: 20th Century Directions and Dilemmas* (Camden, Maine: Penobscot Press, 1992), 226.

[64]Ibid., 224.

This view can motivate, teach, and sustain all who voluntarily belong. The church should guard against a relaxation of the distinction between itself and "the world," the peril of the established and comfortable churches. It also must avoid the theocratic temptation of "the elect" to gain control of the world's centers of power and thus seek to do some apparent good by governing the world as though it were the church. Instead, the church is to be a freed and a freeing body that makes all the difference to those within and can make the same difference for others because it determines to exist as its reconcilingly distinctive self.

Believers in Jesus Christ need to be freed to be God's people doing ministry as agents of the gracious and present reign of God. This means at least these two things:

> 1. All believers should be taught that they are called, gifted and, in baptism, ordained to the Christian ministry. This requires teaching and discipling after the pattern of Ephesians 4:11-12. It means understanding that leadership grows out of discipleship, but also that ministry is much broader than what we commonly call leadership.

> 2. Believers also need to understand what Kingdom ministry really is. It is much more than church work, so called. On the other hand, if the church truly is the community of God's people, there is no higher nor more strategic work than nourishing the internal life and the outward witness of believers. In this sense, pastoral ministry may be thought of as the highest calling, for it involves freeing and equipping believers to be agents of the Kingdom of God.[65]

Being faithful to such a concept of Christian ministry will lead to an effective addressing of the greatest of all the church's challenges today. This challenge does not lie primarily in the right religious words or the right structures of ministry. The proof is in the actual being and

---

[65]Howard A. Snyder, *Liberating the Church: The Ecology of Church and Kingdom* (Downers Grove, Ill.: InterVarsity Press, 1983), 222. He adds: "The church has a shortage of 'ministers' only when it fails to see all believers as ministers and thus fails to disciple believers into leaders" (247).

doing of the Christian life. Any renewed confidence in the truthfulness and integrity of Christian convictions will come from the concrete embodiment of the implications of such convictions. Thus:

> …the challenge facing today's Christians is not the necessity to translate Christian convictions into a modern idiom, but rather to form a community, a colony of resident aliens which is so shaped by our convictions that no one even has to ask what we mean by confessing belief in God as Father, Son, and Holy Spirit. The biggest problem facing Christian theology is not *translation* but *enactment*.… No clever theological moves can be substituted for the necessity of the church being a community of people who embody our language about God, where talk about God is used without apology because our life together does not mock our words.[66]

The historic commitment of the Believers Church to nonconformity has continuing significance. Its biblical rootage involves taking seriously Christ's call for an exclusive and costly attachment to him and his Father (Matt. 7:24; 8:18-22; 10:34-39) and Paul's related admonition that believers not be conformed to the negative values and power arrangements of this evil age (Rom. 12:2). Following Christ always means differences from the world. To be authentically Christian, such differences should not be mere ethnic loyalties or cultural incidentals, but basic life orientations that grow out of believers and their congregations being transformed by the Spirit of God into the image of Jesus Christ. Faithfulness to such life orientations is always the key to fulfilling the church's mission in the world and continuing at its best the long and rich heritage of the Believers Church.

---

[66]Stanley Hauerwas, William Willimon, *Resident Aliens: Life in the Christian Colony* (Nashville: Abingdon Press, 1989), 170-171. Emphasis added.

APPENDIX A

Records of Recent Conferences on the Concept and Implications of the Believers Church

For brief historical surveys that give perspective on the recent Conferences of the Believers Church, see:

1. John Howard Yoder, "Introduction," in Merle D. Strege, ed., *Baptism and Church: A Believers' Church Vision* (Grand Rapids: Sagamore Books, 1986), 3-7.

2. Donald Durnbaugh, "Origin and Development of the Believers' Church Conferences," in David Eller, ed., *Servants of the Word: Ministry in the Believers' Churches* (Elgin, Ill.: Brethren Press, 1990), xii-xxx.

3. John Howard Yoder, "The Believers' Church Conferences in Historical Perspective," *Mennonite Quarterly Review* 65 (January 1991), 5-19.

Following is a comprehensive listing of the Believers Church Conferences.

Conference	August 23-25, 1955, Mennonite Biblical Seminary, Chicago, Illinois
Theme	The Believers' Church, for the General Conference Mennonite Church
Published Report	*Proceedings of the Study Conference on the Believers' Church*, North Newton, Kansas: The Mennonite Press, 1955.

Conference	June 8-16, 1964, Earlham School of Religion, Richmond, Indiana
Theme	Historic Free Church Seminar: The Church in the World
Published Report	Franklin H. Littell, "The Concerns of the Believers' Church," Chicago Theological Seminary's *Register* 58 (December 1967), 12-18.

Conference	June 26-30, 1967, Southern Baptist Seminary, Louisville, Kentucky
Theme	The Concept of the Believers' Church
Published Report	James Leo Garrett, Jr., ed., 1969. *The Concept of the Believers' Church*. Scottdale, Pa.: Herald Press.

Conference	June 29-July 2, 1970, Chicago Theological Seminary, Chicago, Illinois.
Theme	Is There a Christian Style of Life in Our Age?
Published Report	Report in Chicago Theological Seminary's *Register*, 60 (September 1970), 1-59.

Conference	May 26-29, 1972, Laurelville Mennonite Church Center, Laurelville, Pa.
Theme	Believers Church Conference for Laity
Published Report	None

Conference	June 5-8, 1975, Pepperdine University, Malibu, California.
Theme	Restitution, Dissent, and Renewal: Concept of the Believers' Church
Published Report	Report in *Journal of the American Academy of Religion*, 44:1 (March 1976), 3-113.

Conference	June 15-17, 1975, Baptist Theological Seminary, Rüschlikon, Switzerland.
Theme	Anabaptists, 1525-1975: The Truth Will Make You Free
Published Report	None

Conference	May 15-18, 1978, Winnipeg, Canada
Theme	The Believers' Church in Canada
Published Report	Jarold K. Zeman and Walter Klaassen, eds., 1979. *The Believers' Church in Canada*. Waterloo, Ontario: Baptist Federation of Canada and Mennonite Central Committee (Canada). Also, Philip Collins, 1982, *The Church of Tomorrow: The Believers' Church* (a study guide). Toronto: Baptist Federation of Canada.

Conference	October 23-25, 1980, Bluffton College, Bluffton, Ohio
Theme	Is There a Believers' Church Christology?
Published Report	J. Denny Weaver, "A Believers' Church Christology," *Mennonite Quarterly Review* 57 (April 1983), 112-131.

Conference	June 5-8, 1984, Anderson University School of Theology, Anderson, Indiana.
Theme	Believers' Baptism and the Meaning of Church Membership: Concepts and Practices in an Ecumenical Context.
Published Report	Merle D. Strege, ed., 1986. *Baptism and Church: A Believers' Church Vision*. Grand Rapids: Sagamore Books.

Conference	September 2-5, 1987, Bethany Theological Seminary, Oak Brook, Illinois
Theme	The Ministry of All Believers
Published Report	David Eller, ed., 1990. *Servants of the Word: Ministry in the Believers' Church*. Elgin, Illinois: Brethren Press.

Conference	March 30-April 1, 1989, Southwestern Baptist Theological Seminary, Fort Worth, Texas
Theme	Balthasar Hubmaier and His Thought
Published Report	*Mennonite Quarterly Review* 65(January 1991), 5-53.

Conference	May 20-23, 1992, Goshen College, Goshen, Indiana
Theme	The Rule of Christ (Matt. 18:15-20): Church Discipline and the Authority of the Church
Published Report	*Brethren Life and Thought* 38 (Spring 1993), 69-107.

Conference	June 1-4, 1994, Ashland Theological Seminary, Ashland, Ohio
Theme	The Meaning and Practice of the Lord's Supper in the Believers Church Tradition
Published Report	Dale Stoffer., ed., 1997. *The Lord's Supper: Believers Church Perspectives*. Scottdale, Pa: Herald Press.

Conference	October 17-18, 1996, McMaster Divinity College, Hamilton, Ontario
Theme	The Believers Church: A Voluntary Church
Published Report	William H. Brackney, ed., 1998. *The Believers' Church: A Voluntary Church*. Kitchener, Ontario: Pandora Press.

Conference	August 8-10, 1999, Bluffton College, Bluffton, Ohio
Theme	Apocalypticism and Millennialism: Shaping a Believers Church Eschatology for the 21st Century
Published Report	Loren L. Johns, ed., 2000 (forthcoming). *The Apocalyptic Vision in Believers Church Perspective*. Kitchener, Ontario: Pandora Press.

Continuation Committee:

Ashland Theological Seminary—Richard Allison, Luke Keefer, Jr.,
   Dale Stoffer
Berlin, Ohio—Marlin Jeschke
Bluffton College—J. Denny Weaver

Note: Parallel planning activity also is now occurring in Canada, especially at Conrad Grebel and McMaster Divinity Colleges in Ontario.

APPENDIX B

Report of the Findings Committee
Conference on the Concept
of the Believers Church
Southern Baptist Theological Seminary
June 26-30, 1967

Excerpts of the larger report as published originally in
James Leo Garrett, Jr., ed., *The Concept of the Believers' Church*
(Scottdale, Pa.: Herald Press, 1969).

What follows is an understanding of the character and contemporary challenges of the concept of the Believers Church as illuminated by the 1967 Conference.

1. **We have found ourselves in agreement that the most visible manifestation of the grace of God is His calling together a believing people.**

    A. The congregation is therefore constituted by the divine call to which men and women respond freely in faith.

    The shorthand label "Believers' Church" therefore points first of all not to the doctrinal content of beliefs held, nor to the subjective believingness of the believer, but more to the constructive character of the commitment in defining visible community.

    We therefore reject any pattern of establishment or any church practice (of which pedobaptism is only the most explicit example) whereby Christian allegiance is affirmed, imposed, or taken for granted without the individual's consent or request.

We are left with uncertainty as to how the reality of regeneration subjectively experienced relates to psychological and social causalities.

We are left with the problem of understanding the child, his possible religious experiences, and his relationship to the believing community, in such a way as to respect the integrity both of his person and of the congregation's discipline.

We are left as well with the problem of understanding our relation to those pedobaptist traditions which by virtue of thorough nurture, meaningful confirmation, and faithful discipline may affirm that they also are constituted of freely committed believers.

B. The believer in Jesus Christ manifests a new quality of life which many of us have preferred to call discipleship.

Discipleship is brought about by the regenerating and sanctifying work of the Holy Spirit, who enables and sustains a life otherwise impossible. Its model is the perfect humanity of Jesus Christ, especially in His servanthood and His cross. It is sustained by the mutual discipline of the congregation, which supplies discernment, admonition, moral solidarity, and forgiveness.

We therefore reject any pattern of indiscriminate membership not conditioned upon commitment to discipleship, whatever be the age of the person admitted to membership, or any pattern which does not provide to the new members the needed resources for growth in maturity and obedience.

We are left with the danger of locating Christian perfection in the believer rather than in Christ and His Spirit.

We are left as well with the danger of imposing our vision of obedience upon the unconvinced, or of defining it legalistically without reference to changes in the ethical context.

C. Every believer participates in the full ministry of Christ. Every believer is a priest, every believer is a prophet or preacher. Every believer participates in that servanthood which Jesus revealed as the mode of His rule. Every believer is endowed with a gift, the exercise of which is essential to the welfare of the body.

We reject the concept of ministry as a unique sacramental, professional, or governing caste, and the concept of "laity" as usually defined negatively from that perspective.

We are left with the question whether the subordination of teaching, like other ministries, to the life of the congregation might increase the church's susceptibility to ideological conformity to the world or to alien forms of church life.

We are left as well with the question whether believers' churches, as time passes, can give to new charismatic leaders the same hearing and support which their founders once received.

2. **We have found ourselves in agreement that the particular local together-ness of the congregation is the primordial form of the church.**

A. The congregation is called to a prophetic life whereby, in the exercise of personal gifts, study both of Scripture and of contemporary reality, and Spirit-led group process, the will of God is discerned in a given time and place.

   We reject:

   (1) Administrative processes or patterns of congregational life which either deny the right, or avoid the responsibility and chal-lenge, to exercise this discernment;

   (2) Habits of thought which are slow to believe that God's will may thus be known to the church;

   (3) That laxity in discipline which permits membership to be divorced from participation in this common obedience.

   We are left with uncertainty about the readiness of men in our day, whether in "believers' churches" or elsewhere, to accept the challenge of such openness and mutual responsibility.

B. The congregation is called to a sanctifying, healing life whereby in praise, confession, forgiveness, and reaffirmation of covenant men grow in live-liness, and in the authenticity of their communion with God. The instru-ment of this healing is not so much a professional service or an intellec-tual illumination of the meaning of selfhood, as it is the actual experience of redemptive personal relationship in admonition and acceptance and mutual caring. The structural separateness of the voluntary community is the indispensable form; these loving relationships are the substance.

   We reject the routinization of patterns of worship which hamper the believer's freedom to share and to receive.

   We are left with the dangers of prescribing or routinizing particular new patterns of worship or of personal experience.

C. The congregation is called out of the wider society for a communal exis-tence within and for, yet distinct from, the structures and values of the rest of the world. This distinctness from the world is the presupposition of a missionary and servant ministry to the world. At times it demands costly opposition to the powers of the world.

We reject any view of the world which fails to reckon with its fallenness and any view of the church which simply identifies her membership or her goals with the world in its rebelliousness.

We are left with the danger of misunderstanding separation from the world in terms of geographic or social distance or of a merely ethical or cultural nonconformity, and with the further danger of precipitately applying the concept of separation from the world to other Christians from whom we differ.

We are left as well with the task of interpreting ecclesiologically the significance of the corpus christianum, that acculturated Christianity or Christianized culture which is both the progeny and the parentage of the restoration churches. Some would hold that the case for the Believers' Church, or for movements of restoration, is refuted by these churches' arising from, or degenerating into, forms of "Christendom."

D. The centrality of the congregation dictates a specific Believers' Church style of ecumenical relations. This is not the spiritualized concept of a purely invisible unity. Nor need it be denied that councils, boards, conventions, associations, and synods may have any ecclesiological significance. The import which congregationalism has for these other agencies means rather that their authority is that of the "congregational" character, procedures, and unity of conviction which is given them as they meet. They cannot authoritatively bind other local congregations, which meet more frequently, whose members know one another better, and whose responsibilities are for the total life of their members.

We reject that vision of the ecumenical task which seeks to relate the "faith" or the "order" or the administrative structures of entire "denominations" or "communions" and which makes decisions by instructed delegates, proportional representation, and majority votes, and processes which are not congregational in character.

We reject as well the assumption that the visible unity we seek would take the form of one agency (board, convention, association, council or "Church") seeking or claiming to gather, represent, or lead all Christians.

We are left with the dangers of anarchy, competitiveness, and isolationism which threaten when the rejection of "high" or magisterial
visions of unity is not coupled with an equally statesmanlike vision and
an equally passionate commitment to a freer, more fluid, more missionary, and more costly manifestation of the unity of Christ's body.

3. **We have found ourselves in agreement that the Word of God creates,
   judges, and restores the church.**

A. It belongs to the particular, historical character of Christian faith that its
   foundation and therefore its norm is fixed in the events to which the
   Apostles testify. The church exists where these events are reported and
   their meaning interpreted by believing witnesses to believing hearers.
   The recognition of the New Testament canon fixes the normative authority of the apostolic witness.

   We reject the concept of continuing traditional development as a
   norm independent of Scripture. We reject as well any historical interpretation which would fail to read the Old Testament as interpreted by
   the New or the New as testifying to Jesus Christ.

   We reject as well any narrowing of the listening community by the
   claims of hierarchical authorities or expert interpreters.

   We are left with the danger of so oversimplifying the doctrine of the
   perspicuity of Scripture as to bypass the necessary historical and con-
   textual requirements of correct interpretation.

   We are left as well with reticence and difficulty in recognizing and eval-
   uating those changes in teaching, emphasis, and interpretation which
   arise within our own history.

B. Since the life of churches is—like the gospel events—historical, particular, and contingent, the church may be disobedient. If the church persists
   in disobedience and hears and follows alien spirits, she may become
   apostate. In this event, the Holy Spirit calls men to the restoration of faithful belief and practice according to the New Testament norm.

   We reject any concept of the indefectibility of the church which would
   by definition make apostasy impossible and restoration unnecessary.

   We are left with the temptation to exaggerate the possibility or desirability of imitating in particular details the cultural forms of New Testament church life.

   We are also left with the recurrent temptation to justify separation
   when every effort has not been made to bring about acceptance of the

truth by the larger body, or to justify as "restoration" what is simply schism.

C. Jesus promised His disciples that by the Holy Spirit He would continue to lead them into all truth, to instruct them in the meaning of what they had already heard, and to renew that meaning in new situations. This continued instruction and guidance are limited by, but not limited to, the verbal content of canonical Scripture.

We reject any concept of the closing of the canon which would limit valid Christian witness to the repetition of words of Scripture.

We also reject any concept of "New Light" which would not be subject to the "testing of the spirits" by the norm of the New Testament witness to the Incarnation and Lordship of Christ.

We are left with semantic uncertainty as to whether this continued guidance and instruction beyond the apostolic age should be called "revelation."

4. **We have found ourselves agreed that the mission of the church in the world is to work out her being as a covenant community in the midst of the world.**

A. The visible community is the organ of missionary proclamation. Integration into its fellowship and style of life is the goal of the evangelistic call to individuals.

We reject the concept of evangelism which is limited solely to moving individuals, in their self-concern, toward a sense of forgiveness, self-acceptance, and assurance.

We are left with the danger that the congregation might understand its proclamation as recruitment of support for its institutional program.

B. The visible community is the organ of witness to the surrounding society. As discerning community it is led by the Holy Spirit to develop criteria of moral judgment in social issues. As forgiven community she brings to bear the qualities of compassion and love. As paradigmatic community the church is the pilot agency in the building of new patterns of social relations. The democratization of the power structures of society and the development of welfare concerns are pioneered and preached by the covenanted community.

We reject the idea that the churches' primary role in social changes is to call upon the larger social order to accept some immediately available change in power structures or to call for the maintenance of the social status quo.

We reject as well the idea that it is not the concern of the church to speak to issues of public morality as these arise in social, economical, political life.

We are left with the unmet need for the church to think about her social witness in forms which run ahead of rather than behind the world's own efforts to solve its structural problems.

Signers of this Report (August 10, 1967) were nine members of the Findings Committee, from Canada and the United States, in addition to the Committee's three officers: John Howard Yoder, Goshen Indiana, Chair; William L. Lumpkin, Norfolk, Virginia, Vice Chair; and John J. Kiwiet, Oak Brook Illinois, Secretary.

SELECT BIBLIOGRAPHY

General: Books

Basden, Paul, and David Dockery, eds., *The People of God: Essays on the Believers' Church*. Nashville: Broadman Press. 1991.

Bowman, Carl F., and Stephen L. Longenecker, eds. *Anabaptist Currents: History in Conversation with the Present*. Bridgewater College, Bridgewater, Virginia: Forum for Religious Studies, Penobscot Press. 1995.

Brackney, William H. *Christian Voluntarism: Theology and Praxis*. Grand Rapids: Eerdmans. 1997.

Brown, Charles E. *When Souls Awaken: An Interpretation of Radical Christianity*. Anderson, Ind.: Gospel Trumpet Company (Warner Press). 1954.

Brown, Dale W. *Understanding Pietism*. Nappanee, Ind.: Evangel Publishing House. 1978, rev. ed. 1996.

Burkholder, John, and Calvin Redekop, eds. *Kingdom, Cross, and Community: Essays on Mennonite Themes*. Scottdale, Pa.: Herald Press. 1976.

Callen, Barry L. *God As Loving Grace: The Biblically Revealed Nature and Work of God*. Nappanee, Ind: Evangel Publishing House. 1996.

Clapp, Rodney. *A Peculiar People: The Church As Culture in a Post-Christian Society*. Downers Grove, Ill.: InterVarsity Press. 1996.

Durnbaugh, Donald F. *The Believers' Church: The History and Character of Radical Protestantism*. Scottdale, Pa: Herald Press. 1968, 1985.

Estep, William R., Jr. *The Anabaptist Story*. Grand Rapids: Eerdmans. Rev. ed. 1975.

Friedmann, Robert. *The Theology of Anabaptism*. Scottdale, Pa.: Herald Press. 1973.

Garrett, James Leo, Jr. Editor. *The Concept of the Believers' Church*. Scottdale, Pa.: Herald Press. 1969.

Goertz, Hans Jürgen, *The Anabaptists*, trans. Trevor Johnson. N.Y.: Routledge, English ed. 1996.

Hauerwas, Stanley. *Christian Existence Today*. Durham, N.C.: Labyrinth. 1988.

Hauerwas, Stanley, and William Willimon. *Resident Aliens: Life in the Christian Colony*. Nashville: Abingdon Press. 1989.

Klaassen, Walter, ed. *Anabaptism Revisited*. Scottdale, Pa.: Herald Press. 1992.

Kraus, C. Norman. Ed. *Evangelicalism and Anabaptism*. Scottdale, Pa.: Herald Press. 1979.

Littell, Franklin. *The Anabaptist View of the Church*. 2nd ed. Boston: Starr King Press, Beacon Hill. 1952, 1958, 1964.

Littell, Franklin. *The Free Church*. Boston: Starr King Press. 1957.

Littell, Franklin. *A Tribute To Menno Simons*. Scottdale, Pa.: Herald Press. 1961.

Loewen, Jacob A., and Wesley J. Prieb. *Only the Sword of the Spirit: Perspectives on Mennonite Life and Thought*. Hillsboro, Kan.: Kindred Productions. 1997.

Longenecker, Stephen L., ed. *The Dilemma of Anabaptist Piety: Strengthening Or Straining the Bonds of Community?* Bridgewater College, Bridgewater, Va.: Forum for Religious Studies, Penobscot Press. 1997.

Murch, James DeForest. *The Free Church*. Louisville, Ky.: Restoration Press. 1966.

Pipkin, H. Wayne, and Yoder, John H., trans. and eds. *Balthasar Hubmaier: Theologian of Anabaptism*. Scottdale, Pa.: Herald Press. 1989.

Snyder, C. Arnold. *The Life and Thought of Michael Sattler*. Scottdale, Pa.: Herald Press. 1984.

Snyder, C. Arnold. *Anabaptist History and Theology*. Kitchener, Ont.: Pandora Press. 1995.

Snyder, Howard A. *Liberating the Church: The Ecology of Church and Kingdom*. Downers Grove, Ill.: InterVarsity Press. 1983.

Snyder, Howard A. *A Kingdom Manifesto: Calling the Church to Live Under God's Reign*. Downers Grove, Ill.: InterVarsity Press. 1985.

Snyder, Howard A. *Signs of the Spirit: How God Reshapes the Church*. Grand Rapids: Academie Books, Zondervan. 1989.

Trueblood, David Elton. *The Company of the Committed*. N.Y.: Harper & Row. 1961.

Weaver, J. Denny. *Becoming Anabaptist: The Origin and Significance of Sixteenth-Century Anabaptism*. Scottdale, Pa.: Herald Press. 1987.

Williams, George. *The Radical Reformation*. Philadelphia: Westminster Press. 1962.

Yoder, John H. *The Politics of Jesus*. Grand Rapids: Eerdmans. 1972, rev. ed. 1994.

Yoder, John H. *The Priestly Kingdom*. Notre Dame, Ind.: University of Notre Dame Press. 1984.

General: Journal Articles

Bainton, Roland H. "The Left Wing of the Reformation," *Journal of Religion* XXI (1941), 125-134.

Bender, Harold. "The Anabaptist Vision," *Mennonite Quarterly Review* 18:2 (1944), 67-88.

Brown, Dale W. "Tension and Reconciliation in a Split Society or Strategies of Witness for the Believers' Church in a Revolutionary Age." The Chicago Theological Seminary *Register*, September 1970, 21-46.

Brown, Dale W. "Communal Ecclesiology: The Power of the Anabaptist Vision." *Theology Today* 36:1 (April 1979), 22-29.

Gross, Leonard. "Recasting the Anabaptist Vision: The Longer View." *Mennonite Quarterly Review* 60:3 (July 1986), 352-363.

Littell, Franklin. "The Historic Free Church Defined." *Brethren Life and Thought* IX, Autumn 1964, 78-90.

Littell, Franklin. "The Concerns of the Believers' Church." Chicago Theological Seminary *Register*, LVIII, December 1967, 18.

Littell, Franklin. "The Contribution of the Free Churches." The Chicago Theological Seminary *Register*, September 1970, 47-57.

Ruether, Rosemary, "The Believers' Church and Catholicity in the World Today," The Chicago Theological Seminary *Register*, September 1970, 1-9.

Specific Topics: Books and Journal Articles

Brackney, William H., Ed. *The Believers' Church: A Voluntary Church*. Kitchener, Ont.: Pandora Press. 1998.

Callen, Barry L. *Faithful in the Meantime: A Biblical View of Final Things and Present Responsibilities*. Nappanee, Ind.: Evangel Publishing House. 1997.

Eller, David. Editor. *Servants of the Word: Ministry in the Believers' Church*. Elgin, Ill.: Brethren Press. 1990.

Hauerwas, Stanley. *The Peaceable Kingdom*. Notre Dame, Ind.: University of Notre Dame Press. 1983.

Klaassen, Walter. *Living at the End of the Ages: Apocalyptic Expectation in the Radical Reformation*. Lanham, Md.: University Press of America. 1992.

Klaassen, Walter. *Armageddon and the Peaceable Kingdom: Prophecy and Mystery True To the Gospel*. Scottdale, Pa.: Herald Press. 1999.

Kraus, C. Norman. *Jesus Christ Our Lord: Christology from a Disciple's Perspective*. Scottdale, Pa.: Herald Press. 1987, 1990.

Kraus, C. Norman. *The Community of the Spirit: How the Church Is in the World*. Scottdale, Pa.: Herald Press, rev. ed. 1993.

Littell, Franklin. "The Discipline of Discipleship in the Free Church Tradition." *Mennonite Quarterly Review*. April 1961.

Sider, Ronald J. "Evangelicalism and the Mennonite Tradition," in C. Norman Kraus, ed., *Evangelicalism and Anabaptism*. Scottdale, Pa.: Herald Press. 1979.

Stoffer, Dale. Editor. *The Lord's Supper: Believers' Church Perspectives*. Scottdale, Pa.: Herald Press. 1997.

Strege, Merle D. *Baptism and Church: A Believers' Church Vision*. Grand Rapids: Sagamore Books. 1986.

Strege, Merle D. "Demise (?) of a Peace Church: The Church of God (Anderson), Pacifism, and Civil Religion." *Mennonite Quarterly Review*. April 1991, 128-140.

Weaver, J. Denny. "Discipleship Redefined: Four Sixteenth Century Anabaptists." *Mennonite Quarterly Review* 54:4 (October 1980), 255-279.

Weaver, J. Denny. "Reading Sixteenth-Century Anabaptism Theologically: Implications for Modern Mennonites as a Peace Church," *The Conrad Grebel Review* 16:1 (Winter 1998), 37-51.

Zeman, Jarold K., and Walter Klaassen. Editors. *The Believers' Church in Canada*. Waterloo, Ontario: Baptist Federation of Canada and Mennonite Central Committee. 1979.

Specific Books: Denominational Personal Profiles

Allen, C. Leonard, and Richard T. Hughes. *Discovering Our Roots: The Ancestry of Churches of Christ*. Abilene, Tex.: Abilene Christian University Press. 1988.

Bittinger, Emmert F. *Brethren In Transition: 20th Century Directions and Dilemmas*. Bridgewater College, Bridgewater, Virginia: Forum for Religious Studies, Penobscot Press. 1992.

Callen, Barry L. *Contours of a Cause: The Theological Vision of the Church of God Movement (Anderson)*. Anderson, Ind.: Anderson University School of Theology. 1995.

Callen, Barry L. *It's God's Church!: The Life and Legacy of Daniel Sidney Warner*. Anderson, Ind.: Warner Press, 1995.

Cooper, Wilmer A. *A Living Faith: An Historical Study of Quaker Beliefs*. Richmond, Ind.: Friends United Press. 1990.

Durnbaugh, Donald F. *Church of the Brethren: Yesterday and Today*. Elgin, Ill.: Brethren Press. 1986.

Durnbaugh, Donald F. *Fruit of the Vine: A History of the Brethren 1708-1995*. Elgin, Ill.: Brethren Press. 1997.

Hughes, Richard T. *Reviving the Ancient Faith: The Story of Churches of Christ in America*. Grand Rapids: Eerdmans. 1996.

Kauffman, J. Howard and Harder, Leland. *Anabaptists Four Centuries Later: A Profile of Five Mennonite and Brethren in Christ Denominations*. Scottdale, Pa.: Herald Press. 1975.

Keim, Albert. *Harold Bender, 1897-1962.* Scottdale, Pa.: Herald Press. 1998.

Kent, Homer A., Sr. *Conquering Frontiers: A History of the Brethren Church.* Winona Lake, Ind.: BMH Books. Rev. ed., 1972.

Kraybill, Donald, and Niemeyer, Lucian. *Old Order Amish.* Baltimore: Johns Hopkins Press. 1993.

North, James. *Union In Truth: An Interpretive History of the Restoration Movement.* Cincinnati: Standard Publishing. 1994.

Ruether, Rosemary, "The Free Church Movement in Contemporary Catholicism," in Martin E. Marty and Dean G. Peerman, eds., *New Theology No. 6.* N.Y.: Macmillan. 1969.

Smith, John W. V. *The Quest for Holiness and Unity.* Anderson, Ind.: Warner Press. 1980.

Snyder, Howard. *The Radical Wesley.* Downers Grove, Ill.: InterVarsity Press. 1980.

Stoffer, Dale R. *Background and Development of Brethren Doctrines: 1650-1987.* Philadelphia: Brethren Encyclopedia, Inc. 1989.

Toews, J. B. *A Pilgrimage of Faith: The Mennonite Brethren Church in Russia and North America 1860-1990.* Hillsboro, Kan.: Kindred Press. 1993.

Webb, Henry. *In Search of Christian Unity: A History of the Restoration Movement.* Cincinnati: Standard Publishing. 1990.

Wittlinger, Carlton O. *Quest for Piety and Obedience: The Story of the Brethren in Christ.* Nappanee, Ind.: Evangel Publishing House. 1978.

Dissertations

Bowman, Carl F. *Beyond Plainness: Cultural Transformation in the Church of the Brethren from 1850 to the Present.* University of Virginia. 1989.

Burkholder, John L. *The Problem of Social Responsibility from the Perspective of the Mennonite Church.* Princeton Theological Seminary. 1958.

Clear, Valorous. *The Church of God: A Study in Social Adaptation*. University of Chicago Divinity School. 1953.

Durnbaugh, Donald F. *Brethren Beginnings: The Origins of the Church of the Brethren in Early Eighteenth-Century Europe*. University of Pennsylvania. 1960.

Frantz, Nadine Pence. *Theological Hermeneutics: Christian Feminist Biblical Interpretation and the Believers' Church Tradition*. University of Chicago. 1992.

Keefer, Luke. *John Wesley: Disciple of Early Christianity*. Temple University. 1982.

Russell, Jane Elyse. *Renewing the Gospel Community: Four Catholic Movements with an Anabaptist Parallel*. University of Notre Dame. 1979.

Smith, John W. V. *The Approach of the Church of God (Anderson, Ind.) and Comparable Groups to the Problem of Christian Unity*. University of Southern California Graduate School of Religion. 1954.

Stoffer, Dale. *The Background and Development of Thought and Practice in the German Baptist Brethren (Dunker) and the Brethren (Progressives) Churches (c.1650-1979)*. Fuller Theological Seminary. 1980.

Weaver, John Denny. *The Doctrines of God, Spirit, and the Word in Early Anabaptist Theology, 1522-1530: A Comparative Study in the Swiss and South German Lines of Anabaptism*. Duke University. 1975.

Encyclopedic Works

The Brethren Encyclopedia. Philadelphia, Pa.: The Brethren Encyclopedia, Inc. 1983-1984 (vols. 1-3).

The Mennonite Encyclopedia. Scottdale, Pa.: Herald Press. 1955-1959 (vols. 1-4), 1990 (vol. 5).

Journeying Together. Anderson, Ind.: Leadership Council of the Church of God. 1996.

Records of Recent Believers' Church Conferences

See Appendix A.

INDEX